FOR ARGUMENT'S SAKE

A GUIDE TO WRITING EFFECTIVE ARGUMENTS

FOR ARGUMENT'S SAKE

A GUIDE TO WRITING EFFECTIVE ARGUMENTS

Katherine J. Mayberry
Rochester Institute of Technology

Robert E. Golden
Shippensburg University of Pennsylvania

SCOTT, FORESMAN/LITTLE, BROWN HIGHER EDUCATION
A Division of Scott, Foresman and Company
Glenview, Illinois   London, England

Acknowledgments

Cover illustrations courtesy of The Newberry Library, Chicago.

Acknowledgments are listed at the back of the book on pages 191–193, which constitutes a legal extension of the copyright page.

Library of Congress Cataloging-in-Publication Data

Mayberry, Katherine J.
    For argument's sake: a guide to writing effective arguments /
    Katherine J. Mayberry, Robert E. Golden.
       p.   cm.
    ISBN 0-673-39826-9
    1. English language—Rhetoric.   2. Persuasion (Rhetoric)
3. Logic.   I. Golden, Robert E.   II. Title.
PE1431.M39   1990   808'.042—dc20   89-39555
                                                    CIP

1 2 3 4 5 6—MPC—94 93 92 91 90 89

Preface

For Argument's Sake provides the key information students need in order to improve their written arguments. It discusses the four most common types of arguments—factual arguments, causal arguments, practical recommendations, and evaluations—and how to support each type. It also treats in detail crucial matters such as motivation, audience, focus, style, revision, and logic.

For Argument's Sake was written in response to our need for a practical, flexible, and thorough text appropriate for both freshman composition and upper-level argumentative writing courses. We found existing argument books either too sketchy to be useful or so elaborate that mastering the text itself would become the challenge of the course. We also found most existing books somewhat stale in their approach to written argument, occasionally mixing different approaches in ways bound to confuse students. *For Argument's Sake* is the result of our effort to create an introduction to written argument that is relevant to students from a variety of disciplines, new in its approach to some fundamental issues, and detailed enough to be useful without being overwhelmingly complex.

Organization

This text is structured around three major phases of writing: formation, support, and review. Chapters 1 through 6 discuss the formation of arguments, including motivation, audience, focus, and style; Chapters 7 through 10 discuss how to support factual arguments, causal arguments, practical recommendations, and evaluations; and Chapters 11 and 12 treat reviewing and revising arguments, including a section on openings and closings. We have presented these writing phases in the order that students typically follow when writing arguments, but we are fully aware that there are exceptions to this order. Like most writing teachers and scholars, we recognize the recursive nature of writing, where changes in one phase or aspect of writing lead to changes throughout an argument.

Special Features

The discussion of motive in *For Argument's Sake* is unique to argument texts. Asking why people create written arguments is a basic and legitimate question that can lead to the creation of more meaningful and effective arguments. Motivation is given serious attention in Chapter 2.

The discussion of style in Chapter 6, which includes the all-important matter of a writer's image, is placed *before* our discussion of support; we wish to stress that style is not an afterthought or frosting on the cake but an integral component of argument. Furthermore, the view of style we propound encourages more stylistic richness than most current writing texts.

Placement of the discussion of traditional logic in the "Revising" chapter is also unique. We believe that traditional logic, including a list of logical fallacies, is more valuable to students when they review their arguments than when they create early drafts.

For Argument's Sake contains examples from the humanities, the social sciences, and the physical and biological sciences, plus many examples from college life, business, and the professions. This range of applications helps students see the importance of writing effective arguments not only during college, but after college.

Because improvement in writing only comes with practice, virtually all of the activities throughout the text require some kind of writing. Students are asked to produce many types of written arguments, from brief paragraphs to more fully developed essays.

Acknowledgments

Many people deserve our gratitude for their valuable suggestions at various stages in the preparation of this text, including George Ball, a consultant for Xerox Corporation; Sarah Collins and Joseph Nassar, faculty in the Division of Language, Literature and Communication at the Rochester Institute of Technology; and manuscript reviewers Nevin Laib, Franklin and Marshall College; David Jollife, University of Illinois at Chicago; Carolyn Miller, North Carolina State University; Paul Sawyer, Bradley University; Patricia Graves, Georgia State University; Christopher Gould, University of North Carolina at Wilmington; and Marti Singer, Georgia State University. We also thank the Rochester Institute of Technology for granting a leave to Robert E. Golden to work on this text. Our thanks as well to the many people at Scott, Foresman/ Little, Brown who helped this project go smoothly, and a special thank you to Acquisitions Editor Constance Rajala, whose enthusiasm, support, and patience is appreciated.

Katherine J. Mayberry

Robert E. Golden

Contents

Chapter 1

An Overview of Argument 1

ARGUMENT—A DEFINITION 1

LEVELS OF ARGUMENT 2
    The Manifest Argument 2
    The Implied Argument 4
    Argument by Image 7

COMBINING LEVELS OF ARGUMENT 7

THE ARGUMENT PROCESS 9
    Forming the Argument 9
    Supporting the Thesis 10
    Reviewing Your Argument 11

MARY CHARLES REVISITED 11
Summary: An Overview of Argument 12
Suggestions for Writing (1.1) 12

Chapter 2

Where Writing Begins: Motives and Audience 14

MOTIVES FOR WRITING 14
    The Value of Dissonance 15
    Writing Arguments That are Meaningful to You 16
Activities (2.1) 17

THE IMPORTANCE OF AUDIENCE 17
    Who is the Audience? 18
Activities (2.2) 19
    Why Will the Audience Read the Argument? 20

Activities (2.3) 22
> What Should the Audience Be Able To Do After Reading
> the Argument? 22

Activities (2.4) 23

Summary: Where Writing Begins 24

Suggestions for Writing (2.5) 24

Chapter 3

Focusing Your Position: Theses and Definitions 26

THE THESIS 26
> Generating a Thesis 27
> Keeping Your Working Thesis Flexible 29

Activities (3.1) 30

POSITIONING THE THESIS 31
> Thesis Stated in the Introduction 31
> Thesis Stated at the End of Argument 32
> Other Placements of the Thesis 33
> Unstated Thesis in a Manifest Argument 33

Activities (3.2) 33

DEFINING YOUR TERMS 34
> Types of Definitions 35

Activities (3.3) 37

Summary: Focusing Your Position 37

Suggestions for Writing (3.4) 37

Chapter 4

The Classes of Manifest Argument 39

FACTUAL ARGUMENTS 39
> Representative Factual Theses 41

Activities (4.1) 41

CAUSAL ARGUMENTS 42
> Representative Causal Theses 43

Activities (4.2) 44

PRACTICAL RECOMMENDATIONS 45
> Representative Theses for Practical Recommendations 45

Activities (4.3) 46

EVALUATIONS   46
>   Representative Evaluative Theses   48
Activities (4.4)   49

COMBINATION THESES   49
>   Representative Combination Theses   51
Activities (4.5)   51
Summary: The Classes of Manifest Argument   52
Suggestions for Writing (4.6)   52

Chapter 5

An Argument's Support   53

AN INTRODUCTION TO SUPPORT   53

ARRANGING YOUR ARGUMENT'S SUPPORT   55

ADDRESSING THE COUNTERARGUMENT   56
Summary: An Argument's Support   58
Suggestions for Writing (5.1)   59

Chapter 6

Image and Style   60

THE ROLE OF VOICE   61
>   The Importance of Ethos   61
Activities (6.1)   63

THE VIRTUES AND LIMITATIONS OF PLAIN WRITING   63
Activities (6.2)   65

METAPHOR AND ANALOGY   65
>   Some Cautions About Metaphor and Analogy   67
Activities (6.3)   67

CONNOTATIVE LANGUAGE AND SLANTING   68
Activities (6.4)   69

THE MUSIC OF LANGUAGE   69
Activities (6.5)   71
Summary: Image and Style   72
Suggestions for Writing (6.6)   72

Chapter 7

Making Factual Arguments   73

SUPPORTING PERSONALLY EXPERIENCED FACTS   73
Describing the Experience   74
Establishing Your Own Credibility   74
Activities (7.1)   75

SUPPORTING FACTS REPORTED BY OTHERS   75
Determining the Reliability of Your Source   75
Citing the Source in Your Text   77
Activities (7.2)   77

SUPPORTING FACTUAL GENERALIZATIONS   78
Grounds for Generalizations   79
Activities (7.3)   81

STATISTICS   82
Activities (7.4)   84
Summary: Supporting Facts   85

A SAMPLE FACTUAL ARGUMENT   85
Suggestions for Writing (7.5)   88

Chapter 8

Making Causal Arguments   89

CAUSAL CONSTELLATIONS   89
Causal Chains   90
Activities (8.1)   91
Necessary and Sufficient Causes   92
Central Causes   93
Contributing Factors   93
Deciding Which Causes to Argue   94
Activities (8.2)   94

DETERMINING CAUSALITY   95
Method of Agreement   95
Method of Difference   96
Method of Proportional Correlations   96
Activities (8.3)   97

CAUSALITY IN HUMAN ACTIONS   98

Activities (8.4) 98

Summary: The Nature of Causality and Determining Cause 99

SUPPORTING CAUSAL ARGUMENTS 99
    Establishing Factuality 100
    Reporting the Process of Determination 100
    Identifying an Acceptable Motivation 101
    Qualifying Your Argument 102
Activities (8.5) 103

Summary: Supporting Cause 103

ARGUING EFFECTS 104
    Determining and Supporting a Probable Effect 105
    Comparable Situations 106
Summary: Determining and Supporting a Probable Effect 107
Activities (8.6) 107

A SAMPLE CAUSAL ARGUMENT 108
Suggestions for Writing (8.7) 110

Chapter 9

Making Practical Recommendations 111

ASSUMED VALUE IN PRACTICAL RECOMMENDATIONS 112

WHEN YOUR VALUES DIFFER FROM ASSUMED READER
VALUES 113
Activities (9.1) 115

RECOMMENDATIONS EMPHASIZING THE PRESENT 116
    Evaluating the Situation in Terms of Assumed Needs
    and Values 117
    Evaluating Through Causal Argument 117
    Demonstrating the Probable Results of No Change 118
Activities (9.2) 118

RECOMMENDATIONS EMPHASIZING THE FUTURE 118
    Presenting the Recommendation 119
Activities (9.3) 120
    Arguing the Effects of Your Recommendation 121
Activities (9.4) 121
    Judging Effects in Terms of Assumed Needs and Values 122
Activities (9.5) 124

RECOMMENDATIONS WITH EQUAL EMPHASIS ON PRESENT AND FUTURE   124

Summary: Making Practical Recommendations   125

A SAMPLE PRACTICAL RECOMMENDATION   126

Suggestions for Writing (9.6)   129

Chapter 10

Making Evaluations   130

Activities (10.1)   131

ESTABLISHING THE DEFINITION OF THE EVALUATIVE TERM   131
    Proposing the Definition   132
Activities (10.2)   133
    Arguing the Definition   133
    Ranking the Qualities in Your Definition   135
Activities (10.3)   135

APPLYING THE DEFINITION TO YOUR SUBJECT   136

FURTHER METHODS OF SUPPORTING EVALUATIONS   137
    Identification of Effect   137
    Appeal to Authority   138
    Comparison   138
Activities (10.4)   138

THE VARIETIES OF EVALUATIONS   139
    Ethical Evaluations   139
    Defining the Evaluative Term in Ethical Arguments   140
    The Argument in Ethical Evaluations   140
Activities (10.5)   140
    Aesthetic Evaluations   141
Activities (10.6)   143
    Functional Evaluations   143
Activities (10.7)   144
    Interpretations   145
Activities (10.8)   148
Summary: Supporting Evaluations   149

SAMPLE ETHICAL EVALUATION   149

SAMPLE INTERPRETATION   152

Suggestions for Writing (10.9)   154

Chapter 11

Openings and Closings   155

INTRODUCTIONS   155
    Tactics for General Introductions   156
    Introductions in Professional Writing   158
    General Suggestions About Introductions   159
Activities (11.1)   160

CONCLUSIONS   161
    Types of Conclusions   161

SUMMARIES   164

Summary: Openings and Closings   167

Suggestions for Writing (11.2)   168

Chapter 12

Revising   169

WRITING A FIRST DRAFT, REVISING, AND EDITING   169

SOME SUGGESTIONS FOR SUCCESSFUL REVISING   170
    Suggestion 1: Give Yourself Some Breathing Space   170
    Suggestion 2: Avoid the Red Pen   171
    Suggestion 3: Review Your Original Purpose
    and Audience   171
    Suggestion 4: Review Your Overall Organization   171
    Suggestion 5: Review Your Argument's Coherence   172
    Suggestion 6: Review Your Style   173
    Suggestion 7: Use a Word Processor   173
    Suggestion 8: Review Your Support for Adequacy,
    Appropriateness, and Logic   174
Activities (12.1)   174

PRINCIPLES OF LOGIC   174

INDUCTIVE AND DEDUCTIVE REASONING   175

SYLLOGISMS   176

LOGICAL FALLACIES   179
    Ad Hominem Argument   180
    Circular Argument   180
    Distraction   180
    Either–Or   180
    Hasty Generalization   181
    Oversimplification   181
    Non Sequitur   181
    Post Hoc Ergo Propter Hoc   181
    Straw Man   182
Activities (12.2)   182
Summary: Revising   183

AN EXAMPLE OF REVISION   183
Activities (12.3)   188
Suggestions for Writing (12.4)   189

Chapter 1

An Overview of Argument

Mary Charles was confused. She had spent nearly a month researching and writing a term paper for Professor Jameson's class. The assignment had asked students to analyze potential energy resources for the United States in the twenty-first century. Mary was confident she had prepared a first-class essay— carefully researched, clearly written, and neatly presented. In representing a variety of expert opinions on the question of future energy resources, Mary felt she had directly met the demands of the assignment. Yet Professor Jameson was not enthusiastic when he read the report. Although the professor praised the thoroughness, neatness, and clarity of the paper, he told Mary that she had misunderstood the assignment. "You've given the reader a lot of information," explained Professor Jameson, "but you haven't imposed your point of view on the information; you haven't drawn any conclusions from the material. When I asked for this analysis, I was looking for more than facts and the opinions of others; I wanted you to take a position on the question based on what you've learned about the topic." What the professor was looking for, and what Mary failed to give him, was an argument, not just information.

ARGUMENT—A DEFINITION

The subject of this book is writing effective arguments. To some people, *argument* is a negative term, meaning any dispute governed by emotion, not reason. It is synonymous with *quarrel* or *disagreement*. Baseball players argue with umpires, children argue on long hot car trips, and married couples argue over the family budget. This popular understanding of *argument* is different from the original and still primary meaning of the term. Associated with reason and objectivity, argument is more accurately defined as the process of demonstrating, through reason, the likelihood or certainty of a given proposition (a statement that can either be affirmed or denied). Through the process of argument, a preliminary, tentative proposition becomes a reasoned conclusion. Argument is writing or speaking to convince, using methods of reason. More simply, argument is making a point.

Most of us write because we have points to make, but often we fail to clarify those points in our minds before putting them on paper. The result is loose, uninteresting, and ineffective writing, like Mary's paper on energy resources. To avoid following Mary's example, you need to realize (as many writers do not) that argument operates, or should operate, in virtually all writing: business correspondence, college essay-examinations, instructional manuals, term papers, letters of application, travel brochures, even fiction. Skill in argument is necessary to writers in all fields, not just to trial lawyers and members of Congress or to contract negotiators and editorial columnists.

When we say that argument should prevail in most writing, we don't mean that everything you write should sound like a logic textbook, filled with a prescribed series of premises and conclusions. The following chain of reasons is obviously inappropriate for a Chamber of Commerce travel brochure on the state of Michigan:

> Michigan has pure air and wide open spaces.
>
> Michigan is the land of lakes.
>
> Campers love pure air, lots of space, and
>   fresh water to swim in.
>
> Therefore, if you're a camper, you'll love
>   Michigan.

Such an argument is probably embedded somewhere in the words and pictures of Michigan's brochure, but it is presented more subtly.

LEVELS OF ARGUMENT

It is easier to appreciate the prevalence of argument if you recognize the three distinct levels on which argument—the process of convincing—can operate.

The Manifest Argument

The most obvious kind of argument—the *manifest argument*—proves or demonstrates as probable an identifiable proposition through a series of supporting reasons. Readers of a successful manifest argument should have no doubt about the fundamental purpose of the writing—to argue a particular proposition—or about what proposition is being argued. The majority of manifest arguments contain a *thesis statement*: a one-to-three sentence summary of the central point or conclusion of the argument. The thesis statement both raises certain expectations for a reader and reminds a writer to meet these expectations.

A manifest argument *can* lack a thesis statement, so long as the thesis or proposition itself can be clearly identified on the basis of its supporting reasons. You may choose to omit the thesis statement if your argument's central point is likely to be highly controversial or objectionable to your readers, or if it follows so obviously from the argument itself that stating it would be redundant.

The following excerpt from a book by Primo Levi on the Nazi holocaust of World War II is a good example of a manifest argument:

> Human memory is a marvelous but fallacious instrument. This is a threadbare truth known not only to psychologists but also to anyone who has paid attention to the behavior of those who surround him, or even to his own behavior. The memories which lie within us are not carved in stone; not only do they tend to become erased as the years go by, but often they change, or even grow, by incorporating extraneous features. Judges know this very well: almost never do two eyewitnesses of the same event describe it in the same way and with the same words, even if the event is recent and if neither of them has a personal interest in distorting it. . . . Some mechanisms are known which falsify memory under particular conditions: traumas, not only cerebral ones; interference from other "competitive" memories; abnormal conditions of consciousness; repressions; blockages. Nevertheless, even under normal conditions a slow degradation is at work, an obfuscation of outlines, a so to speak physiological oblivion, which few memories resist. Doubtless one may discern here one of the great powers of nature, the same that degrades order into disorder, youth into old age, and extinguishes life in death. Certainly practice . . . keeps memories fresh and alive in the same manner in which a muscle often used remains efficient, but it is also true that a memory evoked too often, and expressed in the form of a story, tends to become fixed in a stereotype, in a form tested by experience, crystallized, perfected, adorned, installing itself in the place of the raw memory and growing at its expense.

The thesis of this argument is its first sentence: "Human memory is a marvelous but fallacious instrument." The rest of the passage supports and explains this statement through references to different experiences attesting to memory's unreliability and through explanations of memory deterioration. Because Levi is arguing a phenomenon familiar to his readers, he has not had to include rigorous documentation of his thesis.

Another less obvious example of a manifest argument is a typical letter of application—a critical writing task that few of us escape. Every letter of application should argue one central proposition: the writer of the letter is a strong candidate for the position in question. Whether or not this proposition is directly stated in the letter, every piece of information provided, as well as the letter's style, grammar, and even physical appearance, should support and develop that proposition. Your chief task in writing an application letter is to convince the reader, through appropriate supporting evidence, of the probability of this proposition. You can recognize a manifest argument within the following application letter.

> Dear Ms. Miller:
>
> In the April issue of *The Camp Innisfree Newsletter*, you advertised an opening for a senior counselor. I would like to apply for that position. My own experience as a camper and junior counselor, as well as my college minor in elementary education, convinces me that I am well qualified for the job.
>
> Having been a camper at Innisfree for four consecutive summers (1974–77), I am familiar with the physical layout of the camp, as well as its regulations and philosophy. My experience as a junior counselor at Camp Wantabet during the summer of 1980 served as a useful introduction to the duties and responsibilities of a camp counselor. I enclose a reference letter from Mr. Bill DeRitter, the director of Wantabet.
>
> My strong interest in young children led me to pursue a minor in Elementary Education at Pacific College, where I am currently a sophomore. As a requirement of this minor, I have interned as a student teacher for fifth and sixth graders this entire academic year. The knowledge I have gained through this experience of supervising eleven- and twelve-year-olds should be extremely valuable to me as a senior counselor at Innisfree.
>
> I hope you will consider me seriously for this position. If you would like more information than that included in the enclosed résumé and reference letters, please let me know. I look forward to hearing from you.
>
> > Sincerely,
> > Chloë Carlson

The thesis of the argument is contained in the final sentence of the opening paragraph ("I am well qualified for the job"), and the supporting evidence (relevant experience) is contained in the second and third paragraphs.

In manifest arguments, argument operates at its most obvious level. Other levels of argument function in most written texts, but college students and professionals who write on the job are most frequently called upon to write manifest arguments. For this reason, the focus of this book will be manifest arguments.

The Implied Argument

In an *implied argument*, the purpose of arguing a particular proposition lies behind another more obvious purpose—to inform, describe, or explain, for example. While the argument may be detected by alert readers, it is not the obvious purpose of the writing. As well as providing information to readers, writers of implied arguments are also implicitly asking their readers to agree with unstated propositions. Much descriptive and technical writing both serves a straightforward purpose (for example, to provide information) and argues an implied thesis.

Implied arguments are the foundation of advertising, which almost always implies the central proposition "Buy this product" behind less obviously self-serving material. The advertisement on the following page for Saab automobiles, for example, is simply entitled "A Thorough Explanation of the 16-Valve Saab 900 Engine." The advertisement then describes the engine in glowing terms. Nowhere are we told to buy a Saab, but we all recognize the unstated proposition that underlies the explanation.

A great deal of advertising works in this way, from pictures of sun-filled beaches in advertisements for vacation resorts to pictures of cars negotiating mountain highways in advertisements for automobiles. Such advertising is based on the principle that the soft sell—the implied argument—is more effective than the direct approach.

In addition to its straightforward purpose of providing information, technical writing often contains implied arguments. Robert Wright's seemingly straightforward explanation of the interplay between DNA and the human brain is a good example of implied argument in technical writing:

> In their ability to process information—to turn inputs into outputs, reports into instructions—brains are much like the DNA that created them. In fact, what the DNA has essentially done is build a guardian information processor that is faster, more flexible, and more capacious than itself. Both DNA and the human brain exist because it takes information processing to defy the spirit of the second law [of thermodynamics], but the brain is capable of more facile defiance than is DNA; in the time it takes bacterial DNA to receive information about an energy shortage, order the construction of a flagellum, and be transported to more hospitable climes, the human brain can make a whole series of decisions that are, like the DNA's "decision," aimed at keeping its vehicle intact: put hands in pockets to shield them from the freezing wind, head toward a warm building, and, if possible, make it a building with food in it. (Meanwhile, the brain is unconsciously orchestrating all kinds of intricate internal patterns that keep the vehicle running smoothly, somewhat as bacterial DNA oversees everyday functioning.) These two great organic information processors—human DNA and the human brain—are utterly dependent on one another; without genes, the brain could not exist, and without the brain, the genes would not last long enough to get their information sent to the next generation. It is a case . . . of true symbiosis.

Behind the explanatory function of this passage is an unstated proposition that might be summarized as follows: "Alone and in cooperation, DNA and the human brain are phenomenal agents. The complexity of their work is awe-inspiring." By word choice and metaphor, Wright is doing more than explaining his topic; he is passing a judgment on it, evaluating it. Words like *facile defiance*, *decision*, and *orchestrating* suggest that DNA and the brain possess human characteristics like free will and spirit—a suggestion that makes the process described seem utterly remarkable.

A THOROUGH EXPLANATION OF THE 16-VALVE SAAB 900 ENGINE.

This is for all those people who were not far-sighted enough to take Auto Shop as an elective in high school.

Where do we start? Well, let's begin with the familiar: the car you're presently driving.

The overwhelming odds are that for each cylinder your car has, it has two valves. One to let the fuel in and run the engine; the other to let the gases out after they've been burned.

Hence the rule: Make the valves bigger and you increase what's called the *volumetric* efficiency. (In plainer English, the larger the valve, the easier it is for gas to come in and exhaust to go out.)

Unfortunately, the bigger you make the valves, the farther away you move the spark plugs from the center of the combustion chamber. And that starts to wreck what's called the *thermal* efficiency.

The problem: How to increase one efficiency (the volumetric) without decreasing the other (the thermal).

Engineers had been solving that problem for years in their competition and rally cars. Instead of just making the valves bigger,

they simply doubled the number of valves.

Each cylinder, then, gets two valves to ingest the fuel and two valves to throw off the exhaust.

Getting back to your

1986 SAAB 900S	
Power output:	125 HP/92 kw @ 5500 rpm
Max. torque:	123 ft. lbs./166 NM @ 3000 rpm
Compression ratio:	10.1:1
Fuel injection:	Bosch LH electronic
Ignition:	Bosch electronic with knock detector

1986 SAAB 900 TURBO	
Power output:	160 HP/118 kw @ 5500 rpm
Max. torque:	188 ft. lbs./255 NM @ 3000 rpm
Compression ratio:	9.0:1
Fuel injection:	Bosch LH electronic
Ignition:	Bosch electronic, Hall effect

car. If it has a four-cylinder engine, it probably has eight valves.

Whereas a Saab 900S or Turbo (the descendants of rally and competition cars) has sixteen.

Back in the days of cheap gas and free glassware, none of this engineering cleverness was needed. (Well, it *was* needed; it just wasn't called for.)

All you had to do then was worry about performance (V-8 engines and the like) and throw efficiency to the wind.

Today, Saab throws nothing to the wind.

Engine weight: On a football field, 180-pound cornerbacks are faster than 290-pound defensive tack-

les. They have less weight to carry around. So, too, the four-cylinder, two-liter Saab engine block. Everything is attuned to keeping that weight down: The cylinder head, camshaft cover, and intake manifold are built from lightweight aluminum alloys instead of clunkier materials.

Fuel injection: The fuel is not burned mindlessly; the computer-like Bosch fuel injection always maintains the most efficient mixture of gas and air.

Even the stroke the piston makes is only this long:

_____

3.07 inches. So hours and hours and hours and hours of high cruising speed don't create unnecessary wear and tear on the engine.

Saab offers both turbocharged and 16-valve naturally aspirated engines.

In the legendary Saab Turbo. And the not-yet-legendary new Saab 900S.

They prove that there are more ways than one to achieve what is more appropriate to poets than to engineers: the picture of driving exhilaration you see on the right.

SAAB

The most intelligent cars ever built.

Saabs range in price from $12,285 for the 900 3-door 5-speed to $18,695 for the 900 3-door 5-speed, 16-valve Turbo. Manufacturer's suggested retail prices. Not including taxes, license, freight, dealer charges or options. There are a limited number of Turbo models available with Saab's Exclusive Appointments group, which includes: leather upholstery, fog lights, and electric sunroof at additional cost.

Argument by Image

The third level of argument is the least obvious to readers and, unfortunately, to many writers. This is the argument made not by specific supporting reasons but rather by the total impression that is projected—*argument by image*. Every conceivable kind of writing, whether a billboard, an annual report for a multimillion dollar corporation, or directions for putting together a child's toy, projects an image of the individual or organization behind the writing.

Image is the total impression that a reader gets by reading your writing. It is created by a number of different elements. One of these elements is the writing *style*, which is a product not only of your choice of specific words and types of sentences and paragraphs but also of the impression of your character and intellect that you present to a reader—what we'll later refer to as your *voice*. Other elements of image include attention to grammar, neatness, the spacing of text and sometimes of visuals on the page. Together, these elements will constitute an impression of you and your work that will strongly influence a reader's final acceptance or rejection of the entire document. As a writer, your purposes will always be well served by carefully creating a positive and suitable image through these elements. The projection of image, then, becomes a third level of argument, the means by which you can quietly argue that you (or your organization) merit a reader's confidence, respect, and attention.

Take the case of Betty Weiss, a new management trainee at Upstate National Bank, who is asked to evaluate the tellers' weekly balancing system. This assignment is, in fact, twofold. As well as evaluating the system to the best of her ability, Betty must demonstrate, through her writing, certain qualities that her employers value. She must project an image of being thoughtful, educated, and attentive to detail. The content of her manifest argument will help to establish these points, of course, but so too will certain quieter but equally influential elements of her writing, such as her diction, tone, sentence length, grammar, and spelling. If she projects the proper image, her employers will feel justified in having hired her; if she does not, they may reconsider their decision.

COMBINING LEVELS OF ARGUMENT

These three levels of argument do not operate alone. For example, argument by image always works in concert with a manifest or an implied argument. The typical college research paper is an example of a manifest proposition and a projected image working together to create a desired reaction on the reader's part. The obvious task of most college research papers is to support convincingly the central proposition or thesis of the paper. A history paper on World War I might have as its primary thesis the assertion that the war would have erupted even without the assassination of Archduke Francis Ferdinand in Sarajevo. The manifest argument would consist of a presentation of those facts and reasons that would convince the reader of the probability of the thesis.

Less obviously, the assignment requires each student to reveal certain personal qualities. The professor must be persuaded not only that the primary thesis is reasonable, but also that each student has understood the assignment, done sufficient research, and thought carefully and at length about the content and presentation of the paper. That is, the paper must project the image of a thoughtful, conscientious student to the reader. For most instructors, the satisfactory projection of this image is nearly as important as the content of the paper.

Writing tasks in business and industry often combine implied argument and argument by image. Instructional and reference manuals, for example, contain no direct proposition that seeks the reader's agreement. Yet good instructional and reference manuals contain an implicit proposition that the product purchased is superior to its competitors and that the steps outlined in the manual are simple and sensible. Good manuals also give us an image of the publisher or company as knowledgeable in its field, straightforward, and concerned about the needs and desires of the consumer.

The following passage on multiple-image lenses from an Eastman Kodak booklet entitled *Filters and Lens Attachments* is an example of how a reference manual can argue an implied proposition *and* an image of the company:

MULTIPLE-IMAGE LENSES

Multiple-image lenses offer an exciting dimension in creative interpretation with both still and movie cameras. These lenses are specially designed pieces of glass that fit on the front of your camera lens. Since they transmit nearly 100 percent of the light, there is no need for exposure compensation. Multiple-image lenses are multi-surfaced in such a way that they can divide a single subject into several identical images. Depending on which multiple-image lens you choose, you have the capability of recording these repeating images in concentric, radial, or linear patterns.

With a single lens reflex camera, you can see the effect the lens produces right in your viewfinder. Simply rotate the lens accessory until your multiple subjects appear in a pleasing composition. A subject with a simple background takes on a dreamlike quality, while a busy scene can split into a wild, nervous collage.

The passage is intended not only to inform us about multiple-image lenses, but also to make us want to use them. The implicit proposition is that using these lenses is easy, fun, and even artistic, and that proposition is supported: you can be "creative" in making images that are "dreamlike" or that form a "wild, nervous collage."

Eastman Kodak Company also presents itself as friendly and informal, addressing the reader as "you" rather than using the more formal "the photographer" or dropping all reference to a human agent. The "you," of course, also suggests that you, the reader, not someone else, can be doing this kind of photography; you are welcomed into an activity, not just given a seat on the sidelines. This passage, like most of the booklet, uses sentences that are no longer than approximately twenty-five words. The booklet in which this passage appears has two columns on each page and mostly short paragraphs; it has the look, with all its attractive, carefully produced photographs, of an expensive magazine, not a reference manual.

Kodak does not manufacture multiple-image lenses. In this passage it is selling the art and science of photography, not a specific Kodak product. In doing so, however, it is certainly sending readers a message about the company's knowledge of and concern for its primary business. Kodak, like any successful company or organization, like any successful writer, knows that it must maintain its image in all of its written communications, from advertising to strictly technical documentation to combinations of the two.

THE ARGUMENT PROCESS

In one form or another, then, argument informs most of the writing tasks performed by students and professionals. But recognizing the prevalence of argument is only a beginning in making your own writing more effective. As with all effective writing, successful arguments result from a cooperative process of writing and thinking that begins a long way from the ultimate polished product. While there is no set order to this process—different writers undertake it in different ways—it is possible to identify certain broad phases that every writer must work through: forming an argument; supporting the argument; and reviewing the argument. Within each of these phases, which are usually roughly sequential, a number of crucial considerations arise. This book will help you, as writer, recognize these considerations and make the choices most likely to yield an effective argument. At this point, we offer a brief explanation of each phase to give you an overview of the creation of effective manifest arguments.

Forming the Argument

Forming your argument consists of discovering a motive for writing and identifying an audience to write to, discovering and sharpening the central point to be argued, and developing an appropriate style.

A successful argument is usually one that is important to its writer, that is born of strong personal interest, often an interest in changing things. As much as possible, you should try to enliven your writing assignments with the energy of your own interests, your own experience. In other words, find a personal motive for writing your assignment.

Identifying your audience is another important task in forming an argument. *Audience* is an inescapable element of writing, yet one that is often underestimated or misunderstood by writers. While usually a solitary act, writing is the act of writing *to* someone: friends, business associates, professors, relatives, the general public. Even writers of private diaries have an audience in mind, although the audience may be merely themselves in the future. When writing does not work, one of the most common causes is the writer's failure to understand sufficiently the needs of the audience. Without this attention to audience, even the most brilliant prose can be wasted on uncomprehending and indifferent readers. Before writing, you need to ask yourself three basic questions about your audience: Who are my readers? Why will they read what I have written? What should they be able to do after reading what I have written?

You cannot write an effective manifest argument without a very clear understanding of the central point you are arguing. While discovering a motive for writing is very helpful, you must still discover, or at least clarify, the informing proposition of your argument. In some instances, this proposition will come to you early and easily; more frequently, you may have to labor through much reading and thinking before arriving at a reasonable and interesting proposition. In most manifest arguments, this proposition is summarized in a one- to three-sentence statement called the *thesis statement*. A critical element of manifest arguments, the thesis statement requires considerable attention: it must be absolutely clear, interesting, and representative of the argument as a whole.

As we have noted, the image you project through your writing subtly yet powerfully influences the overall effect of your argument. While virtually everything you do in creating your argument has some effect on your image, the *style* of your writing is the most revealing reflection of you. As you write, you must be aware that all the choices you make about language—diction, figures of speech, even the sound of the words—will work together to create an impression on the reader. Obviously, you want this impression to be positive—to suit the occasion and advance your argument. Broadly speaking, a style that uses language fairly, intelligently, and sensitively will project an image that the reader will trust and respect.

Supporting the Thesis

Having formed your argument, it is time to consider how best to support your thesis. An argument's support is all the material that turns a tentative thesis into a justified conclusion; it is the evidence for the thesis or theses. *Support* is the meat of argument; it is the single most important component, the defining component of argument. Without support, a thesis is purely speculative and hypothetical; with appropriate support, it becomes a sound, credible conclusion.

Manifest arguments can be classified into four groups: (1) factual arguments; (2) causal arguments; (3) practical recommendations; and (4) evaluations. Some basic principles of support are applicable to all four classes of argument, but each also has its own requirements. Knowing these requirements will help you argue effectively in a wide variety of situations. A tentative thesis allows you to identify the class of argument you intend to create, helping you to select supporting material appropriate to that class of argument and to sustain a focus as you write.

As well as selecting the most suitable support, you must present and arrange it effectively, remaining sensitive to your reader's disposition toward your argument and maintaining a style that works with and not against the argument you are developing.

Reviewing Your Argument

With a first draft written, one that is well formed and supported, you will want to take a step back and review what you have created. As you look at the argument whole, knowing what you have argued and how, you will probably want to add an introduction and conclusion. Introductions, which are the reader's first impression of you and your argument, should be informative, engaging, and representative. Conclusions and summaries (and there *is* a difference between the two) are the final impression of your argument; they must round it off, creating a sense of closure and completion that will satisfy the reader.

In all the arguments you write, you should treat your first draft as a true *draft*, leaving yourself plenty of time to come back to your writing and *revise* it, to make whatever changes need to be made in the paper's content, organization, and style. In the revision stage, you will review your entire argument, asking yourself basic questions about purpose, audience, style, organization, and adequacy and logic of the support. At this stage, an awareness of the principles of logic will help you detect any basic errors in reasoning.

Effective revising means a willingness to make major changes if necessary; it should not be confused with *editing*, the review of your argument for correct spelling, grammar, usage, and format. Revision can mean redesign; editing should be the final spit and polish on a nearly finished product.

MARY CHARLES REVISITED

Remember confused Mary Charles? If she had read this chapter before she started her report, she would have realized that most writing goes beyond the simple purpose of transmitting information; on some level, it makes a point as well. She would know that every aspect of her writing, from the spelling and the format through the structure of the argument itself, plays an important role in winning over her readers. She would be ready to start her next writing assignment with a sharper focus and a clearer sense of purpose. Yet she still would have plenty of questions, including questions about effective theses, appropriate style, strong and weak arguments, and meaningful revision. We cannot answer all of Mary's questions, but we hope that by the time she has finished this book she can begin her next writing project with a clearer focus and a greater understanding of how to write effective arguments.

SUMMARY

An Overview of Argument

- Argument is the attempt by the writer to convince the reader of a point of view, using methods of reason. Most effective writing contains some kind of argument.
- A *manifest argument* demonstrates that an identifiable proposition is probable by a series of supporting reasons.
- In an *implied argument*, the proposition being argued lies behind another more obvious purpose, such as to inform, describe, or explain.
- *Argument by image* helps convince the reader through the impression the writer creates. This image is created through style, correct spelling, punctuation, grammar, and physical appearance.

  In successful writing, argument by image works in concert with a manifest or implied argument.
- While the process of creating arguments varies from writer to writer, the following three phases should be worked through: (1) forming an argument, which can consist of discovering a motive for writing and identifying an audience to address, discovering and sharpening a position, and developing an appropriate style; (2) supporting the argument; and (3) reviewing the argument, which can include adding an introduction and conclusion and revising the entire argument.

Suggestions for Writing (1.1)

1. Write a job application letter that is an effective manifest argument. Your first paragraph should state the position desired and announce your primary qualification for the position. The second paragraph should expand upon this primary qualification, while the third paragraph—and other paragraphs if

needed—should develop your other qualifications. Your concluding paragraph should state your willingness to answer additional questions or to be available for an interview.

2. Analyze an advertisement in a newspaper or a magazine. Does the advertisement contain a manifest or an implied proposition? How does image support this proposition? Does the advertisement give supporting reasons for purchasing the product, and do these reasons seem plausible to you? Address these questions in a two-to-three-page essay.

3. Analyze an editorial in your local newspaper. What is the editorial's manifest proposition and what kind of support is given for this proposition? Do you find this support convincing? Why or why not? Write a two-to-three-page essay on these questions.

Chapter 2

Where Writing Begins:
Motives and Audience

All of us often write from sheer compulsion, because authority or policy or necessity requires a written document from us. A student writes a research paper because a professor has assigned it; a sales representative writes a monthly report because a supervisor requires it; a mother writes a note about her child's absence because a school's policy insists upon it. Yet we all know or suspect that the best writing springs from some source other than mere necessity and that even when necessity is present, in good writing there are also other motives at work. Shakespeare wrote *Hamlet* to earn a living, but earning a living was hardly his sole motive for writing.

MOTIVES FOR WRITING

What are these other motives for writing? They can vary enormously, from a desire to create a record for posterity to a desire to express love or joy to a yearning to get a strong feeling out of our system, to purge it. One very common motive for writing, especially for the writing of arguments, is an attempt to resolve dissonance in our lives. *Dissonance* is a musical term meaning an inharmonious arrangement of tones that suggests tension and therefore requires resolution, but it can also mean lack of agreement or disparity. It is a good way to describe the mismatch between the way we want life to be and the way it is. Dissonance energized Socrates' questioning of the conventional wisdom of his time, the angry voice of the prophets in the Old Testament, and the writing of *The Declaration of Independence* and *The Communist Manifesto*.

And it drives much that is written in private diaries, editorials, and general-interest essays.

The Value of Dissonance

If you do not know what to write for an assignment, dissonance can be a good starting place. What bothers you? What do you wish were different from what it is? What change would make this situation better for you? The cause of the dissonance could be anything from parking problems on campus to the status of women in large corporations to the chemistry experiment that did not work the way it was supposed to. The field could be English composition or sociology or history or physics.

Looking for dissonance can lead to discovering a specific focus, since all of us can point to events or conditions that cause discomfort or disagreement. In an English Composition class, for example, if you were asked to write about the impact on your life of a recent technological development, you might begin to narrow the topic by considering a development that has complicated your life instead of simplifying it. Once you have settled on a focus—compact discs, let's say—concentrating on the problems of these discs rather than praising their virtues will give your paper a sharper edge. This approach has many advantages, one of which is its uniqueness: most students assigned this topic would concentrate on the benefits of technology. And in writing, an unusual approach, so long as it is intelligent, is often effective. Finally, focusing on problems is more useful and productive than ignoring them; neither you nor your readers can improve a situation until you have identified its problems. Whether you are writing a report at work or a letter to the editor of your local newspaper, your readers will often be in a position to do something about the problem.

We don't advocate your turning every writing assignment into an occasion for pointless complaining; such an approach is rarely effective. Searching for dissonance does not mean becoming a professional cynic; you can be critical without being negative, discerning without being a whiner. The student who recognizes that compact discs do have *some* advantages needs to be balanced in the overall view: "Compact discs are a boon to music lovers because they offer durability and recording accuracy superior to both records and tapes, but the price of discs is a major obstacle for many purchasers. Although the price of discs may decrease in the future with advances in technology, discs are now so expensive that many people cannot afford them." The student who writes this thesis will concentrate on the actual problems of disc prices, but will also have given compact disc technology credit for its real advantages.

Sometimes balance and fairness are not appropriate—*The Declaration of*

Independence would be much less effective if it presented a balanced view of the British government—but extreme situations calling for one-sided appeals are relatively rare.

Writing Arguments That are Meaningful to You

Not all writing is based on dissonance and not all your writing can originate in or gain energy from your own emotions or beliefs. Nevertheless, even when the assignment you are given is narrowly defined, when you have little room to maneuver, to search for areas of dissonance, keep in mind these simple suggestions to help make the writing meaningful to you:

1. To the degree that you can, write about what is important to you. Projects originating in personal interest and strong feeling are almost always more vital and compelling to writers and readers than those that writers care little about. Even if you don't care about the Civil War and you have to write about it, try to find the one aspect of the Civil War that is at least potentially more meaningful to you than anything else. Discovering this aspect may require some research, but the time spent will be rewarded by your more positive attitude toward the topic. If you are interested in medicine, for example, you may be able to write about the medical treatment of the wounded in the Civil War, comparing and contrasting it with contemporary practice.

2. Don't lie. Express only those opinions you can honestly believe in. If you are unsure of your thesis despite your best efforts to become comfortable with it, don't hesitate to use qualifiers such as "perhaps," "probably," "usually," or "likely." Never be lukewarm when you can be hot or cold, but don't take a position simply for the sake of taking it. That ground is too slippery. A qualified thesis, such as "Athletes who train diligently will usually perform better than athletes who do not," is preferable to the unqualified statement "Athletes who train diligently will perform better than athletes who do not" because there will be some exceptions to this rule. On the other hand, try to avoid the risk—common in much student writing—of overqualifying your thesis to the point that it is virtually meaningless. A thesis such as "Some athletes who train diligently may perform better than athletes who do not" is too qualified to be useful or interesting.

3. Don't be pompous. Much ineffective writing is done by students trying to write like their professors, and some of the worst writing in business comes from people who believe they have to leave their humanity behind when they write at work. Pomposity is partly in the eyes of the beholder, of course, and there is no foolproof way to guard against it, but ask yourself one key question about your writing: "Does it sound as though *I* wrote it?" A title such as "An Examination of Personality Traits of the Central Character in Jane Austen's *Emma*" is stuffy and vague. A title like "Emma's Pride in Jane Austen's *Emma*" is more direct and certainly less pretentious.

These suggestions apply not only to college assignments, but to any assigned writing: a monthly sales report, a memo on improvements in office procedures, a technical report on which brand of copier to buy. You may not have chosen to do the writing in the first place, but to the degree you can, you need to make the project your own, not simply a task assigned you by someone else.

Activities (2.1)

1. Look at the last four things you have written: letters, reports, essays, memos, etc. What were your reasons for writing them? Were any of them written merely because you had to write them? Would any of them have been improved if you had tried to write about what is important to you? Write a one-to-two-page essay addressing these questions.
2. List four aspects of your life or of the world around you that you wish were different. From these four aspects derive tentative topics for essays.

THE IMPORTANCE OF AUDIENCE

When Laurie Sands began her new job as a computer software specialist for Ace Computer, she thought she would have no trouble with any writing she had to do. After all, she had graduated from college with honors and had done well on all her written assignments. She thought of herself as a good writer and an even better software specialist. Her self-assessment was not inaccurate, but many of her reports came back with question marks in the margins and with requests that certain sections be rewritten. She was first shocked, then annoyed, and finally puzzled. Only gradually did she recognize, through reviewing written comments on the reports and through conversations with some of the reports' readers, that her reports contained what *she* knew, not what her audience knew or needed to know. The content of the reports was technically correct, but the reports were too specialized for the needs of the audience.

Laurie's difficult transition from college writing to professional writing is not unusual. College writing assignments sharpen many writing skills and increase your knowledge of the subject you are writing about, but these assignments give you little practice in the critical skills of assessing and addressing a particular *audience*. The audience you will face in a professional setting may differ markedly from your college audience. When you write in college, you are usually writing for a professor who is a specialist in the subject of the paper, who knows very well the purpose of the paper, and who is obligated to read the paper through to its end. Not only are you writing *to* a specialist, you are also encouraged to write *as* a specialist, demonstrating your facility with the concepts and terminology of a particular field or discipline.

This emphasis on specialization has the unfortunate effect of giving many writers a false sense of audience. These writers usually assume that the audience for their professional writing will be people much like themselves or their professors. They do not realize that their audience may not be specialists in their field, may not be familiar with the original purpose for writing, and may have no compelling reason to read the writing all the way to the end. In fact, audiences of most writing—technical, professional, and general writing—frequently know less about the subject than the writers. Only by assuming this fact can a writer appeal to and satisfy the largest possible audience.

Developing an accurate sense of audience depends in part on experience, but you can sharpen this sensitivity by considering the following questions each time you prepare to write: *Who* is the audience? *Why* will the audience read your argument? *What* should the audience be able to do after reading your argument? You must keep these three questions in mind both before you write and while you are writing. Unlike speaking, where a listener is almost always present, writing is a solitary activity, with the writer often tempted to ignore the eventual recipient of the writing. But good writers keep the image of a reader constantly before them: they know a reader's interests, extent of familiarity with the subject, and probable attitude toward the argument, as well as what they expect a reader to do after reading the argument. To good writers, a reader is always present as a necessary partner in the act of writing.

Who is the Audience?

The composition of your audience can determine what you say and how you say it, so make sure you know to whom you are writing. Sometimes this question about the composition of the audience will be answered in terms of specific individuals that you know, but more often it is answered in terms of categories or groups of readers, such as the readers of a certain newspaper or magazine, or the users of a certain product, or the students in a particular class. Most college essays, for example, are written for professors as the primary audience; most memos are written to members of the same department or unit as that of the writer. Whoever the audience may be, you must identify them *before* you begin to write.

Once you are sure you know your audience, you must consider how much they know about the subject. Readers usually know much less than you, the writer, about the subject in question; even readers in the same organization with similar education and experience may be unfamiliar with the content of your report. You should take care to provide any necessary background information, and explain all specialized vocabulary, basic concepts, and assumptions that may be unfamiliar to even *part* of your audience. The risk of ignoring the needs of some of your readers is more dangerous than the risk of providing too much explanation.

The composition of your audience will have a marked influence on the presentation of your material. Knowledgeable audiences can grasp a complicated presentation; nonspecialist audiences will require simplicity. Take the example of Maxwell's Demon. According to the laws of physics, faster-moving molecules create more heat than slower-moving ones. When two connected containers are filled with gas—one with hot gas and one with cold—their temperatures will eventually converge. Through random motion, the faster-moving molecules of the hotter container will move to the colder container, while the slower-moving molecules will wander to the hot side. Ultimately, the temperatures of both containers will be the same. The British scientist James Clerk Maxwell, however, hypothesized an imaginary person—the demon—who violates the laws of physics by allowing the fastest-moving molecules of the colder container to move to the warmer one, yet stopping all other exchanges, thereby raising the temperature of the warmer container and lowering the temperature of the colder one. (Maxwell's hypothesis is an impossibility, by the way.) A writer addressing a general audience would have to explain the concept of Maxwell's Demon in great detail. The same writer writing to a group of chemists or physicists could simply refer to Maxwell's Demon, confident that the audience knew the term and the scientific principles on which it is based.

The success of many arguments depends on an accurate assessment of readers' beliefs and values as well as their familiarity with your subject. An argument written for the *New Left Journal* favoring the reciting of the Pledge of Allegiance in public schools could only succeed if it appealed to a value held by the *Journal*'s readers. Clearly, these readers would not be moved by a "Your country: love it or leave it" approach. But if you rested your claim on the principle of free choice, arguing that every student should have the choice of saying the pledge, your argument might succeed.

Activities (2.2)

1. Examine a copy of *four* of the following and try to identify the probable audience for each. Estimate the level of education and the kinds of occupations each audience would probably have. Example: *Publications of the Modern Language Association* (PMLA). Level of education: usually at least some graduate education. Occupations: primarily graduate students in English or foreign language and literature and college-level instructors in these subjects. Describe the results of your investigation in a one-to-two-page essay.
   a. *The Wall Street Journal.*
   b. *Time* Magazine.
   c. *Cosmopolitan.*
   d. *People* Magazine.
   e. *The New England Journal of Medicine.*
   f. *Popular Mechanics.*

    g. *Soldier of Fortune* Magazine.

    h. Instructor's Manual for the Apple Macintosh Computer (or some other personal computer).

    i. *Mad* Magazine.

    j. *The New York Times.*

2. The following passage is from a brochure on how employees can use statistics to improve the quality of their organization's products. The intended audience for this brochure is company employees with a seventh-grade reading level and with no previous knowledge of statistics. How well does this passage communicate with its intended audience? If you believe that the passage would be difficult for its intended audience, can you suggest ways to change it to make it more accessible to them? Write a one-to-two-page essay addressing these questions.

> Quality can be best maintained by preventive action in advance of complete tool wear or predictable machine maintenance. If we check characteristics of parts on a sampling basis as they are produced, it is better than sorting through a bin of hundreds of parts looking for the defective parts and then trying to determine which parts can be salvaged.
>
> Collecting and analyzing data on current operations is essential in supplier and company plants. By studying the data, the causes of defects for each main quality characteristic can be investigated and determined. Appropriate solutions, including redesign or reprocessing, can be developed. Once problems are identified, a decision can be made whether to analyze past data, to collect new information, or a combination of both.

Why Will the Audience Read the Argument?

Writers rarely ask themselves *why* readers will want to read their report, often assuming that the reader has the same interest in the subject as they do. Unfortunately, the level of interest is usually not as high; the reader's interest must be captured and held. Even in business, where the reader often must read a report as a part of work, the report competes with all the other reports that must be read and with other responsibilities. Because a reader at work is a busy person, the report should contain something that will get the reader's attention and hold it. A good introduction and thesis help to win over the reader, but before you can write a good introduction and thesis you must understand what is interesting and important to the reader.

In a sales report, for example, what is the one item that is going to be most important to the district sales manager, who is the primary reader of the report? What is the one way to phrase the thesis that will catch this reader? If sales in the district seem to be going well because they were up 10% last month compared to a year ago, but the situation is actually far less promising because sales of the most profitable items were down 15%, the writer must be precise in word choice. An opening such as "Although overall sales for August were up 10%

when compared to a year ago, the district must address the problem of a 15% decline in the sales of our most profitable merchandise" would alert the district manager to the basic facts and the crucial problem that needs to be solved. The opening shows an awareness of the particular audience and its needs and interests.

These same issues are even more pressing in writing outside of a business or professional context, because then the readers are under no compulsion to read what is written. Writers who write daily or weekly columns in newspapers are under continual pressure to find a "hook" that will catch the readers' attention. These writers need to find, in a subject important to them, the topic or angle that will also interest their readers. What aspect of the nuclear arms race will interest readers who have been reading and perhaps having nightmares about the subject for years? If readers are tired of hearing about the potential destruction, perhaps they will be interested in an essay on the present costs. Or if readers' interest in the subject seems to be exhausted, but you feel compelled to bring the issue to their attention once more, what about a "hook" such as "Why is the bomb so boring?" You need to be constantly aware of what is likely to catch your readers' attention by asking yourself such questions as "What will appeal to the readers' self-interest?", "What are people talking about right now?", "What don't the readers know about this subject that they should?", or even "What is currently unfashionable or unpopular that I can make people look at in an entirely new way?" You can address these questions while still writing about what is important to you; good writing is always a successful marriage of the writer's commitment and the reader's interest.

Our hypothetical article about the arms race points out the importance of the audience's attitude toward the subject. In the case of the arms race, you could assume that few believe the arms race is a good thing (though many may see it as unavoidable) and that no one favors the possible outcome: nuclear destruction. You may also suspect, however, that most people are tired of hearing about the topic. If you write about the arms race, you may have to tread carefully between your readers' fear of nuclear destruction and their apathy about an issue that has been intensely discussed for years.

In other cases, you may be faced with an audience overwhelmingly in favor of your thesis, which simplifies and almost eliminates the need to convince but which can make the task of writing almost too easy. Flaccid, cliché-ridden sermons, political speeches, and essays often result from situations where a writer tells the already converted what they already know in language with which they are already too familiar. In these cases, you need to combat triteness, perhaps by assuming the position of someone opposed to your view and then refuting that position, but only after giving your views—and your audience's—a thorough working over.

In still other cases, you may have to convince an audience decidedly hostile to your thesis—a very difficult task. Although ways to win over a hostile audience vary, they all give the audience credit for their views. If you were trying to convince an American audience very suspicious of the Soviet Union that the arms race must be slowed down, you might argue something like "The Soviets may not be well-intentioned, but they'll be around for the forseeable future, and it's too expensive and dangerous for us to keep inventing new ways to blow them to smithereens." With a thesis like this, which concedes that the audience is not wholly wrong in their views of the Soviets and which tries to appeal to the audience's self-interest, you have at least a chance of winning over your audience. You would have no chance at all if you argued that your readers were wrong because they were simpleminded and pigheaded.

When you know that some in your audience hold a view contrary to your own, or when an opposing view is well known, you will often have to include a *refutation* of the opposing argument in your own. (We discuss refutations in Chapter 5 of this book.) Even if you don't directly refute this opposing argument, you will at least have to acknowledge its existence—thus making your readers know that you are sensitive to their knowledge and beliefs.

Activities (2.3)

For the following audiences, identify the audience's motivation for reading the type of writing listed. Motivations could include entertainment, general information, information necessary for work, or information necessary for personal finances. Example: a secretary—instructions on how to use a word processor. Information necessary for using equipment at work.

1. An electrical engineer—a biography of Abraham Lincoln.
2. A financial adviser—a brochure on Individual Retirement Accounts.
3. A self-employed businessman—a brochure on Individual Retirement Accounts.
4. A sales manager for a large corporation—the monthly report of sales in her district.
5. A lawyer—a mystery novel.
6. A college student—a brochure on Fort Lauderdale, Florida.
7. A high school teacher—the evening newspaper.
8. A literature professor—a paper by a student in one of his classes.
9. New owners of a stereo—instructions on how to set up the equipment.
10. A stockbroker—the listing of prices of stock on the New York Stock Exchange in the local newspaper.

What Should the Audience Be Able To Do After Reading the Argument?

When you write, you should ask yourself if you expect your readers simply to agree with your argument, or if you expect them to take some action based on their agreement. If you were trying to convince readers that stray dogs on campus are a problem, you should give evidence of the seriousness of the situation, such as raided garbage cans or vicious dogs. If you want your audience not simply to agree that there is a problem but also to take action to solve the problem, you must include specific steps they can take, such as writing letters to the college's president and reporting stray dogs to the campus safety patrol. You should also convince your readers that their taking these actions will probably have the desired consequences: the college's president will take steps to solve the problem, and the campus safety patrol will follow up on reports of stray dogs. Arguments that end with a request for action on the part of the reader should be specific about the proposed action, show the connection between the argument and the proposed action, and convince the reader that the action will lead, or at least probably lead, to the desired changes.

Your expectations of the readers largely determine the tone of your writing. If you intend to convince gently, the tone can be mild: "The citizens of this community need to consider an alternative to the property tax as a way of raising money for education." If you intend to exhort, the tone should be more forceful, as in Winston Churchill's famous address to the British people in their darkest days of World War Two: ". . . we shall fight on the beaches, we shall fight on the landing grounds, we shall fight in the fields and in the streets, we shall fight in the hills." If you intend to command, you can be very blunt: "No smoking is allowed in the computer room. Those caught smoking there will be asked to leave and will have their right to use the room suspended for two weeks."

Activities (2.4)

For each of the passages below, identify the main purpose of the passage: to inform, to entertain, to instruct the reader in how to perform a specific action, or to request the reader to consider some issue of social, cultural, or philosophical importance. If the passage seems to combine two or more purposes, which purpose is predominant? Write a one-page essay discussing your analysis of these four passages.

1. BEIRUT, Lebanon—Three Egyptian Embassy staff feared kidnapped by gunmen in west Beirut today have turned up safe, an Egyptian spokesman said.

   Police said the embassy had told them the men were dragged at gunpoint from a taxi near the seafront in broad daylight.

   The spokesman said the three, all Egyptian nationals, returned safely to the Egyptian Interests Section at the French Embassy.

2. Mistakes enliven American life. Some, of course, are caused by pomposity and make those responsible for them appear ludicrous. About others there is an innocence that it would be a shame to lose. In arguing for a civil tongue, I am arguing for naturalness, even when it leads to mistakes. There is no reason that naturalness cannot be joined to correctness, but even when it isn't, clarity and genuineness can come together. More than this, we Americans don't have as much fun as we could with English. The fun is there to be had, but it requires some knowledge (which need not be formal), some imagina-

tion, and a sense of delight in what language can do. (Edwin Newman, *A Civil Tongue*, pp. 280–281)

3. We recommend the following:
   a. A thorough inventory should be conducted by the warehouse staff.
   b. This inventory should be overseen by external auditors.
   c. The results of the inventory should be sent to management.
4. It is one of the blessings of old friends that you can afford to be stupid with them. (Ralph Waldo Emerson, *Emerson in his Journals*, p. 195)

SUMMARY

Where Writing Begins

- Dissonance—the mismatch between the way we want life to be and the way it is—can be a motive for effective arguments.
- When you write, try to write about what is important to you, expressing only those opinions you honestly believe in and avoiding pomposity.
- Before you write, consider these three questions:
  Who is the audience?
  Why will the audience read the argument?
  What should the audience be able to do after reading the argument?

Suggestions for Writing (2.5)

1. From your list of topics from Activity 2 at the end of the first section of this chapter, "Motives for Writing," select one of the topics and write a two-to-three-page essay proposing a solution to the problem that bothers you.
2. Write a two-to-three-page essay trying to convince a hostile audience of the appropriateness of a certain action. Two possibilities are writing to college students about an increase in tuition or writing to homeowners telling them that the road in front of their homes is going to be widened. You may think of some other possibility.
3. Examine the last report or essay that you wrote and write a two-to-three-page essay on who your audience was, why they would have read what you wrote, and what you expected them to do after they had finished reading. How well does that report or essay, when looked at in light of these questions, communicate with its intended audience? Are there any changes you would make in it now that you have looked carefully at these questions about audience?

4. Write a one-page essay to students in one of your classes evaluating the effectiveness of that class's instructor. Then write a one-page essay to the instructor about the same topic. Make a list of the differences in the two essays. (One possible structure for each essay is to begin with a thesis sentence and then support it with two brief paragraphs.)

5. Write a two-to-three page evaluation of a speech you have heard given by a politician or other public official. Who is the audience for the speech? Why would the audience listen to the speech? How does the speaker appeal to this audience? What does the speaker want the audience to do after hearing the speech? How effective do you believe the speaker was in achieving this goal? If it is possible to obtain a printed transcript of the speech, give your instructor a copy of it.

Chapter 3

Focusing Your Position:
Theses and Definitions

Having discovered a motive to argue from and identified an audience to address, you are ready to begin focusing your argument. Every step in the writing process—from discovering a motive to revising a final draft—should sharpen the focus of your argument. This chapter covers two critical points in the focusing process: formulating your thesis and defining your terms.

Some writers do not write a word before devising a thesis; others let their theses evolve during an exploratory first draft, focusing and modifying as they write. But whether you come to your thesis early or late in the writing process, your argument is not sufficiently focused until you can succinctly summarize its principal claim or claims. The first part of this chapter discusses the processes of formulating, modifying, and positioning a thesis statement.

Clarifying your argument's central terms—both to yourself and your readers—is a way of sharpening your argument to a fine point. You can only argue your thesis effectively when you are certain of its meaning and clear about the territory cut out by your terms; your readers cannot be moved by your writing unless they too are certain about the meaning of critical words and concepts. Knowing when and how to *define* your terms contributes to a well-focused, thus effective, argument. The second part of this chapter will address these issues of definition.

THE THESIS

The *thesis* of a manifest argument is a short summary of the argument's central proposition. All manifest arguments have at least one thesis, and some longer arguments more than one. Usually, the thesis is stated directly, but occasionally it is only implied by the material chosen to support it. Regardless of its placement within the argument, regardless even of whether it appears at all, the thesis informs and propels the argument, giving it energy and structure.

Theses (or thesis statements) can be short and highly condensed, as in the statement "America's youth is becoming insular and self-absorbed"; or they can be long and intricate, reflecting the structure of the entire argument: "Because a capitalist system rewards aggressiveness, competitiveness and intelligence, offering little recompense to the timid and the weak, it is an almost perfect economic extension of Darwinism. In a capitalist society, the 'fittest' get rich, the unfit stay poor."

Because it summarizes the argument's central point, a thesis statement can be extremely useful to readers. Whatever their levels of interest, knowledge, and intelligence, all readers approach an unfamiliar manuscript ignorant of its content and direction. An unequivocal, succinct statement of a document's chief point or points alerts readers to the goal of the argument and equips them to understand the relationship of the parts to the whole.

A good thesis statement also helps readers evaluate an argument. Knowing exactly what central point a writer has intended to make, readers can judge whether the point has been made successfully. A thesis such as "The United States should not attempt to protect dying industries with high tariffs" provides a benchmark against which readers can judge the supporting argument, but a thesis such as "Free trade has a role in international commerce" is too vague, too unfocused to serve as a meaningful benchmark.

While theses can be discovered or changed at virtually any point in the first draft, formulating a tentative, working thesis early in the process can help you generate ideas, focus your writing, and direct your structure. A preliminary thesis will determine the kinds of evidence you will need to support your argument, and it will serve as guide and reminder about the content of the argument, its organization, and its ultimate direction.

Generating a Thesis

For inexperienced writers, the most critical question about the thesis is, "Where does it come from?" Writers who do not feel they have a wealth of ideas and experiences to draw from are often very insecure about coming up with an arguable position. Unfortunately, thesis statements rarely spring fully polished from the brain at the touch of some magical switch; more frequently they evolve gradually from the writers' early reading and thinking about the subject or from their own vague discomfort with a particular situation or issue.

Sometimes the invention process can be short-circuited. In some situations, theses are actually assigned. Students in beginning college writing courses are often assigned a particular thesis to develop ("Write a two-page essay supporting your view of the effectiveness of student orientation at this college"). Essay examinations can offer students at least the germ of a full-blown thesis statement. For example, the question "Was the dropping of the atom bomb in August of 1945 on Nagasaki and Hiroshima necessary to achieve Japan's surrender? Support your answer with specific reasons" dictates the rough form, though not the content, of the thesis that will begin the answer: "The dropping of the bomb was/was not necessary for the following reasons."

Some writers, moved to argue a position that they strongly believe in, come to their work with their main point already firmly set in their minds. Yet the passion of their initial conviction can prevent them from reasonably examining the evidence for and against their position. In Chapter 2 we noted the value of dissonance in giving writers a starting point for their writing, but strong feelings about a subject do have a certain risk. Writers who begin an argument in the white heat of commitment to some unscrutinized position can blind themselves to its weaknesses or to the strength of its opposition. They would be wise to treat such a preconceived thesis as tentative, as a guide to the preliminary research and thinking. Such a tentative thesis, or hypothesis, serves as a starting point, a basis for further investigation; it is flexible, even expendable in the face of contradictory material.

Many arguments originate in a vague topic and little direction about specific conclusions to be reached. A literature student asked to write a fifteen-page analysis of the early poetry of William Wordsworth is almost certainly going to begin with little focus or sense of purpose. And a new employee asked to evaluate the product quality and cost effectiveness of one of a company's suppliers would probably be equally adrift.

In cases such as these, how do writers move from a vague assignment to a working thesis that will give the evolving argument some direction and discipline? There are many answers to this question, because generating a thesis or position—indeed, the entire writing process—is a highly idiosyncratic process. Some writers logically deduce a thesis from the evidence in Sherlock Holmes fashion, while others have their thesis come to them unexpectedly while daydreaming or jogging or listening to music. Theses can be slowly and painfully dredged from the earth or they can come like lightning from the sky. Either kind of thesis can be sound, provided it can be convincingly and reasonably supported.

For those times when you have difficulty arriving at a thesis, we offer these three suggestions:

1. Don't press to arrive at a thesis prematurely. More time is wasted following up a forced, dead-end thesis that eventually has to be scrapped than thinking, reading, and taking notes as preparation for deciding exactly what your position is going to be.

2. Instead of rushing the thesis during the preliminary research phase (and research can mean nothing more than tapping the contents of your own brain without ever opening a book), concentrate instead on gradually narrowing your topic. For example, if you're preparing to write the paper on the poetry of

Wordsworth, your research might lead you originally (and accidentally) in the direction of thematic content, then to the narrower concern of images of nature, then still more narrowly to the recollection of nature as an inspiration to poetry. By the time you have gathered material on this focused subject, you will not be far from imposing a particular point of view on the subject. This point of view on a focused topic will be your thesis, which might be something like "Wordsworth as a poet was inspired by nature, but nature sifted through memory, not nature as it is immediately perceived." While you may have accumulated a lot of seemingly useless notes along the way, you should be saved the agony of distorting your paper to fit an unworkable thesis hit upon with too little consideration. As you are closing in on a thesis, keep in mind that good thesis statements are rarely too narrow; poor ones are often too broad.

3. In the early stages of writing, don't spend too much time polishing and refining your thesis statement. At this stage a thesis needs a narrow topic and the expression of a definite attitude toward that topic. A good working thesis could be no more than "Smoking in public places is harmful to everyone." Later, after the first draft, you can refine and shine, adding a summary of supporting reasons, if necessary.

Keeping Your Working Thesis Flexible

As you proceed with a rough draft that works from a tentative, working thesis, you may discover that the preliminary thesis needs modification. Perhaps the thinking and research you have done on the subject have made you realize that your thesis does not apply as widely as you thought, that there are significant exceptions to your position. Be flexible enough to accept these discoveries and change your thesis accordingly. Writing is not simply the recording of previously established thoughts but also a way of clarifying your thoughts, of discovering if what you meant to say can be said in a coherent and defensible way. Take advantage of the guiding service offered by a thoughtful thesis statement, while remaining open to those discoveries to which writing and thinking can lead you.

Let's say you begin the composition process with a thesis that arises easily out of your own strong opinions about the issue of affirmative action. Your preliminary or working thesis is "Jobs should be given to the most qualified applicant, not to the most qualified minority applicant. To reject the best candidate on the grounds of his or her majority status is unjust and inequitable." This thesis statement summarizes not only your position against affirmative action, but also points to the main support for that position—that affirmative action is unjust and inequitable. In order to argue your thesis convincingly, to convince your audience that one's minority or majority status is irrelevant to considerations of merit, you will need to demonstrate the injustices of affirmative action.

So far, so good, you think. Even though you aren't personally aware of a wide range of cases, it should be easy to come up with examples of the basic unfairness of affirmative action. In the course of your reading, however, you keep coming up against the stubborn argument that majority candidates are often more qualified for jobs and educational opportunities because they have had far more educational and economic privilege than members of minority groups. To reward the most qualified, this argument continues, is to perpetuate this tradition of unequal opportunity. You find this position persuasive and reasonable, though it doesn't change your central view that qualifications, not race, should determine one's success in the job market. Gradually, you realize that this is a more complicated issue than you had recognized; a hardline position is not completely defensible.

You consider ignoring the counter-argument and sticking to your original thesis, but you conclude that your argument will actually be stronger if it refects the ethical complexity of the issue and your awareness of the unfair advantage long given to the majority group. So you rewrite your working thesis to read "Although affirmative action laws were designed to redress the tradition of unequal educational and economic opportunities, they are not the ideal answer to the problem. Hiring on the basis of race and gender with secondary consideration to qualifications is unfair; only the victims of inequity have changed." This new working thesis is richer and more balanced than the first, reflecting your new understanding of the issue as well as your continuing disagreement with affirmative action laws.

The primary lesson to be learned from this example is that working theses should be seen as starting points, not as immutable conclusions; the thinking and writing processes will inevitably influence the starting point of an argument, shaping and modifying and in some cases even reversing the original position. Your final argument will benefit if you remain flexible about the original thesis, being prepared to alter it in the face of contrary evidence or new ideas.

Activities (3.1)

For five of the following topics, first narrow the topic to one that could be dealt with in a seven-to-ten-page essay; then from that topic derive a working thesis for such a paper. Your working thesis is the thesis with which you would begin to write your essay, though it may be refined or changed as you write. Example: topic: the risks of cigarette smoking; narrower topic: the health effects of cigarette smoking in public places; working thesis: Cigarette smoking in public places is harmful to everyone.

1. Japanese automobiles.
2. Jogging.
3. Women's rights.
4. College education.

5. Television.
6. Central America.
7. Presidential elections.
8. New York City.
9. Careers.
10. Popular music.

POSITIONING THE THESIS

Another crucial decision you will have to make about your thesis is where to place it in your argument. This decision can be made at any time—before you write a paragraph or after the first draft is completed and the exact thesis determined. It is a decision that should be thoughtfully made, because the position of your thesis can influence your audience's reaction to the entire argument.

Theses appear most commonly in the early part of arguments, but there are perfectly legitimate reasons for placing them elsewhere. A thesis placed at the beginning of the argument can have a very different effect from one delayed until the conclusion. The points to consider as you are determining the best placement for your thesis are the function of the thesis and your audience's probable attitude toward your argument. In the following paragraphs, we offer some guidelines (please do not mistake them for inflexible rules) for placing your thesis.

Thesis Stated in the Introduction

Theses are often contained within an argument's introduction, usually for the sake of clarity. If your argument is likely to be difficult for your readers—complicated or highly specialized—placing the thesis early in the argument will help them follow the paths of your reasoning. Theses are also commonly placed within introductions when the proposition is one with which readers will be comfortable, one that will not alienate them from the argument at the outset. A thesis that will seem especially curious or intriguing to readers, so long as it is not immediately objectionable, can be placed early in the writing to lure them into the argument.

In the following essay on vice presidential politics, Michael Oreskes states his argument's major claim—an intriguing correction of the common understanding of the function of the vice presidential office—immediately after his introduction:

> In selecting a running mate, Barry Goldwater once explained, a Presidential nominee has one objective: "To get more votes."
>
> Any day now, Michael S. Dukakis will select his running mate and then present

him (there are apparently no women on the list) to the Democratic Convention when it convenes here next week. Vice President Bush will study the Massachusetts Governor's choice and then make his own selection.

They will pronounce profoundly that their principal objective was to select someone who would be ready from Day One to be President. They will probably even mean this when they say it, both being the sort of politicians who actually have an interest in government.

But the reality . . . is that the Vice President's purpose is not so much to succeed the President as to help him succeed at *becoming* President [emphasis added].

Thesis Stated at the End of Argument

Delaying the thesis statement until the end of the argument can be effective, particularly when readers are likely to find the thesis objectionable. If readers are presented with strong support for a position before they realize exactly what that position is, they will be less likely to reject the thesis once it is stated; they will have been exposed to the evidence before their defenses are raised. An argument recommending a course of action unwelcome to readers might first present all the current problems, concluding with the recommendation for change (the thesis). Convinced of the seriousness of the problems, readers will be more likely to accept a writer's recommendation, even though unwelcome.

When the evidence for your argument builds directly and inevitably toward your thesis, with no detours or missed steps, you might consider letting your thesis statement serve as the argument's conclusion. A causal argument identifying the chronological chain of causes producing a given effect might reveal the chain link by link, starting with the effect and moving backward, or starting with the first identifiable link and moving forward. Only after the final link has been identified would the thesis appear. It might read:

> Mid-life psychological crises do not erupt from nowhere. As our hypothetical case reveals, they result from a long series of inefficient steps an individual takes to avoid pain or loss suffered in early childhood. But with each attempt to avoid a reenactment of early loss, the individual only perpetuates that loss, until finally the coping system breaks down and the original pain must be faced and accepted.

In Chapter 12, which contains a discussion of the central principles of traditional logic, we will introduce the sequential steps of reasoning required for deductive and inductive reasoning. In both *deductive* logic (moving from general facts to particular conclusions) and *inductive* logic (moving from particular facts to general conclusions), conclusions *follow* preliminary assertions; they do not precede these assertions. If you are writing an argument that recognizably fits these patterns of reasoning (for example, in induction, $a + a + a + a + a = b$), you can present the argument according to that pattern, with the conclusion (or thesis) at the end.

Other Placements of the Thesis

A thesis can be placed virtually anywhere in an argument, provided you have a good reason for that placement, one that is based upon your readers' probable reception of the thesis and of the argument as a whole. If your argument requires you to provide considerable background information to your readers—a long history of the problem of toxic waste, for example—you might delay your thesis statement until you have provided all the necessary background information. Or, in another argument, you might choose to lead up to your thesis statement with your most persuasive and logical support, then move from the thesis to a discussion of its significance (which, in fact, would constitute a *secondary argument*—an interpretation of your position).

Unstated Thesis in a Manifest Argument

On rare occasions, you can strengthen your argument by omitting your thesis altogether. If a bold statement of your position would be so shocking or unacceptable to your readers that they would refuse to consider any of your evidence, then you would be wise to leave it out, supplying instead clear statements of the individual pieces of evidence that might gently lead your readers into the vicinity of your unstated proposition. If you wished to convince homeowners of the need for increased commercial zoning in their quiet residential town, you might focus on the current financial difficulties of that town, discussing the advantage to homeowners of an increased tax base. It is likely that they would agree with such a position, but would see red at the mention of rezoning.

A word of caution about omitted theses: make sure you have a very good reason for using this tactic. Arguments lacking an identifiable position statement are often ineffective because they seem to lack a point and structure.

Activities (3.2)

For two of the following, consider where in the argument the thesis statement could be effectively placed. Then write a paragraph justifying your choice.

1. Thesis: Dog owners should receive tax credits for neutering their dogs.
   Audience: subscribers to *Dog World Magazine*.
2. Thesis: Despite his enormous popularity with students, Coach Stern's consistently poor record warrants his immediate dismissal.
   Audience: students with whom Coach Stern is enormously popular.

3. Thesis: As the evidence demonstrates, ant colonies are enormously well organized systems in which the good of the whole always takes precedence over the good of the individual.
   Audience: undergraduate biology students.

4. Thesis: John Locke, like his predecessor Hobbes, understood human knowledge, however complex, to derive from the basic knowledge originating in experience, in sensation.
   Audience: undergraduate philosophy students. (From Art Berman, *From the New Criticism to Deconstruction*, University of Illinois Press, 1988, p. 13).

5. Thesis: Because all the women I know are more interested in personal relationships than any of the men I know, I conclude that women in general attach greater importance to relationships then do men.
   Audience: male readers.

DEFINING YOUR TERMS

As the concise statement of your argument's central position, your thesis cannot afford to be vague or obscure. If readers have only a fuzzy sense of *what* you are arguing, they aren't likely to find the execution of your argument meaningful or effective. As you draft, modify, and position your thesis, make sure that all its terms, as well as its overall meaning, will be clear to your audience.

The importance of clarity, of course, does not stop with the thesis statement. Any term or concept in your argument that has the slightest chance of being misunderstood by your readers should be carefully defined. Since your readers can only agree with your argument if they understand it, you must ensure that understanding by defining any potentially puzzling terms. You do not want to leave readers guessing your meaning, because they may guess the wrong meaning or may simply be annoyed and refuse even to guess. If you are in doubt about whether to define a term, define it.

The following types of language, whether in your thesis or in the body of your argument, need clarification through definition:

1. Unfamiliar terminology. Any specialized or unusual terms that could be unfamiliar to your readers must be explained. If it is unlikely that your readers have heard of Maxwell's Demon, define it.

2. Nonspecific language. In general, avoid vague, fuzzy terms, particularly in statements of evaluation and measurement. If you claim that "Ajax Motors is the world's largest corporation," consider how little that statement tells the reader. In what way or ways is Ajax the largest? Does it have the most employees? Earn the most income? Have the highest profits? A more specific statement, such as "Few people realize it, but Ajax Motors now employs more people than any other corporation in the world," is far more useful to the reader. When you do use such nonspecific words as "poor," "excellent," "talented," "large," "grand," or

"minimal," make sure you explain the meaning of your modifier as precisely as possible. If you call someone a talented artist, define your use of "talented." (We discuss the importance of defining evaluative terms more fully in Chapter 10.)

Types of Definitions

Terms requiring clarification can be defined briefly or extensively, depending on the needs of your audience and the importance of a particular term to your argument. The three types of definition you will use most commonly are the shorthand definition, the sentence definition, and the extended definition.

Writers often resort to shorthand definitions when the term in question requires only a quick explanation. A *shorthand* definition explains an unfamiliar term with a more familiar one, as in the following example: "Acetylsalicylic acid (aspirin) is an effective medicine for most headaches."

A *sentence* definition, similar to a dictionary definition but written as a grammatical sentence, consists of the term to be defined (the *species*), the general category to which it belongs (the *genus*), and those characteristics that distinguish it from all other members of that general category (the *differentiae*). A sentence definition has the following structure:

SPECIES = GENUS + DIFFERENTIAE

An example of this form of definition is "A heifer is a young cow that has not borne a calf." In terms of the structure just described, the sentence definition works in this fashion:

HEIFER = YOUNG COW + THAT HAS NOT BORNE A CALF
SPECIES = GENUS   + DIFFERENTIAE

Sentence definitions need to be tight and specific: the genus and differentiae should point to only one species, the species you are defining. If a heifer is the only species that qualifies as a young cow that has not borne a calf, your definition is good. But if the definition read "A heifer is a young cow," it would be too broad because it would include all young cows, regardless of their maternal status. Always try to keep your genus limited; otherwise, no amount of differentiae will distinguish the species from other members of the same class or genus.

An *extended* definition includes this basic sentence definition, but it can include any additional material that would help a reader understand the term being defined. Some elements found in extended definitions are: the history of what is being defined, a comparison and contrast with objects or concepts similar to it, a discussion of its uses or its social significance, a negative definition (statement of what the term is *not*), and an analysis of the parts that constitute it. The following passage is an example of the kind of elements found within extended definitions:

> **Expansion of matter** is the increase in size of a body, be it a solid, a liquid, or a gas, when it is heated. It is an effect which is used in many devices, particularly in those which measure or regulate temperature. For example, the expansion of a liquid is used in the mercury thermometer and the expansion of a solid is the basic mechanism in many thermostats. The expansion of a gas is used in a hot air balloon. When the gas in the balloon is heated it expands and thus becomes less dense than the cooler air outside; hence the hot gas rises, bearing the balloon with it. However, although such uses can be made of thermal expansion, it can also cause problems; and the effects of expansion must always be considered in the design of any object which is going to operate over a range of temperatures.
>
> Uniquely among liquids, water exhibits a strange and exceedingly important behaviour: between 0 and 4°C (32 and 39°F) it contracts on heating; only above 4°C (39°F) does it start to expand. This means that when it is cooled below 4°C it expands, becoming less dense than less cold water and so floating on top of it. The expansion continues until the top layer of water freezes; and it is for this reason that ice always first forms on the surface of water, protecting to some extent the water beneath it, and then extends downwards, whereas in all other liquids it forms from the bottom.

This extended definition, taken from the *Oxford Illustrated Encyclopedia*, includes a sentence definition, examples of uses of this characteristic of matter, and a contrast between the behavior of water and that of other liquids. Other extended definitions could work in very different ways.

A *stipulative* definition is one that for the purposes of a particular argument restricts the meaning of a term to one of the term's possible meanings. Stipulative definitions can be found as sentence, extended, or shorthand definitions. Any term with several possible meanings can be given a stipulative definition: "In this essay I want to discuss politics: not the politics of public life— executives, legislatures, elections, laws, and courts—but the politics of power relations in our jobs, what most of us call 'office politics.' " In this sentence, the writer restricts the meaning of "politics" to the meaning needed for the essay.

Stipulative definitions should normally be given for words that are very general or vague, including adjectives like "artistic," "human," "natural," "realistic" or "classic" and nouns like "freedom," "democracy," and "socialism." All of us use at least some of these very frequently in speech and rarely bother to define them, but successful written arguments demand more precision than everyday conversation, partly because there is no speaker present to clarify meaning to the audience. Giving a stipulative definition also helps writers be sure that they know what they are talking about. For example, if a writer wants to claim that Walt Whitman is more "human" as a poet than T.S. Eliot, "human" must be defined precisely enough to be useful to the writer's argument.

Activities (3.3)

1. Examine an extended definition in an encyclopedia, reference guide, or text-book, and write a one-to-two-page essay that describes what elements (sentence definition, samples, history of the object or concept being defined, comparison or contrast, and so on) have been included in the definition and speculates on why they have been included. Are there other elements that you believe should have been included to help the definition? Are there any elements that could have been omitted?

2. Write a paragraph giving a stipulative definition of one of the following: "love," "friendship," "science," "classical." Then write a formal sentence definition that encapsulates your stipulative definition.

SUMMARY

Focusing Your Position

- Thesis statements help readers understand and evaluate manifest arguments, and they help you, the writer, generate the direction and content of your arguments.

- If you have difficulties coming up with a working thesis, you probably need to do more thinking and reading about your topic. When you are knowledgeable enough, a thesis should come to you.

- Always be prepared to modify a working thesis to fit with new ideas and information.

- Theses can be placed virtually anywhere in a manifest argument. The most effective placement depends on the nature of your argument and its probable reception by readers.

- Any terms in your thesis or the body of your argument likely to be unfamiliar to your readers should be defined by a sentence definition, an extended definition, or a shorthand definition.

- Stipulative definitions, which restrict the meaning of a term to one of the term's possible meanings, should be given for general or vague terms.

Suggestions for Writing (3.4)

1. Take one of the following vague or overused theses and turn it into an interesting thesis with fresh and precise language. Then write a two-to-three-page essay to support this new thesis. As you develop support for your argument, you may have to modify the thesis so that it will fit your support.

    a. Waste not, want not.
    b. Children are not as respectful of their elders as they should be.
    c. America must remain the strongest power in the world.
    d. A little learning is a dangerous thing.
    e. Meryl Streep (or someone else) is a talented actress.

2. Write a two-to-three-page essay that is an extended definition of some concept or object, making sure that your definition also includes a formal sentence definition. Your instructor may have suggestions for this assignment, but we also suggest one of the following: academic freedom; moral relativism; cybernetics; entropy; or feminism.

Chapter 4

The Classes of Manifest Argument

The goal of all manifest arguments is to gain a reader's agreement with the argument's thesis or theses. Yet arguments differ in terms of the level of agreement sought and the means used to achieve that agreement. An argument that Pittsburgh, Pennsylvania grew to be a major metropolis because of its geographical location is very different from an argument that Rembrandt is a greater painter than Rubens. The first argument would rely heavily on factual evidence, while the second would depend, at least in part, on the personal taste of a reader. If carefully made, the first argument could convince virtually any reader, but the second, no matter how reasonable, could not expect such unanimous agreement.

Manifest arguments can be classified according to what you are arguing and how much agreement you expect of your audience. The four most common types, or classes, of arguments are (1) factual arguments; (2) causal arguments; (3) practical recommendations; and (4) evaluations. Knowing what class of argument you wish to write will help you determine the best support for your working thesis. In this chapter we introduce these four classes of argument and give examples of typical thesis statements for each class.

FACTUAL ARGUMENTS

Factual arguments seek to convince an audience that a certain proposition is factual—that a given condition or phenomenon exists or has existed. The fact can be as basic as "Despite appearances, the sun is the center of our solar system, not the earth," or as little known as "Bats find their way in the dark by using their own sonar system." Writers of these arguments would expect their audience to accept their claims as true, although perhaps not as true forever and under all circumstances—in the Middle Ages it was a "fact" that the earth was the center of the solar system—but as true given our current knowledge and the context assumed by the readers and writers.

The concept of arguing a fact may seem a contradiction in terms. You probably think of facts as true and immutable statements about reality, not as provisional propositions requiring support and verification. If it's a fact, why argue it? But a fact only becomes a fact if it is adequately verified, if evidence is presented that proves its existence. Because facts become the cornerstones of so much of what we know and expect about the world, we must subject factual propositions to rigorous scrutiny. We cannot afford to accept on faith statements paraded as facts. In more cases than you realize, facts require verification—sometimes brief, sometimes extensive.

Facts are crucial to argument; indeed, an argument cannot succeed without some reference to fact. In the arguments that you will write, facts will play three roles. Sometimes they will appear as the central thesis of an argument, as in a laboratory write-up reporting that "The addition of sulfur to the compound created sulfuric acid," in an essay exam requiring you to explain the concept of the Consumer Price Index, or in an annual sales report claiming that sales have increased 125% in the last year.

More frequently, facts will function as support for other theses, as secondary theses for a thesis of the same or different class. A general claim such as "All the teachers in the Wildwinds Day Care Center have experience working with preschool children" would be supported by facts about the particular experience of each teacher. In this supporting role, facts are subject to the same principles of verification that apply to facts as central theses.

Facts are extremely useful as examples or illustrations of difficult, unfamiliar, or abstract concepts. In this role, they do not so much prove a point as clarify it. A writer might explain or illustrate the concept that modern physics views time as related to space and the motion of an object through space by offering the fact that a clock in a rapidly moving spaceship actually moves more slowly than a clock on the earth. Concrete facts such as this give a reader a great psychological boost, because they create a comfortable, familiar footing. As with the other uses of facts, illustrative facts must be verified or at least verifiable.

The four types of facts that will figure most commonly in your arguments are (1) common knowledge facts; (2) personally experienced facts; (3) facts reported by others; and (4) factual generalizations.

Common knowledge facts are so universally acknowledged as true that they require no support or proof beyond mere statement. "Men cannot bear children" is such a universally accepted fact, as is the statement "The winter season in Florida is milder than in Vermont."

Personally experienced facts are the events, observations, and conditions cited in your argument that you have personally experienced and thus have verified through that experience. In his essay "Ali: Still Magic," Peter Tauber supports his claim that former world heavyweight boxing champion Mohammed Ali remains strong and vigorous through such personal observations as the following:

> Walking down the driveway he slipped on a patch of ice and almost fell. But he didn't fall. Instead, without taking his hands out of his jacket pockets, he did a kind of modified Ali Shuffle, a quick two-step, and after a small hop, kicked one foot off a flower bed's retaining wall until he was on dry paving. He turned around without breaking stride, to warn me . . . "Careful—ice."

Often it is necessary to bring into an argument facts that do not arise out of your own experience but that do not qualify as commonly acknowledged facts. Such material, *facts reported by others*, is obtained from second- or third-party sources. A second-party source would be the person who ascertained the fact—for example, your manager telling you that sales had declined 5 percent in the last quarter, or a written report containing that information. A third-party source would be a person or document containing facts ascertained by someone else—for example, a biology textbook describing some little-known facts about Darwin's work on the *Beagle.*

Factual generalizations are broad claims made about a large group or time-span. Any class of thesis can be stated as a generalization. A factual generalization claims that a certain condition is true for a large number of subjects or over a long period of time. Factual generalizations are not separate from the three types of facts just identified; any of these could be stated as a generalization, as in the personally experienced generalization "Most of my friends are interested in sports." In formal written argument, general claims must be supported, whether they are the central thesis or reinforcement for that thesis.

Representative Factual Theses

Thesis statements for factual arguments are likely to resemble the following typical examples:

1. New York City is the banking center of the United States.
2. Our solar system is approximately five billion years old.
3. Steel radial tires last longer than tires made with nylon.
4. A healthy diet must include 60 milligrams of vitamin C daily.

Activities (4.1)

1. For each of the factual propositions listed below, identify the category or categories of fact (common knowledge, personal experience, second or third party, generalization) in which the proposition belongs. Example: The Cuban Mis-

sile Crisis occurred in October, 1962. Second or third party for most students;
personal experience for older people.

   a. The disappearance of former Teamster's Union leader Jimmy Hoffa is still
unexplained.

   b. The risk of getting cancer is decreased by a high-fiber diet.

   c. My Communications professor routinely missed her 8:00 class.

   d. Alaska is the largest state in the United States.

   e. An apple a day keeps the doctor away.

   f. I get better grades on the papers I take the time to revise.

   g. Severe air pollution is dangerous for people suffering from lung diseases.

   h. Women under 30 have better driving records than men under 30.

   i. In 1980 Japan became the world's leading producer of automobiles.

   j. In Italy, people take more time to enjoy life than they do in the United
States.

2. Write a thesis for a factual argument on *three* of the following topics; then
develop each thesis into a paragraph: (1) comparative standards of living among
the countries of the world; (2) the popularity of soccer in the United States;
(3) the decline of the railroads as a means of passenger transportation in the
United States in the last forty years; (4) career expectations of women college
students; and (5) skyscrapers. Example thesis: "If you don't know much about
the Chicago skyline, you would probably guess that the world's tallest building is in New York. While the Empire State Building and the World Trade Center are the most well known examples of skyscrapers, the world's tallest
building is actually in Chicago. The Empire State Building is 1250 feet high,
the World Trade Center, 1350 feet high, but the Sears Tower in Chicago, at 1454
feet, is the tallest of the three."

CAUSAL ARGUMENTS

Causal arguments claim a causal link between two events or conditions.
They can argue that A caused B or, more speculatively, that A could cause B
at some future time. Statements such as "Excessive layers of management
have caused the decline of several large American corporations" or "High consumer spending will lead to greater inflation" are examples of this kind of
argument.

Most of us are drawn naturally to the activity of assigning cause. We witness
the careers of prominent public figures and wonder what factors account for
their phenomenal successes. We reflect on a great tragedy like the Holocaust
and want to know how such a thing could happen. We seek the reasons behind
events because we want assurance that the world is governed by certain principles, not simply by random chance. And identifying cause is almost always
instructive. If we know why a certain phenomenon came about, we have a reasonable hope of preventing that effect (if it was an unfortunate one) or of reproducing it (if it was a desirable one) in the future. Airline officials would want to
know what caused a plane crash in order to prevent similar crashes; a sales

manager would want to know what circumstances contributed to a dramatic growth in quarterly sales so the success could be reproduced in succeeding quarters.

In arguing an effect, that A could cause B at some future time, we predict a future occurrence on the basis of certain current or intended circumstances. Stockbrokers must be skillful in this form of argument, as they try to enhance and protect the interests of their clients by predicting market activity. Doctors focusing on *preventive* medicine regularly identify probable effects to their patients: "If you don't eliminate fatty food from your diet, you have a greater risk of heart attack." In business and industry, the long-term health of a corporation often depends on the prediction of future trends and their impact on the business. Eastman Kodak, for example, with its enormously successful traditional business of photographic products, must determine the probable future of photography in the face of competition from electronic imaging products like the camcorder and VCR.

Under carefully controlled scientific conditions, it is possible to identify cause and even to predict effect with such a high degree of certainty that the causality can be established as *factual*. Researchers have determined that smoking increases the risk of lung cancer and that lobar pneumonia is caused by the pneumococcus bacteria. But in the causal arguments that most of us make, arguments that revolve around human behavior—our actions, our successes and failures, our relations with others—certainty is virtually impossible. In these more speculative arguments, the best we can hope for is to establish *probable* cause or effect convincingly.

But because a position cannot be proven with certainty does not mean that it isn't worth arguing. Probable, reasonable positions are extremely sound bases for decisions and actions and are the goal of most of the arguments we write. If we allowed ourselves to be moved by certainty alone, our progress would be slow. Probability is not easy to achieve; in many cases, it requires more skill than establishing certainty in factual arguments. In the case of causal arguments, probable cause or effect cannot be established without an understanding of the many principles governing causality and the variety of supporting material that can be gathered for a causal argument. These principles will be discussed in Chapter 8.

Representative Causal Theses

Following are some examples of theses for arguments identifying probable cause or effect:

1. The decline of Great Britain as an economic power after World War Two was primarily caused by a lack of entrepreneurial spirit in British business leaders.

2. Sally would have gotten that job if she had written a better résumé.
3. America could probably learn a great deal from the Japanese system of education.
4. If he paid more attention to his appearance, John would have more friends and would be happier.
5. American colleges and universities would be better places if they placed more emphasis on informal contacts between students and faculty.

Activities (4.2)

1. For two of the following theses, write a paragraph on each explaining why you believe the thesis anticipates a speculative causal argument or a factual causal argument.
    a. If Abraham Lincoln had not been assassinated, he could have lessened the bitterness between the North and the South after the war.
    b. The widespread use of computers in business and industry will increase total employment, not decrease it.
    c. If it had not snowed, Ohio State could have defeated Michigan in that football game.
    d. For most automobiles, failure to change the oil at regular intervals will damage the engine.
    e. The decline in the percentage of the population attending organized religious activities has caused the rise in the crime rate in the last 40 years.
    f. The use of seat belts decreases the number of fatalities in automobile accidents.
    g. If newlyweds had more realistic expectations about marriage, there would be a decline in the divorce rate.
    h. The children of the affluent would be happier if they had to do more for themselves.
    i. Some cold medicines can cause drowsiness.
    j. The existence of nuclear weapons has prevented the outbreak of World War III.
2. Write a thesis for a causal argument for one of the following; then make a list of all the reasons you can think of that would convince a reader of the cause or effect you identify. Describe these reasons in a paragraph. (1) The cause of a particular war; (2) a team's victory or loss in a certain game; (3) a change in some aspect of the government's social or economic policy; (4) a change in exercise or dietary behavior; or (5) the cause of a person's career success or failure. Example of (3): "There would be fewer homeless people if the federal government increased its aid to cities." Reasons: Money could be used for low-income housing. Money could be used for training programs that would give the poor a means of self-support. Other countries that give substantial aid to cities do not have the problem with the homeless that we do.
    Then write a coherent paragraph giving your thesis and the reasons to support it.

PRACTICAL RECOMMENDATIONS

A common goal of argument is to convince an audience of the need for a particular change in existing circumstances. Some *practical recommendations* seek only to gain an audience's agreement with an idea or a decision, but others have a more practical purpose: they attempt to move an audience to a particular course of action or, more modestly, to convince an audience that a particular course of action should be taken by another person or group. A student in an English Composition course might write a paper calling for the lowering of the legal drinking age, or the same argument might be made in a letter to the editor of a newspaper or to one's congressional representative. A lab technician might write a memo to the supervisor suggesting the purchase of new, more efficient laboratory equipment. And an academic department chairperson might request from the dean an adjustment in the salaries of certain junior faculty. All these arguments are practical recommendations; they recommend that certain actions be taken or that certain new policies or alterations in existing policies be instituted.

Before determining the best type of support for your recommendation, you must identify the emphasis of the recommendation. All recommendations are to some extent concerned with the future, with what should be done at a later time, but implied in an argument of this type is also a judgment about present conditions. Writers almost always propose change because of dissatisfaction with a current situation. In arguing a practical recommendation, you must determine whether you want to concentrate on the current problem, or the improvements resulting from your recommendation, or whether you want to give present and future equal emphasis.

The main goal of recommendations emphasizing *present* conditions is to demonstrate that a current situation is problematic or unacceptable. Because their purpose is more to demonstrate *that* something needs to be done than *what* exactly that something is, they usually do not discuss a proposed change in any detail.

In writing recommendations emphasizing the probable *future* effects of the proposed change, you must do more than identify current problems: you must come up with a new plan, arguing convincingly that your recommendation is feasible and that it will produce desirable effects.

Recommendations with *equal* emphasis on present and future consider at some length what currently exists, what could exist, and what the results of the changes are likely to be.

Representative Theses for Practical Recommendations

Because arguments of practical recommendation argue for an action not currently in effect, words such as "should," "would," "must," "ought," "needs to be," "will," or "might" typically introduce these arguments.

Following are some sample theses for arguments of practical recommendations:

1. Mrs. Carlson's word processor must be replaced immediately. (emphasis on present)
2. We need more emphasis on science and math in our schools to prepare the next generation for a world of international economic competition. (emphasis on future)
3. The county would benefit from a redistribution of tax income. (emphasis on present and future)
4. The city must put a traffic light at that intersection where there have been three accidents in the last month. (emphasis on present)
5. The United States and other nations should explore Mars to increase our knowledge of the solar system. (emphasis on future)

Activities (4.3)

For two of the following situations, write two theses of practical recommendation, one focusing on current conditions and one on the results of recommended improvements. Example: taking a typing course. Thesis with a focus on current conditions: "I need to take a typing course because I can't use the word processor required in my English Composition course." Thesis with focus on future improvements: "I need to take a typing course so that I will be ready for the day when every office has its own word processor."

1. Replacing a television.
2. Requesting a new strict policy on noise in a dormitory.
3. Advocating a freeze on the research for and manufacturing of nuclear weapons.
4. Purchasing a new car to replace your or your family's current one.
5. Increasing the number of police in the most dangerous sections of a city.

EVALUATIONS

Factual arguments and practical recommendations are usually made in fairly formal contexts, as part of professional or academic assignments. But all of us regularly use this fourth kind of argument, known as *evaluations*—the argument that seeks agreement about a particular value judgment made by the writer. When we are arguing an evaluation, we are proposing our own personal judgment about a work of art, a policy, a person, an action, even another evaluation. Informal pronouncements of personal taste—"Your tie is ugly," "That restaurant serves the best chicken wings in town," "I enjoy playing basketball more than tennis"—come under the category of value judgments, although they are so purely subjective, so clearly a matter of personal taste, that there is little point in trying to argue them reasonably. We are all inclined to pass judgment on the world's passing show, and frequently we do not much care whether these judgments are taken seriously.

But when we do care about the impact of these judgments, when we want our opinions to influence others, we must understand how to argue judgments of value. In fact, many value judgments, while perhaps originating as unconsidered personal opinion, *can* be effectively and convincingly argued. Such assertions as "Pornography is an offense to all women" or "The government made major mistakes in trying to trade weapons for hostages," if they are serious, carefully considered judgments, could become useful and important arguments.

Because evaluations tend to work from very personal value systems, they are probably the hardest of all arguments to argue convincingly. It is extremely difficult to change someone's mind about an opinion or judgment. If your concluding judgment is reached by a responsible and reasonable presentation of evidence and if that judgment gains the sympathy of your audience, you will have argued the value judgment successfully, even if it does not change everyone's mind.

Virtually any subject can be evaluated—personal behavior, art, political candidates, automobiles, mortgages, training techniques. But despite the endless range of subjects, the terms in which we make evaluations usually fall into one of four main categories: ethical, aesthetic, functional, or interpretive.

Ethical evaluations judge behavior in terms of an ideal code of moral principles—principles of right and wrong, good and evil. The thesis "Hitler was an evil man" introduces an ethical evaluation. In ethical evaluations, we do not usually argue the definition of the principle by which we are judging a subject—good, evil, right, wrong; rather, we argue that a particular principle or term applies or doesn't apply to a given subject. We would assume agreement about the term "evil" and demonstrate the ways in which the term applies to Hitler.

Aesthetic evaluations make a judgment about a work of art, such as a poem, an opera, or a film: "Sarah Rossiter's novel *The Human Season* is an impressive first novel." While changing aesthetic tastes or opinions is difficult, convincing an audience to appreciate the strengths or weaknesses of a work of art by gaining a greater understanding of it is a feasible and worthy task.

Functional evaluations consider how well a subject performs or functions. The subject can be an individual, in which case we are considering how skilled or effective the person is in a certain role or activity ("Former Secretary of State Henry Kissinger was a brilliant negotiator") or how an object or mechanism performs certain functions ("Nikon makes high-quality cameras"). These evaluations are concerned with practical measurements of function, not with ethical or aesthetic considerations.

Particularly common to college writing assignments, *interpretive* evaluations are explanatory evaluations of a person, event, or object: "The key to Hamlet's character is his Oedipal obsession with his mother"; "Richard Nixon's presidency was destroyed by his inferiority complex." None of these statements is simply factual or descriptive; each gives us a particular explanation of what happened beneath the surface.

None of these statements is verifiable through scientific experiment; they originate in the subjective, particular point of view of one individual, and they can surpass mere opinion only by being supported by facts and reasoned argument. Reasonable, intelligent people can vary in their interpretation of a certain situation, such as the key to Hamlet's behavior in Shakespeare's play, but not all interpretations are equally plausible or illuminating. To argue, for example, that gout explains much of Hamlet's behavior when there is no evidence to support that view is an example of very poor interpretation.

Interpretations are close to arguments identifying probable cause or effect, our second category of arguments, because neither is scientifically verifiable. The major difference is that causal speculations treat an expanse of time, typically from the past to the present, while interpretation focuses on the present. A statement such as "South Africa has reached a crisis because of its apartheid policies" is an example of causal speculation because the statement attempts to explain the causes for the situation in South Africa. The statement "South Africa's apartheid policy is on the verge of collapse" is an example of interpretation because of its emphasis on unfolding the inner reality of the present situation. The dividing line between the two is very fine, however, because interpretation often involves some causal speculation—in the example above perhaps an examination of the roots of apartheid—and causal explanation usually involves some interpretation, such as the view that South Africa is indeed in a state of crisis. You do not have to worry about these fine distinctions, but you need to support adequately either kind of statement.

Representative Evaluative Theses

Thesis statements for evaluations are likely to resemble the following representative theses:

1. The expensive German cars are not as mechanically exceptional as most people assume. (performance evaluation)
2. Many people do not realize that Herman Melville, the author of *Moby Dick*, was also an accomplished poet. (aesthetic evaluation)

3. Former President Jimmy Carter may not have been a great president, but he is an honorable man. (performance and ethical evaluations)

4. Even though our team lost in the final round of playoffs, we have the consolation of knowing that we played a clean, fair game. (performance and ethical evaluation)

5. Mary's constant chatter is an attempt to keep people from abandoning her. (interpretation)

Activities (4.4)

1. Write theses for evaluative arguments for two of the following subjects. Example subject: theft of library books. Example thesis: "The theft of library books is a serious offense not only because stealing is wrong but because the theft of books dramatically increases library costs and deprives other readers of material that is often difficult or impossible to replace."
   a. Military retaliation against terrorism.
   b. Compact disc players.
   c. Pass-fail grading for courses.
   d. Television shows.
   e. The legal drinking age.
   f. Fuel-injected automobile engines.
   g. Teenage pregnancy.
   h. The performance of your student government president.

2. Give an example of an interpretive statement for two of the following topics. Example of topic (a): "The popularity of the film *Platoon* means that Americans are finally coming to grips with both the heroism and the tragedy of America's involvement in Vietnam."
   a. The significance of a play, movie, or short story.
   b. The importance of some contemporary political figure.
   c. The meaning of a current trend in music or fashion.
   d. The attitude of students at a particular college or university toward their future careers.
   e. The attitude of young Americans toward religion.

COMBINATION THESES

Professional writing is full of arguments that do not appear to resemble any of the examples we have presented. As a writer of arguments, you may suspect that there is only a distant relationship between our neat classification of arguments according to function and the cluttered situation you find yourself in when writing. While you may find yourself basing an argument on a thesis statement that bears no resemblance to any of our examples, you should be aware that most theses fulfill one or more of these four functions.

Theses that at first do not appear to fit in any category can be recast so that their place among these four is evident. For example, the famous thesis "The only thing we have to fear is fear itself," which is a perfectly good, lively sentence needing no revision, can be translated to mean "avoid feeling too much fear, because it can paralyze you"—a practical recommendation based on an argument identifying a probable cause. You do not actually have to rewrite the thesis, but if you can discover this bolder, less graceful statement in your original thesis, you should have a clear idea of how to go on to support it.

Often, as this example demonstrates, the context of your thesis will help you categorize it. This quotation about fear is taken from President Franklin Delano Roosevelt's first inaugural address in 1933, in the heart of the Depression, when fear about the future pervaded America. In a less urgent context, "the only thing we have to fear is fear itself" might be an interpretive statement meaning "fear itself is a debilitating emotion apart from any real dangers that may have created the fear in the first place." In the context of Roosevelt's address, however, the remark is part of a broad recommendation to the American people to regain their confidence and begin to plan for the future with new hope.

Some thesis statements actually contain two theses, as in the sentence, "Acts of terrorism are serious offenses against human freedom and should meet with deadly retaliation." The first thesis is the *evaluation* that acts of terrorism are serious offenses, and the second is the *practical recommendation* that they should meet with deadly retaliation. In supporting these theses, you would first have to defend your value judgment that terrorism is a serious offense against human freedom before moving on to the second thesis. The second thesis is a practical recommendation—terrorism should meet with deadly retaliation—that is supported by another value judgment, namely, that retaliation is not only effective but also morally just. Ideally, both theses should be defended, though frequently writers assume that their audience agrees with them on most basic points—for example, terrorism is a flagrant offense and retaliation against it is just—and concentrate on one or two basic points, such as whether retaliation is effective in preventing future acts of terrorism.

Cutting corners in this fashion is frequently desirable because of limitations of space or the necessity of concentrating on just one aspect of a topic, but it can also lead to assuming too much, to thinking only what the crowd thinks. Writers who deal with such controversial topics as terrorism should at least *consider* such basic issues as whether retaliation is morally just, even if they do not write about it in their essays. Reviewing what will be assumed in an essay is one way writers can keep themselves honest.

Frequently, a thesis of fact is combined with one of the other three kinds of theses. When this is the case, as in the statement that "The rise in the divorce rate in the last twenty years may increase the divorce rate in the next generation," you must establish the accuracy of your facts (that the divorce rate has risen) before you go on to speculate about possible effects of this phenomenon. So too with the statement that "Increased credit spending by consumers is bad for the nation's political stability." First, the increased credit spending must be established as a fact, and then the value judgment can be argued.

Reality often escapes our categorizations of it, and theses are no exception. You need to know the different kinds of theses and what they usually look like, but you must be flexible and prepared for the unexpected. You must also be able to create the unexpected when that is needed in your own writing.

Representative Combination Theses

We include below some examples of combination theses:

1. The recent rise in interest rates may contribute to higher inflation. (arguments of fact and effect)
2. No nation is truly free that does not offer its citizens equal opportunity in education and employment. (evaluation and causal argument)
3. If the candidate wants to win votes, he must convince his constituents that his reputation for moral laxness is unwarranted. (practical recommendation, evaluation)
4. Professor Moriarty's lack of publications seriously weakened her chances for promotion. (factual and causal arguments)

Activities (4.5)

Into which of the four main argument types or combination of types do two of the following belong? Write a short paragraph supporting your answer in each case. Example: Automobiles should be designed so that they get a minimum of 30 miles per gallon of gasoline. Type of argument: practical recommendation.

1. Excessive consumption of alcohol can lead to many illnesses.
2. Honesty is the best policy.
3. Cutting defense spending will create a safer world.
4. Tariffs on imports merely raise prices for domestic consumers.
5. Alley cats are a public nuisance in this neighborhood.
6. Politics is the art of the possible.
7. An improved sewer system would solve these flood drainage problems.
8. America should protect its domestic industries with tariffs and quotas.
9. Without a belief in God, life has no meaning.
10. Obesity can help cause heart disease.

SUMMARY

The Classes of Manifest Argument

- The four most common classes of argument are (1) factual arguments; (2) causal arguments; (3) practical recommendations; and (4) evaluations.
- Factual arguments seek to convince an audience that a given object or condition exists or has existed.

  There are four kinds of facts: common knowledge facts; facts experienced by you; facts reported by others; and factual generalizations (which are based on the other kinds of facts).
- Causal arguments claim that one event or condition produces or helps to produce another event or condition.

  In arguing cause, we look for what produced a past or current event or condition.

  In arguing effect, we predict a future occurrence on the basis of certain current or intended circumstances.
- Practical recommendations argue for a particular course of action in order to change existing circumstances.

  Practical recommendations can focus on either present conditions or future effects or a combination of both.
- Evaluations make a value judgment of a person, activity, or object.

  There are four basic types of evaluations: ethical; aesthetic; functional; and interpretive.
- Some arguments and their theses (if they have one) are combinations of two or more of the different classes of arguments.

Suggestions for Writing (4.6)

1. Read an argumentative essay in a magazine like *Harpers* or the *Sunday New York Times Magazine* and write a one-to-two-page essay on what kind of argument it is and why. Be sure to give your instructor a copy of the argumentative essay you are analyzing.
2. Select a familiar document such as King's "I Have a Dream" speech, Lincoln's "Gettysbury Address," *The Declaration of Independence*, or a famous Shakespeare soliloquy, and identify the class or classes of argument it represents. In a one-to-two-page essay, support your identification and discuss the effectiveness of the argument. Be sure to give your instructor a copy of the document you are analyzing.

Chapter 5

An Argument's Support

Knowing the general category of your working thesis will simplify the actual argument process—the task of selecting and arranging the most appropriate material to support the thesis. Broadly defined, an argument's *support* is all the material that transforms your working thesis, or hypothesis, into a justified, credible conclusion. If accurately selected and applied, an argument's support will answer the question all readers of argument pose: "Why should I accept this claim?" Without support, a thesis is purely hypothetical, at best a prospective conclusion. With appropriate and adequate support, it is rendered sensible, credible, and acceptable. Readers will walk away from it convinced.

In this chapter we offer a general introduction to the concept of support, including a discussion of the importance of carefully organizing and presenting your support. We also discuss the questions of whether and where to address arguments counter to your position, as careful consideration of these questions will strengthen the support of *any* argument, regardless of its class.

AN INTRODUCTION TO SUPPORT

We are accustomed to hearing the term *hypothesis* used in connection with scientific research. A hypothesis is an "unproved theory, proposition, supposition . . . tentatively accepted to explain certain facts or . . . to provide a basis for further investigation" (Webster's *New World Dictionary*). A research scientist observing peculiar and surprising behavior in laboratory mice hypothesizes a tentative explanation for this behavior. The scientist then tests the validity of that explanation in many complicated ways, or perhaps simply has an educated hunch to test against a variety of controlled situations. If the tentative explanation or hunch stands up during the experiments, the hypothesis has been proven.

A writer with a working thesis is in much the same situation as the scientist with an educated hunch. Like the scientist, the writer must discover convincing evidence or support for a hypothesis. If this support is available, and if its application to the thesis is in keeping with certain principles of argument, the writer can successfully argue that the thesis, if not absolutely true, is probable and sensible.

As you will learn in Chapters 7 through 10, an argument's support can take many forms: facts, statistics, appeals to shared assumptions and values, authoritative endorsements, comparisons, and refutations of counterarguments can all be used to bolster a thesis, as can any of the four classes of theses just discussed. When a central thesis is supported by another, secondary thesis, the supporting thesis will require its own appropriate support. For example, a practical recommendation like "First-time DWI offenders should have their driver's licenses permanently revoked," might cite as support the argument of effect that "The threat of license revocation would effectively deter many from driving while intoxicated." While not the chief point of the argument, this secondary argument of effect would need its own support.

In most cases, once you come up with a thesis you wish to argue, you will also have in mind, if only dimly, certain material that supports or proves that thesis. Sometimes you will have plenty of supporting material before you have a thesis. The more your thesis emerges from your experience of dissonance and your own interests, the more likely it is that you will have ready at hand some solid support for your argument. (Theses that have no connection with your own experiences, interests, or knowledge are usually difficult to support.)

For example, if your observations of an unhappy grandparent move you to write an argument about age discrimination, you will have at hand some examples of discriminatory practices and their effects. Some of these examples would certainly be useful in a thesis arguing "American society, for all its public attention to human rights, is guilty of systematically depriving its senior citizens of countless 'inalienable' rights." But in order to argue convincingly such a wide-ranging thesis as this, you would need to provide more support than your own personal observations. Further support might include examples of age discrimination obtained from other authoritative sources, statements made by experts corroborating your thesis, or reliable statistics proving the high incidence of forced retirements (a measurable example of age discrimination).

The first step in providing support is recognizing what kind of support your thesis needs. The job of determining the necessary support for a thesis is made much simpler if you know the class to which your thesis belongs. While there is no *one* way to support a particular thesis, each of the four classes of theses generally requires certain types of support. In Chapters 7 through 10 we will discuss how to select and apply the appropriate supporting material for each of the four classes of arguments.

ARRANGING YOUR ARGUMENT'S SUPPORT

Not only is the identification of appropriate support crucial to an argument's success, but also the arrangement of that support—the order in which you present it. You can make strong support more convincing by organizing it effectively, especially by considering the impact your organization is likely to have on your readers.

In most arguments, a number of good organizational strategies exist, but the best organization for any given argument is the one that best suits its particular audience. If you take the time to consider your readers' familiarity with your subject, their ability to follow the course of your argument, and their probable disposition toward your thesis, you should be able to organize your support effectively.

When considering the organization of an argument's support, you will find it useful to view supporting material as discrete units undergirding the thesis in different ways, with different degrees of persuasiveness. Making a brief outline of your argument's main points will help you see your support in this way. A list of supporting points for the thesis that "Bay City needs a convention center to attract visitors to the city" follows.

1. Bay City attracts 30,000 fewer visitors per year than Rock City, a similar city with a convention center.

2. A convention center would add a minimum of $15,000,000 a year to the local economy, which would benefit all the citizens of Bay City, not just those in the food, hotel, and tourist industries.

3. The convention center could be financed by long-term bonds, which would spread the cost over a long period of time.

4. Bay City already has the air, train, and bus facilities to handle more visitors.

5. Experts in the convention business point out that there is a high correlation between convention centers and attracting new industries to a city.

6. Most of Bay City's citizens share a belief in industrial and economic progress, which is the basic value being appealed to here.

Viewing your argument's support as separate units will make it easier for you to determine the most effective ordering of the support.

A good general principle is that the strongest support should be presented first, so that you gain at least provisional agreement from your readers early on. If at all possible, you should save at least one very effective supporting point for the end of the argument, thus leaving your readers with a final impression of your argument's strength. In the outline above, for example, the strongest argument probably is the comparison with Rock City, because Rock City really is comparable to Bay City, and the success of its convention center is well known among Central City's citizens. The last argument—the appeal to shared values—is also strong because this belief in progress is one of the strongest shared values of Bay City's citizens.

What constitutes strong support? To some extent this will depend on your audience. A credulous, inexperienced group and a cynical or expert audience will be convinced by different points. However, relevant factual support— figures, examples, statistics, as in supporting points 1 and 2 above—usually is very strong. Less convincing to a sophisticated audience is more speculative material—an identification of the possible effects of a certain condition. For example, a knowledgeable audience might be skeptical of point 5's claim that a convention center in itself would attract new industry; the claim may be true, yet many readers would hesitate to believe it without further study of the issue. Comparisons, as in point 1's comparison of Bay City with Rock City, can be persuasive so long as you can establish true comparability. Citing expert opinion is usually effective, provided your expert is truly an expert. With point 5, for example, who are the "experts in the convention business" cited in the claim? Do they have a strong bias toward convention centers? What is the basis of their claim? Have they considered other factors, such as the possibility that cities with convention centers usually have strong transportation systems that attract new industry, whereas cities without centers usually do not?

Of course, sometimes you must arrange your support in a certain order. Scientific experiments dictate a certain arrangement. So do causal chains, where Cause A must be discussed before Cause B, Cause B before Cause C, and so on. In these cases, you must make sure that all your support is as strong as possible and that it fits tightly together. With these kinds of arguments, one weak piece can destroy the effectiveness of the entire argument.

ADDRESSING THE COUNTERARGUMENT

As you will learn in Chapters 7 through 10, where we discuss tactics of support for each class of argument, different arguments require different species of support. But regardless of the class of argument you are writing, you must always consider any strong counterarguments, in many cases acknowledging and/or refuting them in your own argument. Because addressing the counterargument can strengthen *any* argument, we regard it as a generic form of support.

As we stated in Chapter 2, you should never write an argument without being aware of other points of view. But carefully considering the possible objections to your argument does not necessarily mean citing and refuting those objections in your argument. In fact, you can use one of three strategies for dealing with counterarguments in your own essay: omission, acknowledgment, or direct refutation. You can omit mention of the counterargument when the argument is neither well known nor compelling. Omission, however, should not mean ignorance. You should have considered this counterargument carefully in constructing your own argument.

Acknowledging the counterargument shows a reader that you are aware of the complexity of the issue and the legitimacy of other positions; it contributes to the impression that you are reasonable and broad-minded. You should especially take care to acknowledge issues when you know your audience will raise them anyway. Near the end of her essay on the advantages of competitive athletics for girls, Margaret Whitney includes a brief acknowledgment of some predictable objections to her argument:

> I am not suggesting that participation in sports is the answer for all young women. It is not easy—the losing, jealousy, raw competition and intense personal criticism of performance.
>
> And I don't wish to imply that the sports scene is a morality play either. Girls' sports can be funny. You can't forget that out on that field are a bunch of people who know the meaning of the word cute. During one game, I noticed that Ann had a blue ribbon tied on her ponytail, and it dawned on me that every girl on the team had an identical bow. Somehow I can't picture the Celtics gathered in the locker room of the Boston Garden agreeing to wear the same color sweatbands.

By pointing out that her views are not universally applicable, the writer actually strengthens the point she is making.

On other occasions, direct refutation of an opposing position is called for. If, for example, you know your readers agree with a position substantially different from yours, you should identify that position and point out its flaws in reasoning, facts, or relevance. Or if you know that a credible, often cited countercase or exception exists, regardless of whether your audience subscribes to that position, you should address it. And finally, if for some reason it is particularly important for you to project a broad-minded, well-balanced image, you should include a refutation in your argument.

As refutations are really a variety of support, they frequently appear along with other supporting material, commonly at the end. If you have a very recalcitrant audience dedicated to an opposing position, you aren't likely to convince them of the weakness of their views at the outset. Readers without strongly held views are less likely to be swayed by a counterargument if it follows an impressive array of support for your thesis. If you include your refutation as the final piece of support, remember that it may linger in your reader's mind for some time, so make it as strong and convincing as possible. Remember also what we said in Chapter 2: some very powerful arguments are no more than refutations of opposing arguments, gaining precision from knowing exactly what they are against and intensity from the energy of this opposition.

As an example of refutation, we cite this paragraph from Martin Luther King, Jr.'s 1963 "Letter from Birmingham Jail," where King responds to criticism from Alabama clergymen about his program of nonviolent resistance to racial segregation:

> You may well ask, "Why direct action? Why sit-ins, marches, and so forth? Isn't negotiation a better path?" You are quite right in calling for negotiation. Indeed, this is the very purpose of direct action. Non-violent direct action seeks to create such a

crisis and foster such a tension that a community which has constantly refused to negotiate is forced to confront the issue. It seeks so to dramatize the issue that it can no longer be ignored. My citing the creation of tension as part of the work of the non-violent resister may sound rather shocking. But I must confess I am not afraid of the word "tension." I have earnestly opposed violent tension, but there is a type of constructive, nonviolent tension which is necessary for growth. Just as Socrates felt that it was necessary to create a tension in the mind so that individuals could rise from the bondage of myths and half truths to the unfettered realm of creative analysis and objective appraisal, so must we see the need for nonviolent gadflies to create the kind of tension in society that will help men rise from the dark depths of prejudice and racism to the majestic heights of understanding and brotherhood.

Note how King specifies the opposition's position and even concedes them a point (they're correct in calling for negotiations) before he then refutes their position and moves to an idealistic statement of his own. This pattern of statement–concession–refutation is typical of effective refutations, though the concession should be included only when it is appropriate.

SUMMARY

An Argument's Support

- An argument's support is all the material that transforms your working thesis into a credible argument.

  Knowing the class of argument you are making will help you determine the appropriate support.

- The order in which you arrange your support depends on your readers' familiarity with your subject, their ability to follow your argument, and their probable attitude toward your thesis.

- When possible, arrange your support to have the greatest impact on your readers, with strong supports placed at the beginning and end of your support section.

- You must always consider counterarguments when constructing your own argument, but in your writing you can deal with these counterarguments in one of three ways: omission, acknowledgment, or refutation.

  You can omit counterarguments when they are not well known or very strong.

  You should acknowledge counterarguments when they are well known.

  You should directly refute the opposing argument when it is held by many of your readers or frequently cited as a powerful argument against your position or if it is especially important for you to appear balanced and open-minded to your audience.

Suggestions for Writing (5.1)

1. Write a thesis that comes out of a position or belief you hold strongly (about a political issue, a policy at your university, or your relationship to your family, for example). Identify the category of thesis and make a list of all the reasons you can think of to support your thesis. In a two-page essay, discuss whether the support you have identified would be sufficient for a general audience, or whether you might need to discover further reasons. Briefly describe where you might look for further support.

2. For one of the following theses, develop the counterargument to your own view on the issue by outlining a counterthesis and at least three supports for that thesis. Then write a two-to-three-page essay refuting this counterargument. The theses:

   a. Women should (or should not) serve in combat roles in the armed forces.

   b. Public prayer should (or should not) be reinstituted in our public schools.

   c. Physical fitness programs should (or should not) be required of all undergraduate college students.

   d. Testing for use of illegal drugs should (or should not) be mandatory for all employees whenever an employer believes it is necessary.

   e. Anyone convicted of drunken driving should (or should not) spend a mandatory thirty days in jail.

Chapter 6

Image and Style

As we noted in Chapter 1, image is a powerful tool of argument. Image—the overall impression a writer makes on a reader—consists of many elements. Most obviously, the quality of the argument itself—its intelligence, honesty, and accuracy—will impress your readers. On a smaller scale, the mechanics of your writing—its grammar, spelling, punctuation, and physical appearance—also help to project an image of you as writer. Stylistic elements contribute to a positive impression as well: word choice, sentence construction, figures of speech such as metaphor and analogy, even the sound of your writing. Your *style* as a writer results from all the choices you make about language in your argument; your style projects an image as do the clothes you choose to wear and the way you decorate your room.

Style is an *essential* component of argument, operating at every phase of the writing process; more than packaging, the frills and ribbons pasted on at the last minute, style informs a work throughout its evolution from idea to finished document. Every good writer has a style—a reflection of character, education, and maturity. Some of this style is unconscious, but a good part of it is consciously developed. Style is not some immutable mirror of the writer; it shoud be flexible, adapting to particular occasions and developing over time as the writer continually experiments and matures.

This chapter will focus on some of the conscious stylistic choices particularly relevant to you as a writer of argument—choices you will have to make about your argument's voice, its level of diction, metaphor and analogy, connotative language and slanting, and about the sound of your prose. As you compose your argument, we encourage you to consider these elements and to make choices about them that accord with your subject, your purpose, and your audience.

THE ROLE OF VOICE

A writer's *voice* is the role that he or she takes for a particular occasion, almost like an actor taking on a part in a new play. To many inexperienced writers, voice suggests insincerity or fakery, but all of us continually "play" different roles. We behave one way in a classroom, another way playing basketball. We talk to our parents in one way and to our friends in another. Voice is simply the manifestation of this adaptability in writing.

The following simple example demonstrates the variability of voice:

> Dear Mr. Jones:
> At the suggestion of Ms. Hawkins, I am writing to inquire about an opening as an electrical engineer in your firm.

> Dear Mom and Dad:
> Hi and help! You won't believe this but I'm broke again. Boy, were my textbooks expensive this quarter!

The same student wrote both these openings and was completely sincere in both cases, though the voices differ markedly. In the first case, the student was formal, polite, restrained. In the second, she was informal and very direct. In cases like these, the choice of a particular voice seems natural; the student did not spend much time or effort choosing these voices. But you can improve your writing by being conscious of the available choices and using them effectively. One crucial choice is between the formal and informal voices—the voices of the first and second letters, respectively. Using an informal voice in a formal situation can have disastrous effects. What would happen to our student if she wrote to Mr. Jones (whom she presumably does not know) in the following manner?

> Dear Mr. Jones:
> Hi and help! I ran into somebody Hawkins—I forget her first name—and she says you've got jobs. Boy, do I need one!

The Importance of Ethos

As the Greek philosopher Aristotle noted, one major element of any successful argument is the establishment of a positive *ethos* (or character)—that is, the portrayal of the writer as a sincere, upright person. Audiences are interested in the source of an argument and trust arguments from people who appear to have the traits they admire, including honesty and a concern for other people. They distrust arguments from people who are known to be dishonest or selfish or whose voice suggests those traits. As a writer, you must be aware of the importance of a positive ethos and demonstrate it in your own writing. In argument, a carefully considered voice can convince an audience that you are a principled person concerned not just with your own self-interest but with the general welfare as well. When your readers believe that you are this kind of person, they are much more likely to accept your argument.

The following letter from an angry student to her campus newspaper does not establish a convincing ethos:

> The grading policies of this college are rotten, just like everything else here at State. How can the administration put a student on probation for failing a course outside of her major? That's just outrageous. When I got an "F" in physics, they put me on probation even though I received at least a "C" in the courses in my major. I didn't want to take physics anyway, and the instructor really stunk. Now I'm not eligible to play on the women's basketball team! When are we students going to force the administration to get rid of this stupid policy?

The reasoning in this letter has many weaknesses, but the writer's failure to establish a convincing ethos also destroys the letter's effectiveness. The writer presents herself as lacking balance (is *everything* at State rotten?) and as concerned only about herself (what about the effect of the grading policy on someone other than herself?). Almost all readers of this letter would dismiss it as a howl of outrage over a personal problem, not an argument for them to consider seriously.

When Aristotle urged creators of argument to establish an effective ethos for their argument, he was not urging hypocrisy. Neither are we. In creating an ethos, you may present your best side, but this side is still part of you. The outraged student who wrote the letter above is presumably capable of balance and of concern for others. Before writing that letter, she should have moved from outrage to a broader perspective, using her own anger as inspiration but recognizing that expressing hurt feelings does not make an argument.

Good writers also create credible voices by being confident about their views but not more confident than their support warrants. A credible voice is neither dogmatic nor apologetic. Readers suspect writers, such as our angry student, who make sweeping claims—such as the one that everything at State is rotten—or forceful statements ("the governor is the dumbest woman in this state") for which they cannot possibly produce adequate support. On the other hand, they also suspect arguments that seem too wishy-washy: "I suspect it is probably true that this policy may lead us in the wrong direction." Student writers, especially when writing about fields new to them, are prone to be excessively cautious, which very quickly undermines readers' faith in the writers and their arguments.

As an example of an argument with a credible voice, let us return to the angry student, who has calmed down and decided to try another version of the letter:

After a painful experience with the policies on probation and suspension here at State, I have concluded that these policies should be revised. The policy states that any student whose grades fall below a "C" average will be placed on suspension, making that student ineligible to participate in athletic teams or many other extra-curricular activities. The policy appears reasonable, but its effect is to place too much emphasis on courses outside of a student's major. Many students, including three of my acquaintances, have found themselves ineligible to participate in these activities even though they were doing acceptable work in their majors. I now find myself in a similar situation, ineligible to be on the women's basketball team yet earning grades of "C" or higher in my major.

The voice in this letter is that of someone who is honest about her own situation but also concerned for others, someone who allows for an apparently reasonable opposing view while remaining firm in her own.

Activities (6.1)

1. Write a one-page letter to your parents or a friend asking for a loan of some money to help with your college expenses. Then write a letter to your college's financial office asking for the same loan. Make a list of the differences in the two letters.
2. Write one or two paragraphs stating why you should be given an award for your many outstanding contributions to your community. Your paragraphs must portray you as deserving this award, but they should not be boastful.

THE VIRTUES AND LIMITATIONS OF PLAIN WRITING

Most writing instructors and most writing textbooks today urge students to make their writing clear and straightforward, without obvious embellish-ments. The British novelist and essayist George Orwell gave the most famous formulation of the rules for this plain style in his "Politics and the English Language":

(i) Never use a metaphor, simile or other figure of speech which you are used to seeing in print.

(ii) Never use a long word where a short one will do.

(iii) If it is possible to cut a word out, always cut it out.

(iv) Never use the passive where you can use the active.

(v) Never use a foreign phrase, a scientific word or a jargon word if you can think of any everyday English equivalent.

(vi) Break any of these rules sooner than say anything outright barbarous.

   The plain style Orwell urges arose as a reaction against the bloated and often dishonest prose of modern bureaucratic society, where military first strikes are called "anticipatory retaliations," visual materials in school curricula become "integrated systems learning designs," and simple sentences and direct expression disappear behind clouds of vague pomposity: "Please contact my secretary about an appointment regarding the project slippages in implementing the new on-line system." The writer could have said "Please see me about the delays in starting the new on-line system," but for too many writers today the first version seems more official, more important. A plain style of writing is an antidote to this swollen contemporary prose.

   But plain writing carries its own risks, as Orwell notes with his sixth rule. Writers who use plain style exclusively risk writing prose that is clear but undistinguished, serviceable but dull. To combat this risk, we suggest the following additions to Orwell's rules:

(i)   Don't be afraid to use metaphors, similes, or other figures of speech, provided they are not overworked.

(ii)   When a long word is the best one, use it.

(iii)   Use long sentences for variety and when they best suit your needs.

(iv)   Dare to try something different.

(v)   Break any of these rules rather than confuse your reader.

These rules do not contradict Orwell's; they are offered as friendly amendments—another point of view to keep in mind, a balance of the delicate scales of an effective style.

   The following passage from the second paragraph of Henry David Thoreau's *Walden* is a good example of writing that succeeds by going beyond the plain style. We have annotated parts of this passage that demonstrate some of our rules for enriched prose.

Clever phrasing — dare to try something different

Use long sentences for variety

Use metaphors, similes

I should not talk so much about myself if there were anybody else whom I knew as well. Unfortunately, I am confined to this theme by the narrowness of my experience. Moreover, I, on my side, require of every writer, first or last, a simple and sincere account of his own life, and not merely what he has heard of other men's lives; some such account as he would send to his kindred from a distant land; for if he has lived sincerely, it must have been in a distant land to me. Perhaps these pages are more particularly addressed to poor students. As for the rest of my readers, they will accept such portions as apply to them. I trust that none will stretch the seams in putting on the coat, for it may do good service to him whom it fits.

Activities (6.2)

Make the following passage more interesting prose by combining sentences, using a more varied vocabulary, adding metaphors or similes if appropriate, and using any other devices that would make this passage more lively.

Baseball is a less suitable sport for television than football. Football has predictable periods of intense action followed by pauses. Many television programs have the same. Baseball does not. The quiet strategy of baseball does not overwhelm us visually. Baseball pitchers make changes in their delivery for different batters. Fielders also move to different places on the field depending on the batter and the men on base. These adjustments are not exciting television.

METAPHOR AND ANALOGY

A *metaphor* is an implicit comparison of two dissimilar subjects so that some aspects of one (usually concrete and familiar) can be used to illuminate aspects of the other (usually more abstract or unfamiliar). "The twilight of her career" is a metaphor comparing something concrete and familiar, the end of a day, to something more abstract, in this case the end of someone's career. The "global village" is another metaphor, where the abstract concept of the globe or world (the entire population of the earth) is compared to the more familiar and concrete idea of a village. A *simile* is a comparison where the act of comparing is made explicit, usually through the use of *like* or *as*: "Falling in love is like getting caught in a warm spring rain." For our purposes, simile can be seen as a type of metaphor. *Analogy* is like metaphor since dissimilar areas are compared, but in analogy the comparison is extended through several points. The "global village" becomes an analogy when the world is compared to a village in several respects, including the need for certain agreed-upon laws and the importance of communication and cooperation among those in the community.

The following passage from the historian Barbara Tuchman demonstrates the value of metaphor in argument. In the first paragraph of "History as Mirror," Tuchman begins her argument by describing history as a mirror where we can see an image of ourselves:

At a time when everyone's mind is on the explosions of the moment, it might seem obtuse of me to discuss the fourteenth century. But I think a backward look at that disordered, violent, bewildered, disintegrating, and calamity-prone age can be consoling and possibly instructive in a time of similar disarray. Reflected in a six-hundred-year-old mirror, a more revealing image of ourselves and our species might be seen than is visible in the clutter of circumstances under our noses.

According to Tuchman, studying the history of fourteenth-century western Europe is like looking into a mirror. In this mirror we can see a clearer image of ourselves than is available from just examining the present; in the present we are too absorbed in current details to get the "big picture." The "big picture" is what makes our lives tick: our motivations, desires, problems, crises, and triumphs. By using this metaphor of the mirror, Tuchman shows us briefly and clearly the value of history to our lives.

In the following passage, the psychiatrist Carl Jung offers us an example of an effective use of analogy in supporting an argument. Jung describes the mind of twentieth-century humanity through the analogy of a building:

> We have to describe and to explain a building the upper story of which was erected in the nineteenth century; the ground-floor dates from the sixteenth century, and a careful examination of the masonry discloses the fact that it was reconstructed from a dwelling-tower of the eleventh century. In the cellar we discover Roman foundation walls, and under the cellar a filled-in cave, in the floor of which stone tools are found and remnants of glacial fauna in the layers below. That would be a sort of picture of our mental structure.

Jung's analogy is effective because it clearly reveals his view of our minds, with the most recent cultural developments being in the most visible upper layers and the more ancient (and instinctive) behaviors being buried below, less visible from the outside but just as important as the upper layers. Of course, Jung could have described these characteristics of our minds in a more abstract language, similar to what we are using here to explain his analogy, but his description would have been less memorable than this picture of a house with a buried cave underneath. This example demonstrates how analogies can crystallize abstract ideas into a sharp picture that both clarifies the ideas and makes them memorable.

Metaphors can also be valuable means of discovery—doors that lead us to important ideas and arguments. All of us are naturally disposed to noticing correspondences, to seeing the threads of similarity that unify experience. We have all had the experience of being spontaneously struck by similarities between two seemingly different subjects. Usually, our minds hit upon such a comparison because it is apt, because it contains a truth that we may not consciously recognize. Upon close examination, these correspondences or metaphors that come to us can reveal important truths about both subjects and can generate and even structure a theory or argument. When the noted MIT computer scientist Edward Fredkin was struck by the correspondences between the operation of computers and the operation of the universe, he followed up that metaphor, creating a controversial but intriguing theory of digital physics from the implications of a seemingly simple metaphor. Like Fredkin and others, you should be alive to the generating power of your natural metaphor-making tendency, letting it work for you in the ideas you develop and the arguments you write.

Some Cautions About Metaphor and Analogy

Metaphors and analogies can illuminate and generate ideas, but they can never *prove* a point. A writer cannot prove that a certian policy should be adopted by using a metaphor or analogy. Calling the world a village does not prove the need for world government. Furthermore, analogies, if pursued too far, inevitably break down because the two areas being compared are not identical; the world may be a village, but it is a village with over five billion inhabitants, speaking thousands of different languages and following an incredible range of customs and beliefs. Some village!

Analogies can be risky if people take them too literally, as they did with the "domino theory" analogy in the 1960s and 1970s. The domino analogy compared countries in Southeast Asia to a row of dominoes. When dominoes are placed on their ends in a row, they will fall down one by one if the first in the series is pushed. According to the domino theory, these countries would fall to communism in the same manner. The domino theory was a major reason for American involvement in Vietnam; American strategists believed that the fall of South Vietnam to the communists would lead to communist control of all of Southeast Asia and perhaps all of Asia. South Vietnam and some other parts of Southeast Asia are now communist, but other countries in Southeast Asia are not and do not seem to be in any danger of falling under such control. The domino theory may not always be this faulty, yet the theory cannot become an excuse for failing to analyze the particular complexities of a specific situation. Real countries are always more complicated than dominoes.

Activities (6.3)

1. For one of the following analogies, write a one-page essay analyzing ways in which the analogy illuminates aspects of the situation and ways in which it does not. Our discussion of the "domino theory" above is one example of this kind of analysis.
   a. Sexual politics.
   b. The family of humanity.
   c. The game of life.
   d. The war of ideas.
   e. The corporate ladder.
2. Write a paragraph that develops an analogy. You may use one of the analogies in Exercise 1, provided it is not the one you used in that exercise. The paragraph by Carl Jung cited above is one model for this development.

CONNOTATIVE LANGUAGE AND SLANTING

Good writers must be aware not only of the *denotations* of words but of their *connotations* as well. The denotation of a word is its explicit meaning, its dictionary definition; the connotation of a word is the meaning or meanings suggested by the word, the word's emotional associations. The denotation of the words "apple pie" is a baked food made with apples. In our society the connotations of "apple pie" are family life, patriotism, and innocence. Writers of arguments need to be sensitive to the connotations of words and use these connotations appropriately; a legislator would not be likely to get a bill passed in the U.S. Congress by labeling it as "Soviet-inspired." A writer urging development of a suburban tract of land for offices and factories is more likely to succeed by describing it as a "High Tech Park" than as an "Industrial Development Area"; the phrase "High Tech" has a certain vogue, while "Industrial Development" smells of factory smokestacks. In Rochester, N.Y., developers of a new suburban office building appealed to the taste for the rural and natural by calling the building "Corporate Woods," though there are few trees anywhere in sight.

The example of "Corporate Woods" points out the risk in a heavy reliance on mere connotation. Beyond a certain point, words used for their connotative value cease to have any meaning at all; there are very few woods in "Corporate Woods" and nothing fresh in "lemony fresh" soap or in "fresh frozen" juice. And what is so natural about many of the products that advertise themselves as "naturally delicious"? Connotation is an inescapable element of argument, but it should not be used without regard to denotation. Some advertising does this and gets away with it, but most readers demand higher standards for other kinds of written arguments.

Writers are often tempted to use not only connotation but also blatantly emotional terms as illegitimate supports for their arguments. Suppose you were arguing for a new recreation center on your campus: you might refer to the necessity of having a place "where students could use their free time constructively, letting off the frustrations and pressures caused by rigorous scholastic demands." Here you are portraying students and their needs in a positive way— we tend to respect anyone subjected to "rigorous scholastic demands." But if you were arguing against the recreation center you could completely alter this impression by using words with negative connotations: "Do our spoiled and spoon-fed students really need another service catering to their already well-satisfied needs?" The respectable students of the first argument have become the undeserving parasites of the second. Words like "spoiled," "spoon-fed," and "catering" are negative words, and their application to the students in question affects a reader's impression of the issue. The words used *slant* the argument, even in the absence of sound evidence. As a writer of responsible arguments, you must not fall into the trap of letting such language suggest conclusions that your argument does not prove.

The temptation to slant is probably strongest in arguments of ethical evalua-tion; of all the arguments you write, these are the most personal, the most self-revealing, and thus the most important to you. For these reasons, they can tempt you to resort to irrational means to convince your audience. You are not likely to invest high emotional stakes in arguing that four-wheel-drive cars are superior to other kinds of cars, but you can be passionately committed to an argument for or against capital punishment or abortion. Slanting, while almost unavoidable in such cases, must not become a substitute for sound support for your argument.

Activities (6.4)

Write two paragraphs describing the same object or activity, but favorably in one paragraph and unfavorably in another. Some possible topics: New York City (or some other city); a particular television show; a book you recently read. Be sure to describe the same qualities in both paragraphs.

THE MUSIC OF LANGUAGE

Any writer who ignores the importance of *sound* in argument is overlooking an enormously valuable method of persuasion. We all know the power of adver-tising's jingles and catch phrases, which linger in our minds even when we wish they wouldn't. Less obvious but perhaps just as powerfully persuasive is prose that holds our attention because of a fresh and pleasing combination of sounds. Such prose contains euphony and rhythm.

Euphony, which comes from Greek roots meaning "good sounds," is a pleasing combination of sounds. We usually think of euphony as a characteris-tic of poetry or some kinds of prose fiction, but it can and should be present in written arguments as well. Euphony, of course, depends on the ear of the reader or listener, but ears can be trained to become sensitive to this quality of prose, just as we learn to be sensitive to different qualities of music.

Rhythm is a recognizable pattern or shape of the flow of sounds through time. In prose, rhythmical units are often divided by grammatical pauses such as commas or periods, though a rhythmical break can also occur at some other place where we would pause to catch our breath if we were reading aloud. "I came, I saw, I conquered" is a simple example of prose rhythm, with three short rhythmical units divided by commas. All of us have a rhythm to our prose just as we have a rhythm to our breathing or walking, and this rhythm can vary with the situation, just as our walking rhythm can. Good prose writers learn to know their prose rhythms, to develop them as they gain experience in writing, and to recognize and use the appropriate rhythm for a specific purpose.

This passage from President John F. Kennedy's Inaugural Address demonstrates a sensitivity to euphony and rhythm:

> To those peoples in the huts and villages of half the globe struggling to break the bonds of mass misery, we pledge our best efforts to help them help themselves, for whatever period is required—not because the communists may be doing it, not because we seek their votes, but because it is right. If a free society cannot help the many who are poor, it cannot save the few who are rich.

The passage demonstrates two key elements of effective prose style: parallelism and emphasis. *Parallelism* is the principle that equivalent thoughts demand equivalent expression, a principle that Kennedy carefully follows with his series "not because . . . not because . . . but because." This series of "becauses" also establishes a noticeable rhythm to the passage. The series is also arranged in order of *emphasis*, the most important point ("because it is right") being placed last.

The passage also contains other devices that enhance its appeal to the ear. The last sentence contains a striking balance of opposites ("many who are poor" and "few who are rich"). And the first sentence even contains just enough repetition of initial sounds to please the listener or reader without being too blatant ("*h*uts . . . *h*alf," "*b*reak . . . *b*onds," "*m*ass *m*isery"). The last point ("because it is right") is also the most briefly expressed, ending the passage on three single syllable words, which helps to stress the importance of this idea.

Developing a sensitivity to language isn't easy, but it can be done, just as most people can develop a sensitivity to tone and rhythm in music. One way to do this is to listen to the sound of your prose as you read it aloud. If this seems awkward, then make an audio tape of your reading, or read to a friend, or have a friend read your prose to you. When you are doing this, listen for spots that seem especially clumsy or difficult and note them for later review. These spots probably need revision. If you practice reading aloud for a while, you should begin to develop a "silent ear" that will give you a sense of how the words sound even without your speaking them aloud.

The sound of your prose *will* affect how readers react to your argument, even if they are not conscious of the role sound plays in written prose and even if they have not developed the skill to create sound-pleasing prose themselves. As the rhetorician Kenneth Burke has noted, audiences tend to identify with skilled speakers and writers and are likely to be carried along simply by the very structure of the prose. Even a reader or listener of Kennedy's Inaugural Address who is suspicious of American aid to other countries is likely to be affected by the rising force of giving aid "not because the communists may be doing it, not because we seek their votes, but because it is right."

Activities (6.5)

Of the following passages, choose the one that you find most striking or memorable as prose. Write a one-to-two-page essay analyzing why you find the prose effective. If you find this assignment hard to do without more information, describe why this is so and what information you need.

1. You know how it is, you want to look and you don't want to look. I can remember the strange feelings I had when I was a kid looking at war photographs in *Life*, the ones that showed dead people or a lot of dead people lying close together in a field or a street, often touching, seeming to hold each other. Even when the picture was sharp and cleanly defined, something wasn't clear at all, something repressed that monitored the images and withheld their essential information. It may have legitimized my fascination, letting me look for as long as I wanted; I didn't have a language for it then, but I remember now the shame I felt, like looking at first porn, all the porn in the world. (Michael Herr, *Dispatches*. London: Picador, 1978, p. 23.)

2. Commercial exploitation and growing population demands will speed destruction of rain forests as well as oceans, grasslands, lakes, and wetlands. *Pleading ignorance of these vital and fragile ecosystems can only spell global disaster. What can you do?*

    You can accept this invitation to support World Wildlife Fund. *We have a plan for survival. We need your help to make it succeed.* (Letter from World Wildlife Fund. World Wildlife Fund, 1987, p. 1.)

3. The stars awaken a certain reverence, because though always present, they are inaccessible; but all natural objects make a kindred impression, when the mind is open to their influence. Nature never wears a mean appearance. Neither does the wisest man extort her secret, and lose his curiosity by finding out all her perfection. Nature never became a toy to a wise spirit. The flowers, the animals, the mountains, reflected the wisdom of his best hour, as much as they had delighted the simplicity of his childhood. (Ralph Waldo Emerson, "Nature," in *Essays and Lectures*, ed. Joel Porte. New York: The Library of America, 1983, p. 9.)

4. Instead of spending your money on a gun to put by your bed, install a phone there. Call the police if you hear a strange noise that you think might be an intruder. By doing so, you can decrease the chances of killing your spouse or child—something that happens all too frequently—if they move around and make noises unfamiliar to you in the night. (Jerry Vaughn, "Think—before you buy that handgun." Rochester, NY. *Times-Union*, Nov. 20, 1987, 10A.)

5. The recently rediscovered insight that literacy is more than a skill is based upon knowledge that all of us unconsciously have about language. We know instinctively that to understand what somebody is saying, we must understand more than the surface meanings of words; we have to understand the context as well. The need for background information applies all the more to

reading and writing. To grasp the words on a page we have to know a lot of information that isn't set down on the page. (E.D. Hirsch, Jr., *Cultural Literacy: What Every American Needs to Know.* Boston: Houghton Mifflin, 1987, p. 3.)

SUMMARY

Image and Style

- Style, a result of the choices about language you make while writing your argument, contributes significantly to the image projected by your argument.
- In arguing, you must establish a voice with the appropriate level of formality for the context, reflecting a positive ethos (moral character) and a reasonable confidence in the position being argued.
- You should write clearly, but you should also use various strategies to enrich your prose, including metaphors, similes, or other figures of speech, long words and sentences when appropriate. In general dare to try something different.
- Metaphor and analogy can be valuable for illuminating and generating an argument, but they can never prove a point.
- You must be sensitive to the connotations of words, but you must defend your position with adequate support, not merely with connotation or open slanting.
- You should be sensitive to, and use, euphony and rhythm in your prose. Two common devices for creating these qualities are parallelism and emphasis.

Suggestions for Writing (6.6)

1. Write a one-page essay describing a friend to another friend. Then rewrite this essay as a speech describing your friend at a ceremony where he or she will be receiving an award. Write a one-paragraph description of the differences between the two versions.

2. Pick a famous brief essay or speech such as Kennedy's "Inaugural Address," Lincoln's "Gettysburg Address," or Martin Luther King's "I Have a Dream." Using this essay or speech as a model, try to capture some of the spirit of the original while using your own words and ideas on some topic of your choice in a two-to-three-page essay. Pay particular attention to frequently recurring patterns of sentences and try to use some similar patterns in your own essay.

Chapter 7

Making Factual Arguments

As we noted in Chapter 4, facts can be argued as central theses, presented as critical support for other theses, or provided as illustrations and explanations of complicated material. However you use facts in your own arguments, you should treat them as theses—as statements that may require support or verification. If the facts you present in an argument appear questionable to your audience, if they need verification yet go unverified, your entire argument will be undermined. An argument that does not get its facts straight is not likely to inspire the confidence or gain the acceptance of its readers.

As we have noted, certain facts require no support. These are the facts that are so familiar ("The first of the presidential primaries occurs in the state of New Hampshire"), or so unprovocative ("My physics teacher is a woman") that no sensible reader would question them. But what of the number of facts provided in arguments that are not so familiar or obvious to readers? Any fact that you think a reader likely to question, either because it is surprising, unfamiliar, or goes against the usual store of traditional information, needs support. Supporting or verifying facts is not particularly difficult; because facts are born of someone's experience, they can usually be verified by presenting the qualifications of the experiencer and, in some cases, by describing or explaining the experience.

SUPPORTING PERSONALLY EXPERIENCED FACTS

There will be times in your writing of arguments when you will need to support a fact that *you* have experienced or observed. You will support personally experienced facts by a credible and objective description of the experience or observation.

Describing the Experience

Let's say you were writing a report for a psychology class on phobias and you wanted to demonstrate how extreme and irrational phobic behavior can be. As evidence for this position you refer to your observations of a friend with a severe flying phobia: "I have seen a friend go into panic on a routine commercial flight." Because this statement suggests extreme, abnormal behavior, it requires some support. The support in a case like this is nothing more than a brief description of the experience—of the pallor, the tremors, the hysteria you observed in your friend. (We are not at this point talking about explaining or interpreting the fact, but about presenting it in such a way that your reader will accept that it happened.)

We have used a simple example to make the point about supporting personal experience—the most basic kind of fact—but the principle holds in more complicated contexts. A chemist reporting results of a laboratory experiment would support his findings by describing the process by which he obtained those results. That is, he would describe his experience, providing the details necessary to demonstrate that the process had not been flawed, that it had been conducted according to certain established rules, and that it really did yield certain results.

Establishing Your Own Credibility

The success of written argument is always a function of a reader's confidence in the writer. Arguments are credible if their writer seems organized, well-informed, and reasonable. The important principle of the writer's image underlies everything we have to say about argument, but it is particularly relevant here. Since *you* are usually the sole support of a personally experienced fact, you must give your readers no reason to mistrust your description of the experience. You must record your description in a manner that reflects honesty and accuracy.

If your readers have any reason to believe that your record of experience is not reliable, your argument, however modest, will fail. For example, if you referred to your 85-year-old grandmother as support for an argument against mandatory retirement, citing her daily five-mile runs, her ability to benchpress 300 pounds, and her current prize-winning research in recombinant DNA, your readers would be very suspicious of such obvious exaggeration, and your credibility as an observer would be seriously questioned.

In presenting facts derived from personal experience, you must also guard against the possibility of your own bias. We often see only what we want to see and ignore what is convenient to ignore. Ask two politicians on opposing sides of an issue their perceptions of a stormy meeting: you will almost certainly get two very different stories about what happened. They are not necessarily trying to falsify evidence, but their biases can color their perceptions. In some contexts, such as sports writing about the hometown team or essays on the opinion page of the newspaper, readers expect and even welcome a certain bias, but they tend to reject open manifestations of it in other contexts, such as front-page news, academic projects, or business reports.

Activities (7.1)

For one or more of the situations below, write a factual thesis and then support it with an accurate, appropriately detailed, unbiased description of the experience or observation.

1. Study habits of your roommate or friend.
2. Lecture style of a professor.
3. Your work environment.
4. Your experience in public speaking.
5. Your observations of a well-known speaker.

SUPPORTING FACTS REPORTED BY OTHERS

Most formal arguments cite facts obtained from second- and third-party sources. It might seem that supporting such facts in your argument is a simple matter of a footnote or endnote indicating the source of your fact. But this is only the last and simplest step in supporting these facts. Before you include any second- or third-party fact in your argument, you must satisfy yourself of the reliability of its source.

Determining the Reliability of Your Source

Whenever you include a fact in your argument, you are tacitly saying to your reader, "I believe this fact to be true." Your decision to include it is in itself a form of support. While you will often lack the knowledge or opportunity to test the fact itself, you can and should scrutinize the *source*, requiring that it be trustworthy, objective, and current.

The most obviously trustworthy sources are those individuals who are acknowledged experts in the field, people with a proven track record in that area. You can probably trust the facts given out by your college career counselor on postgraduate career opportunities, or facts about astronomy contained in an article by the noted astronomer Carl Sagan, because both these people have established professional reputations. But you should be wary of advice on the stock market obtained from your sixteen-year-old sister. Information obtained from non-experts—from eyewitness observers or amateurs, for example—can be reliable, but you should be more skeptical about these sources than about acknowledged experts.

If you can determine nothing about the reliability of the individual presenting the fact, or if the fact appears in an unsigned article in a periodical or in an unsigned entry in a larger volume, you can consider the reputation of the periodical or volume. Reputable journals in a particular field, for example, *The Journal of the American Bar Association* and *The New England Journal of Medicine*, have reputations for reliability, though their inclusion of a given article by no means guarantees its truthfulness. Newspapers like *The Wall Street Journal*, the *Christian Science Monitor*, and the *New York Times* are generally recognized for reporting news events fully and accurately, but again, even these publications can make mistakes. Certainly a report found in *The Wall Street Journal* is more credible than one found in *Star Magazine* or the *National Enquirer*. Reference books like the *CRC Handbook of Chemistry and Physics* or *The Oxford English Dictionary* have long-established reputations for reliability; whenever possible, you should go to works such as these for the facts you need.

In evaluating your sources, you must be satisfied that bias does not cancel out the value of the source. Some bias is almost inevitable in human affairs. Even the most dispassionate and objective scholar is probably biased in favor of the results of his or her own research as opposed to research that contradicts it. In advertising and politics, bias is the norm. When you use a source in an argument, you can assume that it reflects some bias, but you need to determine if the bias is so extreme that it negates the value of what is being claimed. One safeguard here is to see if your source gives you enough particular evidence to make the case credible. An article claiming thinning of the ozone layer that cites specific scientific tests is probably credible or at least worth taking seriously, even if the author is biased in favor of this theory. But an advertisement that claims a twenty-pound weight loss for dieters in three days but offers no independent verification of this claim is almost certainly not credible.

Finally, make sure that the facts reported in your source are current, not outdated. Accepted "facts" are constantly being superseded by newer, more accurate information. In our dizzying age of expanding technology and research methods, the average life span of many facts is brief. Especially in science and technology but in many other fields as well, a fact is of little value if it has not been recently verified. The definition of "recent" depends on the field from which the fact is drawn. A 1978 publication on computer software technology would be of questionable value in 1988 because the technology has developed so rapidly. Yet in the less dramatically changing field of psychiatry, information presented in 1978 would be considered comparatively recent. As you collect facts for your argument, you must determine if they reflect the most recent research available.

Citing the Source in Your Text

Citing the source of second- and third-party facts is necessary even though you have satisfied yourself of the source's reliability. Providing the source is both a courtesy to readers, who might want to examine the subject in more depth, and a safeguard, assuring them that your facts have not been fabricated. In most cases, the citation will take the form of a footnote, an endnote, or increasingly, inclusion of the work in a "Works Cited" list at the end of your argument. Any good college writing handbook will include a section on how to document such sources. As well as a footnote or bibliographical reference, you can also include a brief reference to your source within the text of your argument: for example, "According to *The Oxford English Dictionary*, the word 'flick' at one time meant 'thief.' "

If your readers are not likely to be familiar with your source, it can be very useful to provide credentials briefly within your text: for example, "In his book *The Mismeasure of Man*, Stephen Jay Gould, the noted paleotonologist and popularizer of science, argues that the results of standardized intelligence tests can be misleading and also misused by those in power."

Activities (7.2)

Write a one-page paper analyzing the credibility of two of the following passages. Consider the issues of expertise, bias, and currency of facts. You may need to do some research on the credentials of the author or of the publication in which the passage appeared.

1. Mailer had the most developed sense of image; if not, he would have been a figure of deficiency, for people had been regarding him by his public image since he was twenty-five years old. He had in fact learned to live in the sarcophagus of his image—at night, in his sleep, he might dart out, and paint improvements on the sarcophagus. During the day, while he was helpless, newspapermen and other assorted bravos of the media and literary world would carve ugly pictures on the living tomb of his legend. Of necessity, part of Mailer's remaining funds of sensitivity went right into the war of supporting his image and working for it. (Norman Mailer, *The Armies of the Night.* New York: Signet Books, 1968, pp. 15–16.)

2. **chow chow**, powerful NONSPORTING DOG; shoulder height, 18–20 in. (45.7–50.8 cm); weight, 50–60 lb (22.7–27.2 kg). Its coat has a soft, wooly underlayer and a dense, straight topcoat that stands out from the body. It may be any solid color and is the only breed with a black tongue. A hunting dog in China 2,000 years ago, it was brought to England in the 18th cent. (*The Concise Columbia Encyclopedia*. New York: Columbia University Press, 1983, p. 168.)

3. A SPECTER is haunting Europe—the specter of communism. All the powers of the old Europe have entered into a holy alliance to exorcise this specter: Pope and Czar, Metternich and Guizot, French Radicals and German police spies. (Karl Marx and Friedrich Engels, *The Communist Manifesto*. Ed. Samuel H. Beer. New York: Appleton-Century-Crofts, 1955, p. 8. Originally published in 1848.)

4. The nature of a poet's spiritual evolution is ultimately as mysterious as the nature of the human psyche. However, one aspect of [Theodore] Roethke's growth during this period [1941–46] can be seen in broader daylight. His new awareness of modern poetry and his reorientation toward poetic language had much to do with the impact William Carlos Williams had on him during these years. (Peter Balakian, "Theodore Roethke, William Carlos Williams and the American Grain." *Modern Language Studies*, 17.1 (1987): 58.)

5. Many devices have been used in the attempted measurement of interests. The interest inventory is the most important of these both from the standpoint of the number of counselors using them and the number of investigators working with them. The inventory approach consists of the comparison of likes and dislikes of individuals through questionnaire items. Since the individual is asked to estimate his feeling, the method may be said to be subjective. A complete discussion of interest inventories is given by Fryer [Douglas Fryer, *The Measurement of Interests*. New York: Henry Holt, 1931]. (Harry J. Older, "An Objective Test of Vocational Interests." *Journal of Applied Psychology*, 28 (1944): 99.)

SUPPORTING FACTUAL GENERALIZATIONS

Any thesis, regardless of the class it falls into, can be stated as a *generalization*. The claim "Frank is a successful salesman because his father was also a good salesman" introduces a limited causal argument (with an element of evaluation in the judgment "successful"). The generalized version of this claim would be something like "Successful salesmen tend to have other good salesmen in their families." Similarly, the following comparison based in fact, "*People* magazine and *U.S.A. Today* use much the same format as television news shows," becomes a comparative generalization when the communications scholar Neil Postman tells us that "the total information environment begins to mirror television."

To support any generalization, you need to apply two sets of principles. First, you must demonstrate the reasonableness of the singular claim—for example, that there is a demonstrable *causal* connection between a father and a son who are both salesmen, or that significant similarities do exist between the television news show "20/20" and *People* magazine. In other words, you must rest your claim on the principles of support applicable to the category to which the singular claim belongs. Second, you must also demonstrate that your generalization, regardless of its specific category, has been properly drawn, that there are sufficient grounds for claiming the broad applicability of the specific claim. We will use factual generalizations to illustrate this concept of sufficient grounds, but you should be aware that it applies to all categories of generalizations.

Grounds for Generalizations

All generalizations, even the most informal and sweeping, begin on a specific level. We see something a few times and assume that it happens frequently or even all the time. That is, we move from specific observations to general conclusions; from the particular we infer the general. In traditional logic, this process by which we assume the widespread existence of particular instances is called *induction*. Conclusions drawn by inductive reasoning are always somewhat risky because they are based on incomplete evidence. You assume that because you have never seen or heard of a flying cat, no such creature exists, yet unless you have seen every cat that ever existed, your claim "There is no such thing as a flying cat" has made a rather staggering leap from the particular to the universal. Yet these leaps are the nature of induction.

Supporting a generalization consists of identifying a number of specific verified instances or examples. If you claim, for example, that American films increasingly show the dangers of casual sexual relationships, you would have to cite individual films to support your claim. Or if you write "Many young American novelists find universities a supportive and economically secure place to work," you would need to point to specific examples. If the generalization is a factual generalization, the specific examples will be individual facts, which in some cases may need verification. What makes a factual generalization "factual" is not the absolute truth of the generalization, which can never be proved, but its foundation in singular factual instances.

The most credible generalizations are those with the most and best examples supporting them. You cannot reasonably conclude that all algebra teachers are women if your experience is limited to one or two teachers, but you can reasonably conclude that teenagers like rock music if you have known hundreds of teenagers in many different settings, all of whom like rock music. In supporting generalizations, you need to know how many examples are enough and which examples to include. Unfortunately, no simple formula exists that can supply answers to these questions, but the following general rules of thumb can be helpful.

How Many Examples are Enough? First, the more sweeping your claim, the more examples you will need. Generalizations can be phrased at any point along a continuum of frequency: "*Some* business majors are good in math"; "*Many* business majors are good in math"; "*All* business majors are good in math." Although the word "some" does constitute a generalization, it is a very limited generalization, a safe one to make if you don't have abundant evidence. To support "some," you need only a handful of examples. "Many" requires more than a handful of examples, certainly, but it is far easier to prove than "all." In fact, absolute statements using words like "all," "everyone," "never," or "always," should be avoided altogether in written argument unless every constituent in the group referred to can be accounted for. Otherwise, the claims they make are too grandiose to be credible.

The following passage supports its factual generalization with carefully chosen examples:

> Despite the stereotype of the "yuppie," the young urban professional, as selfish and materialistic, many young professionals that I know are neither selfish nor particularly materialistic. My friend John, a lawyer with a prominent firm, spends part of his weekends doing volunteer work for the Boy Scouts. Another friend, Mary, who is a very successful accountant, spends almost all her weekends with her parents, who live over a hundred miles away and who are having trouble taking care of their house because of illness. And an aquaintance of mine, Chris, who is vice-president of a software development firm, is directing the fund-raising activities for a new building for his church. I could cite other examples as well. Of course, some young professionals are simply out to get all they can for themselves. But many, probably most, have little in common with the greedy, amoral yuppie of popular folklore.

In this passage three examples are given to support the claim that "many" young professionals do not fit the image of the yuppie, and at the end, after giving these three examples and claiming he could cite others, the writer claims that "probably most" young professionals don't fit this image either. In a formal academic argument, we would probably insist on more rigorous proof, such as the other examples the writer claims he could cite, but we would very likely accept these examples as adequate in a short informal essay. As a general rule, three is a good number of examples for a short essay, since one or two examples might seem to be merely exceptions, while four or more examples might be overkill.

The less familiar your readers are with your subject matter, the more specific examples you should supply. If your readers are very comfortable and familiar with your topic, they will often accept sensible generalizations that are only minimally supported. If you refer in an internal business report to the "widespread reliability problems with our new printer," those familiar with the problem will accept the reference and not demand that it be supported. But a reader unfamiliar with this problem may demand evidence that the problem really exists. Of course, some readers unfamiliar with your subject area will accept dubious generalizations simply because they don't know any better. If these readers are misled, however, some of them will probably eventually learn that you were wrong in your generalizations, and they will then suspect your reliability in other situations, even when you are correct in your claims.

Do Your Examples Fairly Represent the Evidence? In selecting which evidence for your generalization to include in your argument, you should make sure that the examples you choose are representative of the ones you have omitted. If, for example, you support the statement "Local elections are controlled by the state capital" with three good examples of this control, but in the course of your research you discovered that there is much evidence contradicting your generalization, you are misrepresenting the evidence by failing to cite this material. True, you may have provided enough examples to satisfy your reader, but you are misleading him by excluding the contradictory evidence. The best way around this error is to qualify the thesis in such a way that the evidence you omit is not contradictory. If you rewrote the claim as "The state capital has controlled a number of local elections in the recent past," your three examples would perfectly support the claim, and the omitted evidence would no longer be contradictory.

Activities (7.3)

1. For two of the following statements, write a paragraph that gives some brief examples to support or refute the statement.
   a. The American people are becoming increasingly aware of and angry about the damage done by drunken drivers.
   b. Most college students look forward to getting married and raising a family some day.
   c. Very few people succeed without hard work.
   d. Country and western music is not very popular with college students.
   e. Fast food restaurants, grocery stores, and other service establishments are finding it harder to hire hourly workers.

2. Write a generalization that is adequately supported by the examples listed for each case below.
   a. John, Susan, and Jim prefer chocolate ice cream, while Jane prefers strawberry and Henry prefers vanilla.
   b. Last Saturday night I sat alone at a showing of the new film *Anxious Hours*, and I saw no line for the film when I walked by the theater just before show time on Sunday.
   c. It is January 15th here in Minnesota and so far this winter we have had two snowfalls that just covered the ground and then disappeared.

    d. There were twenty-five Mercedes-Benz's parked in the lot the night of my
       high school reunion, and as I recall there were only about seventy students
       in my graduating class.
    e. When I returned from winter break to my classes here in Vermont, I noticed
       that Jack, Jeff, Mary, Matthew, Carrie, and Megan all had deep tans.

STATISTICS

Statistics is factual information compiled and reported numerically. Statements like "Thirty percent of the American people believe a woman should
never be president," "The unemployment rate is 11 percent," or "One quarter
of all bridges in this state need repair" are statistics—they indicate the number
of instances in which a given fact applies to a particular group of subjects. In
our world, statistics are an inevitable and integral part of our lives. We judge the
quality of our manufactured products and of many of our services through statistics; we constantly encounter statistics on the health of our economy, our
educational system, our sex lives, our souls. We tend to suspect claims that
lack statistical support and use statistics in virtually every field in our society,
from weather forecasting to managing baseball teams.

    These statistics we depend on are usually generalizations; they infer broad
applicability of a thesis from particular instances. If you read that 80 percent of
high school juniors would rather see a movie than read a book, you can be certain that not *every* high school junior has been contacted. Surveying every high
school junior in the United States is too massive an undertaking to be feasible.
In all probability, a manageable number of juniors has been surveyed and from
the results of that survey, certain general conclusions have been made. In other
words, specific instances (the results of the survey of, let's say, 500 students)
have led to general conclusions (that 80 percent of high school juniors would
rather see a movie than read a book).

    Statistics can be a powerful tool in argument, if used responsibly and in
moderation. Occasionally, you may conduct your own statistical studies and
report the findings in your argument, but more frequently you will include statistics obtained from secondary sources. Whether your statistical generalizations are original with you or cited from another study, you must ensure that
they are conducted and reported according to certain principles. Only then
can they qualify as reliable evidence for your argument. These principles are
as follows:

    First, the smaller group surveyed (or *sample*, as statisticians refer to it)
must be known. If you read that eight out of ten women think they are over-
weight, but no reference is made to the source of the survey or who or how
many were surveyed, you should not accept or use the figure. For all you

know, only ten women were questioned, and they were picked from a list obtained from a Weight Watcher's clinic. Every cited study should be identified and the sample group defined. Without such information, the figures are suspect.

Second, the sample must be *sufficient* in order for you to accept the conclusion drawn from that sample. That both your roommates prefer classical music to rock does not justify the conclusion that classical music is more popular with college students; you need a much larger sample.

And **third**, the sample must be *representative*. If a figure is given about the political inclinations of all Californians, the sample surveyed must represent a cross section of the population. If the 2000 people questioned all have incomes of $40,000 and up, or if they're all over the age of 45, your sample is slanted, not representative of the variety of the population as a whole. Professional polling organizations like Gallup and Harris (groups hired to identify the preferences of large populations based on small samples) choose either a representative or a random sample. A *representative sample* is one that guarantees in advance that the sample will reflect the major characteristics of the population, for example, that the sample will have a percentage of Californians earning over $40,000 that is equal or nearly equal to the percentage of Californians earning over that figure in the total population. In a *random sample* on political attitudes in California, every adult Californian would stand an equal chance of being questioned. When chosen randomly, in 95 out of 100 cases a sample group of 1500 people will be within 3 percentage points of duplicating the answers of the entire adult population. Thus, in evaluating the usefulness of any poll, you should know the method by which the sample was selected.

When you include in your argument statistics obtained from other sources, not only must you test them for the preceding three principles, you must also be certain they satisfy the requirements of second- or third-party facts. The source should have a reputation for expertise in the field and for objectivity; and the figures themselves should be recent. It is unwise to accept as support for your own argument any statistical data not credited to an authoritative source. If you cannot identify the instrument, individual, or organization through which these facts were obtained, chances are good that those facts are not reliable.

When using statistics in your argument, you also need to be aware of the variety of terms used to report large figures and of the way these terms can influence the impact of the figures. A study on high school literacy could report its findings on extracurricular reading habits in a number of ways. It could say that out of 500 high school seniors surveyed, **100** had read at least one unassigned novel in the last year; or the same fact could be reported as **twenty percent** of the students. Of those 100 readers, one could report the **average** number or **mean** of novels read (the total number of novels read divided by the

100 readers), the **mode** (the number of novels most frequently read by individual students), or the **median** (the midpoint of the range of frequency of novels read). The mean, mode, and median for this sample of students are displayed below:

STUDENTS	NOVELS READ	TOTAL NOVELS
25	4	100
10	3	30
45	2	90
20	1	20
TOTAL 100		240

AVERAGE = 2.4 novels (total number of novels read divided by total number of students)

MODE = 2 novels (the most common number)

MEDIAN = 2 (midpoint of the list of number of novels read according to the frequency of the number. Imagine the hundred students standing in a line, starting with all those that read four novels, then those that read three, then two, etc. The midpoint of this line of 100 would occur in the group of students that had read two novels.)

Statistics can be useful in argument, but if scattered profusely throughout a written text, they can have a deadening effect; do not try to bury a reader in statistics. Remember also that a visual display of statistics through a chart or a table can be extremely valuable to the reader in helping to clarify the meaning of the statistics and to reinforce their significance. With statistics it is easy to lose track not only of the " big picture" but of any picture at all; visual displays give the reader the needed picture.

Activities (7.4)

1. For two of the following statements based on statistics, write a paragraph stating the kind of information you would need to assure yourself that the statement was reliable.
   a. Over 50 percent of the doctors surveyed in a nationwide study recommend Brand A medicine over any of the leading competitors.
   b. Brand C: the best built truck in America, according to a survey of truck owners.
   c. Over 60 percent of all Americans favor the President's plan for peace, while 85 percent oppose Senator Flag's call for more offensive weapons.
   d. Despite competition from television and VCRs, moviegoing is still popular in America. When asked how much they enjoyed going to the movies, 88 percent of moviegoers responded that they enjoyed moviegoing a great deal.
   e. A survey of leading economic forecasters indicates that a mild recession will occur in the next six months.

2. Conduct a survey of some of your classmates or of some friends. Ask them one or two questions that can be summarized in statistics, such as how many hours they have studied this week. Compute the mean, mode, and median for these statistics. Write a one-page description of the results of your survey and also present this information in visual form. Also state how representative you believe this group is of some larger but similar group, such as all students who studied last week.

SUMMARY

Supporting Facts

- To support facts founded in your own experience, you must
  describe the experience accurately and clearly;
  establish your own credibility through a responsible, objective, and accurate rendering of the experience.
- To support facts reported by others, you must
  be satisfied of their accuracy;
  provide in your argument brief reference to the source of the fact.
- To support a factual generalization, you must cite a number of the verified facts that have led you to the general conclusion.
  The more sweeping the generalization, the more examples you will need to cite.
  If your readers are likely to be unfamiliar with the subject matter, you should provide several examples as evidence.
  The examples cited must be typical of all the evidence discovered.
- Statistics can be effective support for arguments, provided they are not overused and their significance is made clear.
- When including a statistical generalization, you must be satisfied of its reliability. It is reliable if the sample cited is known, sufficient, and representative.
- You must be aware of the exact meaning of the terms used to report statistical conclusions, particularly average, median, and mode.

A SAMPLE FACTUAL ARGUMENT

The following factual argument, intended for a general audience, presents what to many would be a surprising hypothesis—that the specific language we speak influences how we view the world—and then questions whether this hypothesis will ever become a commonly agreed-upon fact among linguists and other students of language. This brief sample offers a caution to writers of arguments: some plausible hypotheses, even ones that are widely discussed and accepted, turn out to be incorrect or in need of substantial revision before they can be accepted as facts.

THE WHORF HYPOTHESIS

One question that has drawn the attention of twentieth-century linguists is the effect of specific languages on our thoughts and perceptions. Does a speaker of English see the world differently from a speaker of German or Chinese or any other language? And if he does, what are these differences? Are they in specific ideas or in more general patterns of thought? Do speakers of different languages literally *see* the world differently, in the sense of noticing different objects or qualities of objects because their language has words for them?

Languages vary enormously in their sounds, grammar, and vocabulary. In vocabulary, differences are striking. As Carley H. Dodd notes in his *Dynamics of Intercultural Communication*, English has at least seven words for the spectrum of colors from violet to red, but the American Indian language called Shona has four, while another American Indian language, Basa, has two. For our one word ''snow'' Eskimo languages have as many as twenty-five words (p. 136). In grammar, differences are even more striking. The student of language Benjamin Lee Whorf observed that the American Indian language of Hopi contains no past, present, and future tense and uses instead a scheme based on distinguishing between the always true (for example, ''people need food''), occurrences that are observed or could be observed, and occurrences that are not observable or at least not yet observed (Ellis and Beatie, pp. 58-59).

Whorf's study of American Indian languages, which he carried out in the 1920s and 1930s, led to his formulation of what is variously called ''the Whorf hypothesis'' or ''the Sapir-Whorf hypothesis'' (co-named for the linguist Edward Sapir, with whom Whorf studied) or ''the linguistic relativity hypothesis.'' Stated simply, the hypothesis claims that specific languages, especially the underlying patterns of specific languages, play a major role in determining the thought and behavior of a culture. One of Whorf's most famous formulations of this hypothesis is the essay ''The Relation of Habitual Thought and Behavior to Language,'' where he argues that a major characteristic of Hopi behavior, the emphasis on preparation, is a result of linguistic patterns in Hopi (Whorf, pp. 134-159). As Whorf puts it, this emphasis ''includes announcing and getting ready for events well beforehand, elaborate precautions to insure persistence of desired conditions, and stress on good will as the preparer of right results'' (p. 148). Our culture, because of the different view of time implied by English and other major European languages, does not stress preparation as intensely as Hopi culture.

Is the Whorf hypothesis true? Andrew Ellis and Geoffrey Beatie, in their *The Psychology of Language and Communication*, report on studies indicating that humans actually see the same colors even though the number and reference of their words for colors may vary enormously (p. 61). We know that a speaker of English will observe different kinds of snow, even though there is only one ''snow'' in his or her vocabulary. Whorf, however, was mainly concerned with the more subtle and profound effects of language on the basic world view of a culture. Even here, though, Whorf seems to have downplayed the effect society has on language, as a study reported by Ellis and Beatie of the changing nature of Chinese shows: Chinese is becoming more abstract as it moves to accommodate modern science and technology (pp. 61-62). Of course, we are not in a position to observe the social conditions prevailing during the formation of our major languages, but it seems just as plausible to argue that these early societies affected the nature of the language as much or more than the languages affected the society. Certainly today we observe rapid changes in language, at least in vocabulary, as a result of social change.

The Whorf hypothesis does contain some useful insights. We will probably notice different kinds of snow if we have different words for these kinds, and different languages may encourage different kinds of thought. But we do not have much evidence to show that language actually determines a culture's pattern of thought. At least for now, the Whorf hypothesis remains a hypothesis, tantalizing in its suggestive possibilities but unproven and apparently too one-sided in its view of how language and society interact.

WORKS CITED

Dodd, Carley H. *Dynamics of Intercultural Communication*. Dubuque, Iowa: Brown, 1987.

Ellis, Andrew and Geoffrey Beatie. *The Psychology of Language and Communication*. London: Weidenfeld and Nicolson, 1986.

Whorf, Benjamin Lee. ''The Relation of Habitual Thought and Behavior to Language.'' *Language, Thought, and Reality: Selected Writings of Benjamin Lee Whorf*. Ed. John B. Carroll. New York: Technology Press of M.I.T. and Wiley, 1956, pp. 134-159.

Suggestions for Writing (7.5)

1. Write a two-to-three-page essay proving a fact that runs counter to popular opinion. This fact can come from your own experience, from your studies in college, or from your general knowledge. Examples of such surprising facts are: "Despite predictions to the contrary, the increasing use of computers has created more new jobs than it has eliminated existing ones." "In spite of their image as cold and unfriendly places, large cities (or a specific city you know) can be friendly places." This surprising fact can be about yourself, your family, your friends, your hometown, your college, your job, your academic field, or whatever else comes to mind.

2. Stereotypes are misleading factual generalizations that make the false claim that all members of a group have a certain trait: "The English people have stiff upper lips in times of crisis." "American men like to watch football." Take a prevalent stereotype and analyze to what degree the stereotype is true and how the stereotype is misleading. Make sure the stereotype is one you can deal with in a four-to-five-page essay, such as "Engineering students at my college don't get involved in extracurricular activities." You don't have to do a statistical survey to gather data for this essay, but you should carefully examine and present samples to support your thesis.

3. Analyze either a newspaper or a television news show for examples of bias or misleading generalizations (for the television news show you may have to videotape the show so that you can view it two or three times). How objective is the reporting of the news? Are there any examples of misleading generalizations? What kind of news is *not* included? Write a two-to-three-page essay addressing these questions.

Chapter 8

Making Causal Arguments

Making causal arguments is not a simple matter of isolating *the* single cause of a given effect. Causality, like the many-headed Hydra monster of Greek mythology, is multifaceted; every time you think you have isolated a cause, another possibility crops up. In order to create reasonable causal arguments, you must be aware of the complicated nature of the causal beast.

We suggest you be particularly respectful of the complexity of causality in the early stages of your causal analysis, when you are first investigating the possible causes of an effect. Because of the many varieties of cause, you should make your initial list of candidates as inclusive as possible, listing even those factors that seem farfetched. Later, you can apply the principles discussed in this chapter to narrow and rank the entries on the list. But you must not narrow too soon, or you risk overlooking some or all of the causes you are seeking.

CAUSAL CONSTELLATIONS

We find it useful to view the operation of causality as a constellation—a cluster of causes with varying degrees of influence, but all in some way contributing to a particular effect. We use the term *causal constellation* to refer to this entire range of causes—immediate, remote, necessary, contributing—that create and influence a particular effect. The following example illustrates this concept of the constellation.

Suppose you are trying to understand why your best friend Emma decided to drop out of college. Your friend explains her decision simply by saying that she didn't like college, but you know the question is more complicated, and it's important to you to get a fuller understanding. Why didn't she like college?

What circumstances and conditions caused an unhappiness strong enough to prompt this extreme decision? After careful thought, you come up with a number of reasons for her action.

For one thing, Emma was not doing well academically. Although a good student in high school, she found college work extremely difficult. Because she is the kind of person who gets down on herself for failure, her poor academic performance had to have been a blow to her self-esteem; it makes sense that she would want to leave a place where she didn't feel good about herself. Also, Emma was the first person in her family to go to college. Her parents, who were not well educated, had worked very hard so she could have the educational advantages they had lacked. Their ambition for Emma put a lot of pressure on her, which probably made it even harder for her to relax and do her best. Emma's family background worked against her in another way: it deprived her of any close role models to emulate, of any family tradition of success. Graduating from college seemed very foreign to her. Add to these factors Emma's crazy roommate and her distaste for dormitory life, and you begin to wonder how Emma lasted through the first semester.

Your examination of the situation has identified a number of causes for Emma's decision—some very immediate, like the fact that she did not like college; some directly influential, like her poor academic performance, her low self-esteem, and her crazy roommate; some much more remote in time, like her parents' lack of a college degree. But in one way or another, you conclude, all of these factors influenced Emma's decision. Only a thorough analysis like the one you have conducted can fully explain the reasons behind a given effect. The next step would be to determine more precisely the relative influence of each point in the constellation. But in order to take this step, you must know something about the properties of the different points in the constellation.

Causal Chains

Some effects are best understood in terms of a directly related series of causes, like links in a single chain, or a row of sequentially falling dominoes. In these cases, the entire constellation, of which the chain is a part, is less important than an identification of the single *causal chain:* A led to B, which led to C, which ended in effect D.

If someone told you that 'closed captioning' of television shows (where subtitles can be seen on specially equipped televisions) is a result of the rubella epidemic in the United States during the 1960s, you might initially reject the connection as utterly implausible. What you have been given is the first cause and final effect in a causal chain; if the links in the causal chain are filled in, the connection is reasonable. In the 1960s, there *was* a widespread outbreak of rubella, or German measles (at the time, there was no rubella inoculation). Rubella is a relatively harmless disease except to the fetuses of pregnant women; babies whose mothers contract rubella during pregnancy often suffer birth defects, one of which is deafness. Because of the epidemic, huge numbers of babies were born deaf. In the last twenty years, as these children have grown, we have seen increased sensitivity to the needs of the hearing-impaired, one of the most notable being the media's recent provision of closed captioning for television. With all the links in the chain identified, the causal connection between a common virus and the closed captioning service is no longer implausible, though there were other factors at work as well, including the increasing emphasis on the rights of the handicapped in the last twenty years.

The constellation leading to Emma's withdrawal from college contains a causal chain. Beginning with her decision to withdraw, we can move straight back as far as her parents' lack of a college education. The chain works as follows: Emma withdrew from college because she didn't like it. She didn't like it because she felt low self-esteem in that setting. This low self-esteem was a result of poor grades, which at least in part were caused by the enormous pressure she was under to do well. This pressure came from her parents, who, because they had never been to college, desperately wanted Emma to be the first in the family to get a college degree. Not all of the points in the constellation we identified earlier appear in this chain. So while the chain explains much about the evolution of Emma's decision, it does not explain everything, just as the chain linking the rubella epidemic with closed captioning is not the fullest possible explanation of the situation.

Activities (8.1)

1. For two of the following effects, prepare a constellation of probable causes and then discuss in a paragraph or two the amount of influence exerted by each point or cause.
   a. The election of George Bush to the Presidency in 1988.
   b. The success of Japanese products in the American market.
   c. The popularity of American movies throughout much of the world.
   d. The rebirth of feminism in America in the last twenty years.
   e. The increasing interest of college students in liberal arts programs.
2. For two of the following causes and remote effects, write a paragraph describing a plausible causal chain that links the cause with the remote effect.
   a. Cause: the rise of industrialization. Effect: the growth of the conservation movement.
   b. Cause: the invention of gunpowder. Effect: the decline of knighthood.
   c. Cause: Jane's high absenteeism in third grade. Effect: Jane's difficulty with cursive writing.
   d. Cause: the invention of printing. Effect: the growth of democracy in Europe and America.
   e. Cause: Jack's love of parties. Effect: Jack's becoming the mayor of his city.

Necessary and Sufficient Causes

Within any causal constellation, some causes will seem less influential than others—some will shine very brightly as contributors to the effect, others will be dim, though still clearly present. One reason for this variety has to do with time: some causes are more distant from the effect chronologically, and thus seem less important than the more immediate factors. Causes are distinguished from each other in another important way: for every effect, we can expect at least one *necessary* cause and any number of *sufficient* causes.

A *necessary* cause is a cause without which the effect could not have taken place. One cannot get typhus without the introduction of a rickettsia, or gram-negative microorganism, into the bloodstream. This rickettsia is necessary to the contraction of the disease. Thus, you can be certain that anyone who has contracted typhus has been infected by this particular microorganism. But while introduction of the rickettsia is necessary to the contraction of typhus, it doesn't guarantee that the disease will result. People with a vigorous immune system or who have been inoculated against typhus will be safe from the disease.

Necessary causes are usually easy to identify: if we know the effect, we know that certain causes or conditions had to be operating. To use a nonscientific example, if you had not parked your car next to a construction site, it would not have been hit by falling debris. Parking your car in that spot was necessary to the effect. And in the case of Emma, the cause necessary to her withdrawing from college was her unhappiness there. Presumably, if she had been happy and had liked college, she would have stayed.

A necessary cause is not always by itself sufficient to produce the effect. It was necessary for you to park your car next to that building site in order for it to be hit, but your choice of a parking space did not ensure that it would be. Other things had to happen as well—the crane holding the concrete debris had to break, for example. A *sufficient* cause is one that is capable of producing a particular effect. A person's decision to join a health club can have a number of sufficient causes—winning a year's membership in a raffle; wanting to meet new people; wanting to become physically fit. Any one of these motives would be enough to prompt an individual to join a health club, but none of them *has* to exist in order for that decision to be made; that is, they are all sufficient to the effect, but not necessary. In Emma's case, a number of sufficient causes operated: her poor self-esteem, her crazy roommate, her distaste for dormitory life. Any one of these might have been enough to prompt her decision, but none of them was necessary to that decision.

Sometimes a single cause combines the properties of necessity and sufficiency. The example of the rickettsia demonstrates this combination. Not only *must* one be infected with that microorganism to contract typhus (the necessary cause), but this infection is by itself enough to cause the disease (the sufficient cause).

Understanding the concepts of necessary cause and sufficient cause can be extremely useful as you prepare causal arguments. To qualify as a cause for a given effect, a causal candidate *must* satisfy the conditions of a necessary or sufficient cause, or both. If it does not, it is not a direct cause of the effect, though it may well have influenced the effect in some way.

Central Causes

Many causal arguments identify and support a *central cause*—the one that seems to be most powerful in bringing about an effect. The central cause accounts for that effect more than any other cause; its absence minimizes the influence of the other causes, or in some cases, prevents the effect altogether. Usually the central cause is both necessary and sufficient—its presence capable of bringing about the effect, its absence enough to prevent it. Not all effects have such a single dominating cause. To determine whether such a cause exists, you must first be aware of the wider constellation and the relative dominance of each cause.

In arguing a central cause, we run a risk of oversimplifying and even misrepresenting cause, since there is frequently a subtle and complicated interplay of causes. For example, pointing to the rise of Naziism as the central cause of World War Two risks suggesting that other conditions and circumstances— including tensions between the United States and Japan and the worldwide depression of the 1930s—were irrelevant. And pointing to Emma's unhappiness at college as the central cause of her withdrawing doesn't really give us a deep understanding of her decision. Arguing a central cause can be enormously valuable, but you should indicate somewhere in your argument your awareness of the other factors involved.

Contributing Factors

In analyzing causes, we occasionally find a circumstance that is neither necessary nor sufficient yet somehow relevant. This type of circumstance is labeled a *contributing factor*. If Kathy continues to jog even when she is run down, and then catches a virus, her jogging was not a sufficient cause of her illness—the presence of the virus without sufficient antibodies to combat it is the sufficient cause. Nor is the jogging a necessary cause, since she may have gotten the virus even without jogging. Yet her pushing herself while not feeling "100 percent" certainly didn't help and may have made her more susceptible to disease. In this case we can label the jogging as a probable contributing factor.

Emma's situation contains at least one contributing factor: her lack of a close role model. Clearly, this factor was not necessary to the effect, nor was it sufficiently influential to have caused her withdrawal. Yet it made a bad situation worse, depriving Emma of any positive example from which to take heart. Contributing factors are present in most complicated situations; if your goal is a thorough analysis of cause, you need to take contributing factors into account.

Deciding Which Causes To Argue

We have already noted that identifying and arguing the full causal constellation will give the fullest possible explanation of an effect. But it is not always appropriate to reconstruct the full constellation; the ultimate purpose of causal argument is not always thorough explanation. If the point of your argument is to assign responsibility, you would concern yourself only with immediate causes (such as who did what, regardless of why). If your argument has an instructive purpose, and if you want some action taken or avoided on the basis of the causality you demonstrate in a similar situation, you will emphasize those causes, both immediate and remote, that exist in your current situation. If you wish to be as successful in mathematics as Susan is, you might try to reproduce as many of the causes of her success as you can; you certainly can emulate her conscientiousness with homework, her regular class attendance, her active class participation, but a third cause of her success—Susan's family of talented mathematicians—will not help you at all.

In short, never begin a causal argument without first identifying to yourself what purpose you want the argument to serve. Only then can you determine which causes to look for and to argue.

Activities (8.2)

1. For two of the samples below, write a paragraph or two describing what you believe are the necessary or sufficient causes, the contributing factors, and factors that seem to be irrelevant. Indicate briefly why you have categorized each possible cause as you have.
    a. Effect: John's car accident. Possible causes: John was driving at night on a poorly lit road; the road was wet from rain; John had taken a very difficult exam that morning; John was driving ten miles per hour over the speed limit.
    b. Effect: the dramatic increase in the use of VCRs in the last few years. Possible causes: The cost of VCRs is now at an affordable level for most Americans; videotapes of films are increasingly available; the viewer can choose what film he will watch with the VCR; many Americans have a large amount of leisure time available.
    c. Effect: the decline in oil and gasoline prices in the middle 1980s. Possible causes: On the average, cars were more fuel efficient than they were ten years before; there was a growing awareness that petroleum is a nonrenewable resource; the oil-exporting countries were producing more oil than the world consumed.

     d. Effect: Louise's winning an award for the best violin recital at the music festival. Possible causes: Louise practices the violin three hours each day; Louise's parents found the city's best violin teacher for her when she was five; from a very early age it was obvious that Louise was talented musically; Louise prefers Mozart to any other composer.

     e. Effect: Charles's favorite hobby is cross-country skiing. Possible causes: Charles wants to stay in shape, and cross-country skiing is very good for the cardiovascular system; he likes winter and being out-of-doors; he is on a tight budget and cannot afford downhill skiing this year; he was once injured while downhill skiing; in high school he won prizes in cross-country ski races.

2. Do any of the causes you identified above qualify as central causes? If you believe any do, write a paragraph explaining why the cause fits as a central cause.

DETERMINING CAUSALITY

Sometimes in analyzing causes you will discover a number of possible sufficient causes for an effect and not know which were actually operating. In these cases you will need other methods for determining probable cause. The following strategies were formulated by the nineteenth-century philosopher John Stuart Mill to determine cause in such situations. While Mill was looking for ways to establish cause with scientific certainty, his methods have proven to be very useful in situations where certainty is unreachable.

Method of Agreement

This method can be used when you are investigating the cause of two or more similar effects. In these instances you determine what the sets of events preceding each effect have in common; you are looking for a single sufficient cause that operated in all these similar cases.

If you were investigating the reason or reasons for the success of the five bestselling hardbound books of the year, you would list all the factors that might have contributed to the success of each book—that is, the significant characteristics of each. If all the books centered on the subject of personal relationships in the 1980s, you could safely identify subject matter as the leading cause of the books' success. Sometimes you will not discover a factor common to all your effects; perhaps the five bestsellers have no single common characteristic, which means a number of sufficient causes are operating in these instances.

In another example, if you were trying to explain why all your roommates failed the same economics test, and you realized that all of them had had poor grades in high school math, you have discovered a probable cause for their failure on the test: a poor background in mathematics.

The cause you have identified through this and all methods of determination must be linked to the effect through an acceptable principle of behavior. In the case of the economics test, which involves human action, you can only be confident in the cause you have identified if an acceptable linking principle exists. Here, that principle—a poor foundation in a field related and necessary to economics—is perfectly acceptable.

Method of Difference

Mill's method of difference can be applied to determine why two essentially similar situations turned out very differently. If you want to know why one self-help book succeeded while another failed, why one calculus class with Professor Jones was interesting while another was boring, or why the Confederate army lost the battle of Gettysburg but won the battles of Bull Run, you can apply the difference method by looking for the factor present in one case but absent in the other. If the only difference between your two calculus classes with Professor Jones was that the subject matter of the second class was more advanced, that could well be the reason for your unhappiness in the second class.

This method will only work when you are examining truly similar situations that share a number of common factors. If you were trying to account for the difference between your career choice and that of one of your grandparents, the situations would be too dissimilar for the method of difference to tell you anything; your grandparents faced an entirely different range of career choices than you did.

Method of Proportional Correlations

This method is useful in determining the cause of an effect that is continuing and varied—the movement of the Dow Jones Industrial Average, the increase and occasional decrease in the gross national product, the enrollment of college students in certain kinds of majors. In trying to identify possible causes of such measurable trends, you should look for conditions preceding the trends that vary and persist proportionally. In considering the reasons for the rise in the divorce rate over the last ten years, you might discover that there has been a congruent increase in the number of two-income families over the same time period; that is, that there has been an increase in the number of married women who are economically self-sustaining. This fact of increasing economic independence of women is a plausible explanation of the increased divorce rate if it satisfies the following three conditions: (1) if it is truly independent of the effect (not a result of the same cause); (2) if the two trends, with all their fluctuations, are truly proportional; and (3) if the cause and effect are plausibly linked by an accepted behavioral principle—in this case the principle or motive of independence or self-reliance. If these three conditions are satisfied, we would accept that the economic independence of wives is a sufficient cause of divorce.

Activities (8.3)

1. Write a paragraph analyzing which of the three methods of determining cause (agreement, difference, proportional correlation) is operating in two of these examples.
   a. His analysis of sales of luxury items over the last twenty years revealed that sales of luxury items increased dramatically during times of general prosperity and decreased dramatically during times of economic recession.
   b. All great athletes share a burning desire to succeed.
   c. There is increasing evidence linking weather turbulence on the earth to heightened sunspot activity.
   d. The products of Ajax Company outperform those of Ajax's competitors in consumer satisfaction surveys. Ajax performs so well because of its strong quality program that involves employees at all levels.
   e. Optimists get sick less often and recover from illness more quickly than pessimists.
2. Take a group of at least three of your classmates or friends who share a common trait, such as their academic major, a hobby, or some other favorite activity, and try to determine what sufficient cause made each member of the group have this trait. Try to find a common sufficient cause for the entire group, but be prepared to end up with different sufficient causes if a common cause does not reveal itself. Write a one-page essay describing the results of your investigation.
3. Compare two classes you have taken sometime in your education, one that you liked and one that you disliked. The two classes should be as similar as possible in subject matter and level of difficulty. What made the one class likable, while the other was not? Write a one-page essay addressing this question.
4. For the next week, compare fluctuations in two phenomena that you believe might be related, such as the temperature and attendance at one of your classes. Make a chart comparing the movement of these two phenomena and then see if any proportional correlation exists between the two. If there is such a correlation, ask yourself if the two are the result of the same cause and if some plausible behavioral principle links the two. Write a one-page analysis of your study. Be sure to give your instructor the chart you have created.

CAUSALITY IN HUMAN ACTIONS

As we noted in the preceding section, actions carried out by an individual or group are linked to their causes by some universal principle or motivator of human behavior. As an example of how human motivations work in such causal relationships, let's look at the simple proposition that increased fuel prices in the 1970s were responsible for the popularity of fuel-efficient compact cars. This is a simple causal statement, with a fact at the causal end and an action (also a fact) at the effect end.

high fuel prices   popularity of fuel-efficient cars
                (cause)   (effect)

This causal proposition is only plausible if its two sides are linked by some acceptable motive. Why would people buy fuel-efficient cars if fuel prices were high? What motive or need would urge them to react to a particular fact with a particular behavior? In this case, the answer is so obvious that it doesn't need stating in the argument itself: the people who bought compact cars wanted to save money, to conserve their resources; faced with high fuel prices, they bought cars that would use fuel efficiently. Now the fact and behavior are plausibly connected by this universal motivation:

high fuel prices . . . . popularity of fuel-efficient cars
                {desire to conserve their resources}

If you can supply no such motivation between cause and effect, your theory is not plausible, and it's time to look for another cause.

Activities (8.4)

For two of the causes and effects listed below, write a paragraph on each describing a probable human motivation that links the two.

1. Cause: increased leisure time. Effect: more participation in sports like jogging and cross-country skiing.
2. Cause: an abundance of food for most Americans. Effect: a stress on thinness in fashions and in our ideals of beauty.
3. Cause: special incentives that reduce the price of automobiles. Effect: higher automobile sales.
4. Cause: severe economic conditions. Effect: a lowering of the birth rate.
5. Cause: the banning of a book. Effect: increased demand for the book.

SUMMARY

The Nature of Causality and Determining Cause

- Lacking carefully controlled scientific conditions, you can rarely claim absolute certainty for the causes you identify.
- Because causality is always multifaceted, keep your mind open to all possibilities early in your causal investigations.
- A causal constellation is the entire range of causes that create and influence a given effect. Within any constellation, the following points exist:

  causal chain: a series of causes leading in a direct chronological line to the effect;

  necessary cause: the cause without which the effect could not have occurred;

  sufficient cause: a cause that by itself could produce the effect;

  central cause: the single, most powerful cause, usually combining elements of necessity and sufficiency;

  contributing factors: circumstances that are neither necessary nor sufficient causes but that play a role in creating an event of condition.

- The ultimate purpose of your argument (to explain, instruct, or designate responsibility) will determine which points in the constellation are most relevant to your argument.
- When faced with a number of potential sufficient causes for an effect, use the following methods to determine the actual, or at least most probable, cause or causes:

  use the *method of agreement* to find the cause of similar effects;

  use the *method of difference* to determine why two similar situations turned out differently;

  use the *method of proportional correlation* to determine the cause of an effect that varies over time.

- Human actions must be linked to their causes by an assumable motive.

SUPPORTING CAUSAL ARGUMENTS

Most causal arguments are supported through (1) establishing the factuality of the effect(s) and cause(s) you discuss; (2) describing the process (method of difference or of agreement, for example) by which you determine and exclude causes; (3) identifying, if only implicitly, an acceptable motive in arguments involving human action; and (4) stating the degree of certainty of your argument.

Establishing Factuality

Facts are the foundations of causal argument. While in most causal arguments you will write, the causal relationship you propose between two events will rarely be certain and verifiable, there can be no room to doubt the certainty of the events you are linking; they *must* be true in order for your argument to be meaningful and plausible. If you misrepresent the effect through exaggeration, understatement, or inaccuracy, your identification of cause is useless; you are explaining something that didn't actually occur.

Reporting the Process of Determination

Proper use of any of the processes of determination discussed above will provide you with much of the material necessary for supporting your argument. Usually, the best way to convince your audience that your proposed cause is probable is to demonstrate how you arrived at that cause—in other words, to report your application of method to the situation at hand. You don't need to use terms like "method of agreement" or "necessary" or "sufficient cause," but you should provide a summary, a kind of narrative of your investigation.

If your argument identified the reasons for the failure of a number of restaurants in your town, it probably would have relied on the method of agreement, because you are looking for an explanation common to all the restaurant closings. Your report of the process might read something like this:

> From 1984 to 1986, four new restaurants were opened in the small town of East Bay, Wisconsin. None of the restaurants was able to draw enough customers to keep operating; each closed within five months of its opening.
>
> The restaurants had little in common. One specialized in moderately priced Chinese foods, serving lunches and dinners six days a week; one was a diner, with inexpensive diner-style meals served at all hours, seven days a week. *Le Papillon*, an elegant French restaurant, was the most expensive of the four, but the meals were well worth the price. The fourth restaurant, a member of a popular family-restaurant franchise, while serving the least distinctive fare, was well suited to the needs of entire families.
>
> The locations of the restaurants were as varied as their fare and ambience. The Chinese restaurant was located on a busy street just outside central downtown, a street full of strollers and window shoppers throughout the year. The diner was in a converted trolley on the outskirts of a newly gentrified section of town. *Le Papillon* was one of a series of shops and restaurants in the new shopping plaza north of town, and the family restaurant was in an indoor shopping mall.

Located in very different spots throughout town, catering to different classes of customers and offering food ranging in quality from passable to excellent, these restaurants seem to have nothing in common that might explain their almost concurrent failures. But this concurrency was a significant common feature. All four restaurants opened and closed within the same two-year period. All the failures were probably caused more by timing than any other factor.

The years 1984 to 1986 were terrible years for East Bay. In 1984 the ball bearing plant, the town's largest employer, closed. The unemployment rate in East Bay soared to a very high rate of 30 percent. Given the bleak economic picture during this period, it is no surprise that all these restaurants failed. In 1986 the outlook for East Bay began to improve with the opening of a new factory, but this improvement came too late to help these four restaurants.

As indicated in the preceding section on determining cause, some of the methods of determination carry with them particular risks that must be avoided. The difference method, for example, is only reliable if the effects you examine are truly comparable. In addition, when using the method of proportional correlation, you must be sure that the trends you identify are independent—that is, they are neither effects of another cause nor mutually contributing (for example, bad tempers causing quarrels and quarrels exacerbating bad tempers).

In supporting your causal argument, you will be wise to point out that your use of a particular method of determination has avoided the associated risks. For example, if you use the difference method to determine why you like golf but your friend with similar athletic ability and experience in golf does not, you should demonstrate that apparent differences between you and your friend—family background, interest in other sports—are not significant in terms of your argument.

Identifying an Acceptable Motivation

Remember that when the effect you investigate comes in the form of human action, your investigation should penetrate to the level of an acceptable motive. Once you recognize that a motive you find acceptable or assumable connects your effect and its probable cause, you usually do not have to argue the acceptability of that motive, nor in most cases do you have to identify the motive explicitly.

In the simple example cited earlier, where the increased purchases of fuel-efficient cars was attributed to high fuel prices, the linking motive was the desire to save money. In this argument, you would not need to write, "Because people like to save their money, high fuel prices resulted in the popularity of fuel-efficient cars." Once you have identified cause and effect, readers will recognize the operation of this widespread principle without your spelling it out. And that is the point about assumable motivation—it should be so ubiquitous in everyone's experience that readers will immediately recognize and accept it.

You might have to argue the plausibility of a motivation if it does not fit with a reader's understanding of the individual or group in question. If you attributed a friend's decision to go to medical school to a long tradition of doctors in her family, yet she is known for rebellious and independent behavior, the linking motivation—imitation or emulation—is not very plausible, making the cause you have identified, the family tradition of doctors, suspect. If you can demonstrate that she *is* truly motivated by a desire to please her family, despite her seeming independence, you will give important support to your argument. Arguments such as this are most convincing when you have a thorough knowledge of the individual or group involved.

Qualifying Your Argument

Since certainty is rare in causal arguments, you must not mislead your reader and thereby undermine your own credibility by claiming more certainty for your argument than is warranted by its support. You have a wide range of words indicating degrees of causality to choose from, so make sure you use language that accurately reflects your level of certainty. If you are very certain about your causal proposition, you can use such definite words as the following:

necessitated

caused

resulted in

attributable to

produced

created

brought about

was responsible for

But use these words with caution. Without qualifiers like "may have," "probably," "seems to have," and so on, they claim a certainty that can be difficult to document.

The words listed in the following group also indicate causality, but a causality that is clearly qualified:

contributed to

is associated with

is a function of

facilitated

enabled

influenced

increased

decreased

improved

You are better off using words such as these when the causality you propose is not certain. By using such terms, you are both indicating causality and admitting *some* degree of uncertainty.

Activities (8.5)

For two of the examples below, write a paragraph on each indicating what would be needed to make the causal argument more convincing. This additional material could include establishing facts, reporting the process of determination, describing motives, demonstrating the independence of two elements in a proportional correlation, or adding qualifying language, though other steps may also be necessary to make the argument credible.

1. Bill's alleged cheating on the exam was certainly a result of his low grades early in the semester and his desire to be accepted into a reputable law school.
2. The arrest of Hubert Midas, the oil and gas billionaire, for shoplifting a $35 shirt from a downtown department store. Midas must have forgotten to pay for the shirt.
3. As more women have entered the work force, the number of families without children has risen proportionally. The increasing number of women in the work force has caused this rise in childless families.
4. Without Martin Luther King's charismatic personality, the civil rights movement of the 1960s would not have had the impact that it did.
5. The Roman Empire fell because of the moral decadence of many of its citizens.

SUMMARY

Supporting Cause

- To support a cause, you must:
  establish the factuality of cause and effect;
  usually report how you determined the causes;
  identify an acceptable motivation in cases where human actions are at least part of the cause;
  if necessary, qualify your assertions about the certainty of your argument.

ARGUING EFFECTS

As we noted in Chapter 4, because arguments of effect are concerned with the future, with events that haven't yet occurred, their claim to certainty is never absolute. Even the most carefully constructed argument of effect, one firmly grounded in the principles of causality and in experience in the relevant field, can go awry. We have only to look at the accuracy rate of weather forecasters and political analysts to recognize how frequently the future refuses to cooperate with our plans for it. But if executed carefully and according to certain principles, arguments of effect *can* be reasonable and convincing, serving as useful guidelines for many courses of action.

Theses of arguments of effect can be stated in a number of different ways, as in the following:

1. If John continues to drink heavily and drive, it's only a matter of time before he has a serious accident.
2. The number of high school graduates will continue to decline for the next five years, then begin to stabilize.
3. I will not see a woman president in my lifetime.
4. Consumers are so comfortable with certain companies that they will buy almost anything carrying those companies' logos.

While they may seem quite different, these four theses share certain features common to all arguments of effect. Most obviously, all predict that something will happen in the future (or in the case of the third thesis, that something will not happen). Theses 1 and 4—John's heavy drinking, brand appeal—also identify a causal relationship between a current condition and the future event. Theses 2 and 3 do not identify such a condition; to qualify as arguments of effect, the arguments introduced by these two theses must identify certain conditions that have led the writer to draw these conclusions about the future. For thesis 2, those conditions could be certain demographic trends that have persisted over time; for thesis 3, those conditions could be the conservative disposition of most voters, or perhaps a poll indicating strong opposition to a woman president among teenagers and young voters. These current conditions and trends set the ground for an argument of effect. An argument of effect demonstrates that the existence of these conditions and trends is enough to cause a particular future effect. Lacking identified causes, these kinds of theses are nothing more than random predictions, similar to the bizarre predictions on the covers of the sensational magazines found in supermarkets: "Psychic Foresees Economic Collapse Following Landing of Martians on White House Lawn!"

Determining and Supporting a Probable Effect

The processes of determining and supporting a probable effect overlap considerably. If you identify a future effect through sound methods, the best supporting strategy will be to report these methods, which we discuss in the following paragraphs.

Applying the Principles of Causality. To determine whether a projected effect could be created by current or intended causes, you treat both as having occurred and then evaluate whether and how they are causally related. Are the causes currently operating (or that might be set in place) enough to bring about the effect? If you can identify an existing necessary and sufficient cause, your prediction is very likely. If you can identify sufficient cause or causes but no necessary cause, in most cases the absence of a necessary cause will not undermine your prediction.

Let's take the case of a publishing house editor trying to decide whether to publish a book submitted to her on personal relationships. The editor will accept the book if she thinks it will sell well; her job is to decide whether current circumstances would make the book a bestseller. In other words, the projected effect is excellent sales. The circumstances operating are as follows: the market for books on this topic has been very strong; the writer has written popular books on this subject before; the book itself, in the view of this experienced editor, is interesting, original, and provocative. An analysis of these circumstances reveals that all are sufficient causes—in the absence of the other two, one cause alone would be sufficient to create the effect. The editor's experience with bookselling makes her a good judge of the sufficiency of these causes. Our editor knows how important these three circumstances are because she has seen them again and again. In projecting any effect, the arguer must understand the principles of the subject matter.

Missing from this list of current circumstances is a necessary cause, one that has to operate in order for the effect to occur. The absence of necessary cause does not make the projected effect implausible; often it is the sufficient causes that create the necessary cause. In this example, the necessary cause to high sales would simply be that people buy the book, and they will buy the book in the presence of one or more of these sufficient causes.

Causal Chains. In some situations, you can argue a future effect by revealing a chain of causes that plausibly connects cause A with future effect D. To demonstrate the connection between a past or present cause and a future effect, you need to make a series of arguments of effect; if A is the remote cause and D the predicted effect, you will argue that A will cause B, which will cause C, which finally will cause D.

The field of economics often uses causal chains as a basis for future action. A classic example is the government's setting of interest rates on money it lends to banks, which in turn affects the interest rates banks and other financial institutions charge customers on mortgages and other loans and the interest they pay to customers for savings and other deposits. One key step a government can take to reduce consumer spending is to raise its interest rates, which means the banks will raise their rates, and customers will find that it costs more to get a mortgage on a house, finance a car loan, or buy other items on credit. Faced with these rising costs, consumers will decide to spend less. Also, because these same banks are now paying more interest for deposits, consumers have an incentive to save rather than spend—another reason why they will reduce spending. Visually, the causal chain looks like this:

(A) higher government interest rates → (B) higher bank
interest rates → (C) lower consumer spending

This causal chain could be extended, since lower consumer spending could lead to a lower inflation rate or to less importing of consumer goods from other countries. With causal chains, however, the greater the length of the chain, the less predictable become the effects.

Sometimes, causal chains simply don't work the way they are supposed to. When Prohibition became law in 1919, its proponents predicted that alcoholic consumption would decrease and along with it a host of evils, including crime, broken homes, and absenteeism from work. They did not foresee a roaring fourteen years of speakeasies, bathtub gin, and bootleg whiskey before Prohibition was abolished in 1933. Especially when trying to predict human behavior through elaborate causal chains, you should always keep in mind the adage about the road to hell being paved with good intentions.

Comparable Situations

You can also determine the probable future result of current conditions by examining comparable situations in which this cause and effect have already occurred. In trying to raise the educational standards of American primary and secondary schools, teachers, school administrators, and government policymakers look to the experience of other countries. The average scores of students from some other industrialized countries are higher than the average scores of American students on certain standardized achievement tests in areas such as math and science. In some of these countries, notably Japan, children spend much more of the year in school, and the schools place more emphasis on introducing rigorous academic material earlier in the student's academic career. Some proponents of reform argue that the same methods used here will improve students' performance.

This comparison method will only work if the situations being compared are *significantly* similar. In arguing that the United States should follow Japan's example, advocates of these changes also need to look carefully at what each country expects from its schools and how these expectations relate to the general culture. What seems comparable at first view may turn out to be more complicated on closer inspection, since American and Japanese cultures have very different expectations about the role of the individual in society.

The more comparable situations you can find, the more convincing your argument of effect will be. If you can demonstrate that a certain cause has had the same result over and over again, and that the current conditions you are considering are truly similar to these other causes, your identification of effect will be well supported.

SUMMARY

Determining and Supporting a Probable Effect

- To argue an effect, you need to identify a sufficient cause for the effect and prove that this cause exists or could exist.
- You can argue that a certain effect is likely if you can create a causal chain that demonstrates how you can move from one cause to an effect that is the cause of the next effect, and so forth. The longer your chain, however, the less likely it is that the chain will perform as predicted.
- You can demonstrate that an effect is likely in a situation if you can prove that a similar situation produced a similar effect.

Activities (8.6)

1. For two of the following effects, write a paragraph on each describing at least two causes that would contribute to this effect; state whether the causes would be necessary or sufficient. Example effect: obtaining a part-time job. Possible causes: applying for the position (necessary); doing well at the interview (necessary); being the only person available to do the job (sufficient).
   a. Getting an "A" in a course.
   b. Arranging a date with someone you don't know.
   c. Reducing the danger of theft at your college or in your community.
   d. Finding a good place to live.
   e. Avoiding being stopped for speeding by the police.
2. Write a one-to-two-page essay describing a causal chain for some area or activity with which you are familiar. How confident are you that this chain will

work as you have stated? Have you ever seen it work before? Can you think of any circumstances where it might not work?

3. For one of the pairs below, write a one-page essay describing how comparable you find the situations listed. What would be some major differences? Are these differences so significant that the situations should not be compared?
    a. The military strategies of Julius Caesar; military strategies for the United States Army in the 1990s.
    b. Sales techniques for Coca-Cola in the United States; sales techniques for Coca-Cola in France.
    c. The marketing of hockey games in Canada; the marketing of hockey games in southern California.
    d. Being president of a large corporation; being governor of a state.
    e. Teaching elementary school; teaching graduate courses in a university.

A SAMPLE CAUSAL ARGUMENT

The following argument is a sample of causal analysis. Based on an essay written by college student Michele Statt, the essay identifies causes for a recent increase in student interest in liberal arts majors. In her essay Michele establishes the factuality of her effect and of her central cause, reports on the process of determination she used to test this cause (method of agreement), identifies an acceptable human motivation (interest in good jobs), and appropriately qualifies her claims with such phrases as "may have influenced" and "probably associated with." Michele also identifies a causal constellation (without using that term) and a central cause. Michele's essay is not an elaborate and definitive causal argument, but it is a good example of a brief and tentative examination of causes.

THE NEW INTEREST IN THE LIBERAL ARTS

In 1978 only 443 students were enrolled in liberal arts majors at my college. Today, with the recent establishment of new liberal arts majors, 604 students are enrolled in these majors. (In the same period, the total enrollment at my college has decreased by 40 students.) Many other schools have also reported that interest in liberal arts majors has been increasing. According to Michael Useem, Director of Boston University's Center for Applied Social Science, across the nation "the proportion of baccalaureate degrees in the liberal arts in 1986 was the largest in four years, and the proportion of first-year college students reporting an interest in a liberal arts major in 1987 was the highest in 10 years" ("The Corporate View of Liberal Arts," p. 46).

Several causes may have influenced this increase in interest. Many students entering college are unsure of their career choice and gravitate to the liberal arts because such programs typically do not insist on early declaration of a major. Even if the undecided student then chooses to pursue a major outside the liberal arts, she will find that her liberal arts courses can be applied to her new major. However, having started in the liberal arts, she is likely to find a liberal arts major that appeals to her.

Another cause probably associated with this increase is the growing emphasis on career training within the liberal arts majors themselves. At my college the liberal arts majors include such programs as economics, school psychology, criminal justice, and communications—all of which include a significant element of career preparation that appeals to today's college students. Several of these programs at my college are relatively new. Their existence as additional options for students certainly helps to explain the growth in liberal arts enrollment here.

Liberal arts enrollment, however, has been increasing throughout the country, even at institutions that have not added many new liberal arts programs. The central cause for this growth is very likely the increasing demand for liberal arts majors in the job market. Michael Useem's article, based on research supported by the Corporate Council on the Liberal Arts and the President's Committee on the Arts and Humanities, states that since the early 1980s many business leaders have stressed the importance of the liberal arts as preparation for a career in business (p. 46). Useem received responses to his survey from 535 large and mid-sized American corporations. The results indicated that corporations do indeed hire liberal arts graduates, with 44 percent of the respondents recruiting liberal arts graduates on campus and 47 percent hiring such students for internships and cooperative education programs. Twenty-nine percent reported other efforts to recruit liberal arts graduates, and 61 percent have created programs to train liberal arts graduates for jobs in their corporations (p. 47).

Students are becoming aware of this demand for liberal arts graduates. I chose my field of communication both because of my interest in it and because I was aware of job possibilities after graduation. Twelve students that I talked to said that career preparation was one of the two major causes of their choosing a liberal arts major, the other being their interest in the subject. These results are hardly scientific proof, but they are another piece of evidence demonstrating the importance of the job market in rising liberal arts enrollments.

Useem's study also notes that although many companies hire liberal arts graduates, they are often looking for accomplishments in addition to a liberal arts major, including campus or community involvement and a good grade point average. Another important requirement for most of these corporations was exposure to business courses or experience in business before graduation (pp. 47-48, 50-51). The increasing emphasis on career training in at least some liberal arts majors undoubtedly enhances the attractiveness of these majors to employers.

Ten or fifteen years ago, many college students felt that they were forced to make a choice between a liberal arts major or preparing themselves for a career. Because they wanted to find a good job, some of these students chose a program outside of the liberal arts even when they really preferred a liberal arts major. Today's students are more fortunate. They know that in choosing a liberal arts major, they can also prepare themselves for their future after college.

WORKS CITED

Useem, Michael. ''The Corporate View of Liberal Arts.'' *Journal of Career Planning and Employment*, Summer 1988: 46-51.

Suggestions for Writing (8.7)

1. Write an essay describing the necessary and sufficient causes for a major event in your life. Be sure to indicate to the reader how you determined that these causes were the real ones. Make the essay as long as necessary to describe fully the causes of this event.

2. Analyze at least three persons or organizations that share major common traits and determine what similar causes, if any, made them the way they are. As examples, you could analyze successful or unsuccessful teams in some sport, or successful or unsuccessful television shows. Report your analysis in an essay of approximately four pages.

3. Analyze two persons or situations that shared significant traits in common but that have ended up differing in some major way. What caused this major difference? For this essay you might analyze why you and a close friend or a sibling chose different colleges or majors or why you performed differently in two similar classes. Report your analysis in an essay of approximately four pages.

4. Examine two trends that you believe might be causally related to see if there is any proportional correlation between them. An example might be the national crime rate and the national unemployment rate, or the national unemployment rate and the inflation rate. If you expect to find a correlation and you do not, speculate on why the correlation is not present. For this essay you might start with a good almanac, since it will contain many trends with statistical data, but you will probably need to consult a more detailed source such as *Statistical Abstracts of the United States*. Report your analysis in an essay of approximately four pages.

Chapter 9

Making Practical Recommendations

Making *recommendations* (sometimes called *proposals*) is a common assignment for writers in business, education, and government, where major innovations are almost always initiated by a formal written proposal. Many organizations even devise a particular format to which formal recommendations must conform. While these formats can vary considerably in visual details of presentation, the material included is usually consistent. This chapter is concerned not with the varieties of physical format but with the substance of practical recommendations—the material that must be included and the arguments that must be made.

Unlike causal arguments, arguments of practical recommendation are not built upon a singular logical system; instead, they draw on methods and principles frequently used in the other types of argument. For the most part, skill in arguing practical recommendations consists of understanding the particular application of certain familiar methods.

In any recommendation, you must establish a current situation and a probable future situation—you must argue facts and effects. How central either type of argument is to your recommendation depends on the emphasis demanded of the particular situation. If your recommendation emphasizes a *current* problem, much of your argument will be factual; if it emphasizes the probable results of the changes you recommend, your argument will establish the probable effects of the implemented recommendation.

To convince your audience to accept your recommendation, you must base your argument on needs or values to which your audience is committed. To do so, you must know your audience well enough to make accurate assumptions about what they hold necessary and worthy; your recommendation will be based on these assumptions. We call these assumptions the *assumed value* of a recommendation.

ASSUMED VALUE IN PRACTICAL RECOMMENDATIONS

In any recommendation, reasons are advanced to support the suggestions being presented. You recommend that the practice of tripling in student rooms should cease *because* of the discomfort and inconvenience it causes students. A research and development team proposes a new product line *because* it will sell well and use existing manufacturing technology. For a recommendation to succeed, the reasons identified *must* be acceptable to the audience; they will be acceptable if they satisfy needs or values to which the audience is committed.

In recommending that your school's administration add a student parking lot close to campus because of the danger of walking to remote lots after dark, you are claiming that the risks run by students are undesirable; you are judging the situation in terms of the high value most people set on personal safety. Your argument has a good chance of succeeding if your audience accepts the value of student safety.

Similarly, if you recommend that a corporation grant paternity leave to new fathers, and you cite the positive effect on children of increased contact with their fathers, you are making a positive judgment about the effect of this policy change and assuming that your audience shares your view about the value of such an effect.

The *assumed value* of any recommendation is the value or need that will be satisfied if the recommendation is implemented. For the recommendation to have a chance of succeeding, that value or need must be acceptable to your readers; it must be one that is already a part of their value system. In the example of the recommendation for paternity leave, the judgment of the proposed policy was made in terms of the psychological benefits for children of having fathers more involved in child-rearing. This value would be most important to the parents of the children, but would probably not be most important to the upper-level management responsible for accepting the recommendation—not because they are indifferent to how children are raised but because as managers they have other primary responsibilities. To succeed with this group, the argument would need to make a major appeal to management's most pressing values or needs—benefits such as employee morale, increased efficiency, and corporate reputation.

You should never write a practical recommendation without first carefully identifying the probable values and needs of the audience you are trying to move. Recommendations must appeal to the assumed values that the audience believes in and will be moved by. At the least, appealing to an inappropriate value can fail to move your readers; at the worst, it can significantly alienate them. Imagine a group that strongly believes mothers should be the primary child-raisers confronted with the recommendation for paternity leave. Ideas about the value of nontraditional roles for fathers would not only leave them cold, but probably would elicit serious opposition to a recommendation that might have had a chance if it had appealed to other values.

Although your recommendation must appeal to an assumed value or need, you rarely need to identify that value explicitly in your argument. You would certainly have to identify the positive effect of your recommendation—the personal safety of students, for example—but you would not have to convince the audience that this effect is desirable. If you know the audience well, you know they will accept your judgment of the effect. As with evaluative arguments (discussed in the next chapter), you will have little success in trying to convince your readers to embrace a value not currently a part of their belief system. Changing or expanding an audience's values can be done, but at the cost of much space and energy; most practical recommendations cannot afford this expense. Rather than wrestle with this demon of disbelief, cast your judgment in different terms, as was done in the example of paternity leaves, where the basic appeal was switched to one more likely to gain the approval of those making the decision.

WHEN YOUR VALUES DIFFER FROM
ASSUMED READER VALUES

Recommendations actually work with two sets of values—the reader's *and* the writer's. To succeed, a recommendation must appeal to the right reader values, but it actually originates in values held by the writer. In the examples discussed above, we have implied that the assumed values of the audience are identical with the values of the writer. Often, this is the case.

Sometimes, however, the two sets of values are different, particularly when the recommender and reader are members of very different groups—consumer and corporation, for example, or student and faculty. Often, the value that moves you to recommend a particular change is not the value that will move your reader to implement your recommendation. In these cases, you must be aware of what the different values are; so long as they are related and not in conflict, their difference will not weaken your recommendation.

We can observe this principle in the following example of an unhappy customer writing a letter to the local transit authority recommending improvements in bus service. The writer's judgment of the current situation is based on what he perceives to be his rights as a paying customer—primarily the right of good service, which he is being denied. His judgment also originates in more specific needs—physical comfort, the importance of getting to work on time.

However, the value to which he is appealing in his reader is different, although clearly related. If his reader—the manager of customer services at the transit authority—chooses to take action on the strength of the recommendation, he will do so because of the importance to the transit service of the value of *customer satisfaction*. No business, even one that holds a virtual monopoly, as most transit authorities do, can afford to ignore the importance of customer satisfaction; the risks are ultimately too great.

In this example, the values of customer rights and customer satisfaction are not synonymous, but they are *causally* connected: if this customer's rights are being served, he will be satisfied. Not only is there no conflict between the two, but one follows from the other; thus they can happily coexist in this recommendation.

Here is the letter to the transit service:

Mr. John O'Brien
Manager, Customer Services
Metro Transit
Our Town, USA

Dear Mr. O'Brien:

I am writing to complain about the quality of the morning bus service for Bus #15, which runs from the Maplewood Shopping Center to Main Street downtown along Winton Avenue. By the time the bus scheduled to stop at 8:16 gets to my stop at Eleventh Street, it is usually late (in March, by an average of fifteen minutes) and always overcrowded, with standing room only even for elderly passengers. During the month of March, the bus was so overcrowded that ten people at my stop were denied a place: four on March 5, three on March 13, and two on March 20. Many of us have tried to take the earlier 7:44 bus, but the situation is essentially the same for that bus as well. Most of us cannot take a later bus because of our work schedules.

As you might expect, your customers are very unhappy. We feel we are being cheated of the service we deserve for the high fares, and we would like some action taken to improve the situation. To prove to you that I have a lot of company in my unhappiness, I am enclosing with this letter a petition signed by all the regular users of the 8:16 bus. Some of these riders have simply given up and use their cars to get downtown. More will certainly do so in the future if the situation does not improve.

I am sure that now you are aware of this problem, you will take steps to correct it. I look forward to hearing from you about what those steps might be.

Very truly yours,
Patrick Booth

In writing any kind of recommendation, you *must* identify to yourself the values from which you write and those to which you appeal in your readers. Often, these values are the same. But if they are not, they can only coexist in your recommendation if they are directly related and nonconflicting, as they should be in the case of the transit service and its unhappy customers. When you do recognize a conflict, you must find other values on which to base your appeal. When American negotiators make disarmament proposals to their Soviet counterparts, they stress shared values such as a desire to avoid war, not the vigor of free enterprise versus Communist bureaucratic sloth. The American negotiators may hope that the Soviets will eventually abandon Communism, but they are realistic enough to know that this isn't going to happen tomorrow and that they won't get far in their negotiations by attacking the Soviets' basic values.

Activities (9.1)

1. For two of the following, write a paragraph on each describing the assumed value appealed to in the recommendation. Example: "We need a new City Hall for a growing city." Assumed value: importance of progress.
   a. Grading policies at State should be made much stricter.
   b. All young Americans should do two years of national service in the military, the Peace Corps, or some other government-approved organization.
   c. The speed limit near the new elementary school should be lowered.
   d. John needs to exercise at least three times a week and watch his weight.
   e. Women should be allowed to have combat roles in the military.

2. In each case below, the value cited to win the audience's agreement for the recommendation is not appropriate. For two of the following, write a paragraph on each describing another value that would be more appropriate. Sample recommendation: a longer school year for elementary and secondary students. Audience: elementary and secondary teachers. Inappropriate value: more work from teachers. Alternative value: a greater opportunity to ensure student's mastery of skills.
   a. Recommendation: earlier closing of a college cafeteria. Audience: college students. Inappropriate value: shorter hours and fewer headaches for cafeteria staff.
   b. Recommendation: a new federal tax on gasoline. Audience: truck drivers. Inappropriate value: reduced reliance on trucks for transporting goods.
   c. Recommendation: a curfew for everybody under the age of 16. Audience: those under 16. Inappropriate value: those under 16 can't be trusted.
   d. Recommendation: a law requiring motorcyclists to wear helmets. Audience: motorcyclists. Inappropriate value: reduced claims against insurance companies and therefore increased profits for insurance companies.
   e. Recommendation: a shorter work week. Audience: employers. Inappropriate value: more leisure time for employees.

3. For two of the following, write a paragraph on each describing a value these two opposing groups have in common that they can appeal to when they have a dispute. Example: Republicans and Democrats. Common value: concern for the national interest—the country as a whole.

    a. Planners of a new highway; homeowners whose property is in the path of the new highway.

    b. Managers of a company; workers on strike against that company.

    c. Parents planning to take away a child's allowance as punishment for bad behavior; the child in question.

    d. Planners of a large rock concert; neighborhood groups opposed to the concert because of noise.

    e. Proponents of legislation restricting the use of handguns; opponents of this legislation.

RECOMMENDATIONS EMPHASIZING THE PRESENT

Recommendations emphasizing present conditions combine factual arguments, appeals to assumed needs and values, and, often, causal arguments and arguments of effect. Because the main goal of these arguments is to demonstrate that a current situation is problematic or unacceptable, they usually do not discuss a proposed change in any detail. Their function is more to demonstrate *that* something needs to be done than *what* exactly that something is.

To accept this kind of recommendation, readers must first be given an accurate and, in most cases, detailed picture of the current situation. If they don't grasp the situation as it is, they won't be in a position to agree or disagree with your judgment. Your initial presentation of the situation should therefore be a factual argument.

Let's return to the example of the letter to the transit authority. The letter clearly states the reasons for dissatisfaction, and gives details about how this situation affects many people, not just the writer of the letter. In this case, the most effective information is numbers—how late the bus typically is and how many times people have been left behind at the bus stop. To get these figures, the writer had to conduct a little survey over a period of time. The reporting of the circumstances and results of the survey constitute a major part of the letter.

In such a recommendation, inclusion of accurate details is critical. For one thing, readers are going to take exact figures—such as are found in the letter—much more seriously than irate vagueness. Exaggerations like "Huge numbers of people are regularly prevented from riding the 8:16 bus" are far less meaningful than exact figures.

Second, misrepresenting the facts, whether purposefully to strengthen your case, or negligently through sloppy research, will almost always be detected. You can be sure that the recipient of any recommendation is going to investigate the situation before taking action; if the results of that investigation differ substantially from your figures, your recommendation certainly will not be acted upon.

Evaluating the Situation in Terms of Assumed Needs and Values

In writing recommendations emphasizing current conditions, not only must you establish the current conditions, you must also evaluate those conditions according to needs and values important to your audience. While you usually will not have to identify these values directly, you may have to state the judgment itself.

In the example above, an explicit judgment of the situation presented in the letter is hardly necessary. Any reader, whether an official of the transit authority or an occasional passenger, will recognize that the conditions described are undesirable. You could point to this fact for rhetorical emphasis, but the judgment will also be implicit in the presentation.

Recommendations addressed to readers familiar with the current situation but unaware of its problems usually require an explicit evaluation of the situation. As well as describing the situation, you will have to demonstrate why it is unsatisfactory. Readers will accept a situation as problematic if they can be made to recognize that it violates or ignores certain values important to them. Thus, to convince a professor that the schedule of assignments should be changed, you would have to demonstrate that the current schedule goes against a principle important to this professor—perhaps the principle that the students learn as much as possible, or that they be relieved of unnecessary pressure.

Evaluating Through Causal Argument

In demonstrating that a particular situation, practice, or policy is problematic, you may find a causal argument useful. Often the best way to show that a current situation violates the reader's values is by identifying and judging the *effects* of the situation. In recommending changes in the course assignment schedule, you would have a greater chance of convincing your professor if you pointed out the unhappy results of the current schedule—not merely a general reference to the students' dissatisfaction with the schedule, but a reasonable discussion of its concrete results. Perhaps you could identify a series of effects (or causal chain); for example, students have fallen behind in their assignments because of the heavy load; having fallen behind, they do not always understand the lecture material; thus they miss key concepts in the course, which has led to poor performance on tests. You would need to establish the existence of each of these situations as well as their causal relationship to the rigorous assignment schedule. If you can do this, and if your professor recognizes in these effects the violation of an important principle, your recommendation will probably succeed.

Demonstrating the Probable Results of No Change

One way to convince an audience of the need for change is by demonstrating what is likely to happen if the current situation remains as it is. If you can show that maintaining an existing policy or practice will produce undesirable effects not currently obvious, by all means do so; it is an effective strategy. Of course, not all current situations lend themselves to such a strategy; often, maintaining a problematic practice will not create more problems, although it may ensure that current problems will not disappear.

An argument proposing an expansion of the local airport could be supported by a prediction (or argument of effect) of probable effects of the current policy. If you think the airport is too small for the number of flights it handles, you could point out (1) the possibility of an accident resulting from the current heavy traffic, and (2) the legal risk the local government is running if there were such an accident at this seriously overcrowded airport. If you can argue a plausible causal connection between the current policy and these very undesirable results, you will strengthen your recommendation considerably.

Activities (9.2)

For two of the situations below, what kind of evidence would indicate a need for major change? Make a list of this evidence and then write a description of this evidence in a summary paragraph.

1. Traffic at an intersection.
2. Someone's physical appearance.
3. A friend's choice of a career.
4. A student's study habits.
5. The local court system.

RECOMMENDATIONS EMPHASIZING THE FUTURE

Recommendations emphasizing the probable future effects of the proposed changes require more from a writer than those concentrating on a current situation. The biggest practical difference between these two types of recommendations is that in the second, you must do more than identify current problems: you must come up with a new plan. Here you must go beyond the general claim that something must be done; you must also identify, reasonably and convincingly, what that something is—that is, you must propose the actual changes. Your argument will be effective if you can demonstrate (1) that your proposal is likely to produce desirable effects, and (2) that the proposal is feasible, that it can be implemented without tremendous difficulty.

Presenting the Recommendation

The presentation of your proposed plan or recommendation must be clear and immediately intelligible to your audience; readers cannot agree with a plan if they don't understand it. Different situations will demand different degrees of detail in this presentation. Sometimes, a rather general recommendation will be appropriate, as when you are not directly responsible for making the recommendation or overseeing the change. In other cases, particularly when you have some responsibility for the operations of the group in question, a detailed recommendation will be necessary. The following is an example of a general recommendation and a specific recommendation for the same issue:

1. *General* (Written by a group of angry homeowners requesting that the town supervisor take steps to reduce or eliminate the problem of speeding in their neighborhood.)

> Because of the well-known and recurring problem of speeders in the Village Lane neighborhood—a problem we discussed with you two months ago and which you admitted was serious—we recommend that you take more decisive steps than you have taken so far to deal with this problem. We need something more than a patrol car stationed here for two or three nights, which deters speeders only until they realize the patrol car will not be here regularly. We need a more routine presence of the police, more signs posting the speed limit, perhaps even speed bumps in some of the more dangerous places. Since the Village Lane neighborhood consists of narrow streets and shallow front lawns, building sidewalks is simply not possible. For the safety of all in the neighborhood, particularly the children, the town must do more to help us.

2. *Detailed* (Same recommendation as above, written by a chastened town supervisor to the heads of the town police and highway departments after discussions with them on actions to help solve the Village Lane speeding problem. If the town supervisor wants to be reelected, he will send a copy of this memo or at least a summary of it to residents in the neighborhood.)

> At our meeting on May 10 we discussed the problem of speeding in the Village Lane neighborhood and agreed that the following steps should be taken:
>
> - A patrol car will be stationed in the neighborhood at least six hours a week for the next six months, particularly in the evening when the speeding problem seems to be most serious. At the end of six months we will review this policy. A meeting with Village Lane Neighborhood Association officers will be part of this review.
> - The highway department will place five new speed limit signs in the neighborhood at locations mutually agreed upon by the highway supervisor and the neighborhood association. In addition, the speed limit for the entire neighborhood will be dropped from the general town speed limit of 30 mph to 25 mph.
> - The highway department will place speed bumps at the sharp curves on McDonnel and McMurtrie streets, along with very clear warnings to motorists about the presence of the bumps.

These two examples illustrate only two possibilities; recommendations can be more or less detailed than the second example. Generally, the more concrete your recommendation, the more effective it will be, provided your plan reflects a sound understanding of the operations of the group that would accept and implement the plan. You need to remember, however, that there are occasions when a great deal of detail is inappropriate. Most editorials make recommendations without much detail; most politicians give few details in their speeches to general audiences. In deciding how much detail to give, you need to consider the audience's capacity for and interest in the details as well as their role in carrying out the recommendation. In the case of editorials and political speeches, most audiences are not interested in a lot of detail and are not responsible for implementing the recommendation.

Activities (9.3)

1. For one of the general recommendations below, list at least three specific recommendations that would give substance to the general recommendation. Example: We need a city with cleaner air. Specific recommendations: (1) encouragement of "Park and Ride" lots for commuters to decrease automobile traffic; (2) tighter inspection standards for automobiles' exhaust emission systems; and (3) restrictions on the burning of leaves and trash. After you have made this list of recommendations, write a short essay (250–500 words) briefly explaining each of the recommendations and how they relate to the general recommendation.
   a. Our college needs more school spirit.
   b. Americans need to be more tolerant of racial and ethnic diversity.
   c. Adolescents must be made more aware of the dangers of alcohol.
   d. American industry needs to put more emphasis on the quality of its products.
   e. Students and professors must learn to see each other as human beings.
2. For one set of specific recommendations below, summarize these recommendations in a general statement. Sample specifics: Helen should spend more time in the library; she should attend class more regularly; she should finish her assignments on time. General recommendation: Helen should work harder on her courses. Write a paragraph showing the relationship between this general recommendation and the set of specific recommendations.
   a. The shopping mall should expand its parking lots; the lots should have clearly marked spaces for parking and clearly marked lanes for driving; the mall should hire additional traffic and security officers.
   b. George should get moderate exercise at least three times a week, have a checkup from his doctor at least once a year, and watch the cholesterol content of his diet.
   c. Sharon should go to a movie at least once a week, spend one day a week not studying, and spend more time with her friends.
   d. Chuck's car needs an oil change, a new muffler, and new tires. Chuck should also consider having the car painted.

Arguing the Effects of Your Recommendation

At the heart of a recommendation with future emphasis is your identification and evaluation of the probable effects of the new plan. After presenting the recommendation itself, you must demonstrate, through an *argument of effect*, what the results of the implemented recommendation are likely to be.

As with all arguments of effect, this part of your recommendation will be successful if you can show that the changes you propose (the causes) are related to the results you predict (the effects) through established causal principles (as presented in Chapter 6).

If you were proposing that the fees paid to doctors for routine nonemergency visits be increased, you would have to identify the probable results of that change. Suppose you predict the following short causal chain as resulting from this increase: the higher cost will mean that patients will visit doctors less frequently for minor ailments or vague complaints, thus allowing doctors to concentrate on people who really need care. Most readers will accept the argument that people will be hesitant to spend more money for minor problems. There is an acceptable motivational link between raising costs and fewer visits: the link is the common desire to save money.

The second link in the chain also seems plausible: doctors will use at least some of their gained time working with patients who have serious ailments. But if you argued that the patients who visit doctors after the fee increase are the ones really needing attention, you would be on shaky causal ground. While there would probably be fewer frivolous visits to doctors, people with sufficient money might continue visits for minor or imaginary ailments, and some people on tight budgets might be deterred from making even necessary visits. This practical recommendation based on results might break down if the result expected is that only those having genuine need of medical attention will now visit doctors.

Activities (9.4)

For one of the recommendations and projected results listed below, write a short essay of approximately one page in length analyzing how likely you believe the projected results are. You may find some results more probable than others.

1. Recommendation: Increase the price of tickets to films at the college theater from $1 to $1.50. Projected results: no significant decline in attendance; more revenue from tickets to allow the theater to rent better films, which will eventually lead to higher attendance.

2. Recommendation: Allow students to take one course pass/fail. Projected results: Students will feel under less pressure about grades and be more willing to take tough courses. The students will work just as hard in the courses they take pass/fail as they would have if they had taken the course for a regular grade.

3. Recommendation: The United States should spend more on conventional (as opposed to nuclear weapons). Projected results: the Soviet Union will see that the United States is serious about conventional military defense and will be more willing to negotiate reductions in its own conventional forces.

Judging Effects in Terms of Assumed Needs and Values

For your readers to accept your recommendation, they must see as desirable the probable effect you identify. An effect will be desirable if it satisfies or agrees with needs or values important to the readers. In developing a recommendation you will probably identify several probable effects. For al of these effects, you must ask yourself which values that effect would satisfy and whether those values would be important to your readers. If you were to recommend a pass/fail option to faculty by telling them that students would now have more free time, you would probably not appeal to faculty values, since most faculty would not place much value on a decline in student attention to course work. You should not deny this probable effect simply because your audience may not like it, but your major stress for the audience should be on effects that do appeal to their values.

As with recommendations emphasizing current conditions, you may not have to identify the audience need or value to which you are appealing. But *you* must be aware of the values on which your recommendation rests.

When Some Effects Are Undesirable. Few recommendations can promise exclusively positive results. But as long as the desirable effects outweigh the undesirable ones, your recommendation is worth making. When you know that along with the positive effects there may be some less desirable repercussions, you should acknowledge them in your argument. Provided you can demonstrate that the negative effects are less significant than the positive ones, you will not weaken your argument by mentioning them. In fact, an argument that acknowledges and measures its own weaknesses is usually more effective than one that fails to admit what any intelligent reader will recognize.

If you were on a committee recommending the building of a new expressway, you should admit that the building of the new expressway, whatever its ultimate advantages, will cause inconveniences. This is a more effective and responsible approach than ignoring altogether the obvious negative consequences of your recommendation. You will enhance your credibility by admitting what many people will know or suspect anyway.

Implementation. To be successful, your recommendation must pass one further test: not only must it appeal to your audience's values, but also it must be feasible. Even the most brilliant recommendation will be rejected if its implementation is fraught with difficulties. While a detailed implementation plan is not required of all recommendations, some indication of the feasibility of your plan will strengthen your argument. At the least, you must provide a general indication that the recommendation is feasible. There is no point in advancing a recommendation that your audience will see as totally impractical, regardless of how desirable the results might be. Sometimes, your audience will expect from you a very detailed implementation plan, including a list of activities and the name of the person responsible for each activity, the dates for beginning and completing each activity, and the likely costs for each activity.

A crucial element of a general or detailed implementation plan is an analysis of costs. Many great ideas born in the heat of inspiration have failed to become reality because of a lack of cold cash; programs that many judge worthwhile (such as manned exploration of Mars) have been delayed because of their cost. Whenever you present a proposal and outline its benefits, you also need to project its costs as accurately as you can. Remember that these costs often include not only the cost of constructing a new building or starting a new program but also all the continuing costs once the proposal is a reality. Your community may need a new and larger airport or a new bus service for the elderly or new day care facilities, but once these are established, there may be additional costs for just keeping the services going from day to day. The new and larger airport, for example, may need more employees to maintain it and cost more to heat and air condition than did the old one. These continuing costs are easy to overlook or to minimize; the great temptation in making a recommendation that you believe in strongly is to overstate the benefits and understate the costs. You need to fight this temptation, remembering that some of your readers also know that you will have been tempted to do this and will be on guard to assure themselves that you have not succumbed to this temptation.

Partly out of a concern about costs and partly out of a reluctance to change established ways, people accept recommendations that can be implemented within existing systems more readily than those requiring radical changes. Most of us are reluctant to make major changes on the strength of what *might* happen, however convincingly the probabilities are argued. Other things being equal, people usually prefer the least disruptive course of action.

On the other hand, sometimes existing structures need to be shaken up and disruptive measures taken. Much of the world we live in, including the very existence of this country, is a result of radical changes. You should at least consider whether a drastic change will not be ultimately more effective and easier to implement than a piecemeal one. Sometimes piecemeal recommendations are like putting money into an old car that is soon going to break down anyway, or like eighteenth-century Americans hoping King George and the British government would see the error of their ways. One test here, though a difficult one, is whether the piecemeal changes will improve the situation enough to justify the time and cost of the changes: the old car may not be worth keeping; on balance it was easier to leave King George than reform him.

Activities (9.5)

1. Each of the following are recommendations that many people believe are good ideas. Can you think of any drawbacks to these proposals that you would need to admit if you were arguing for these proposals? For one of the following, make a list of possible drawbacks and then write a brief paper (approximately 250 words) summarizing these drawbacks.
   a. Sending astronauts to explore Mars.
   b. Passing elementary and secondary students from one grade to another only after they have passed strict competency tests.
   c. Outlawing smoking in all public facilities.
   d. Increasing the school year by an average of one month for all elementary and secondary school children.
   e. Requiring automobile manufacturers to equip their cars with automatically inflatable air bags that would protect passengers in case of a crash.
2. Prepare an implementation plan for some change you would like to make in your own life, such as studying harder, learning a new sport or hobby, or exploring a possible career. Your implementation plan should include the sequence of activities you will undertake, the dates you plan to begin and end each activity, and the costs, if any, of the project. See the recommendation report at the end of this chapter for a sample implementation plan.

RECOMMENDATIONS WITH EQUAL EMPHASIS ON PRESENT AND FUTURE

The two types of recommendations we have discussed rarely occur in a pure form; most recommendations contain in varying degrees some discussion of both the current situation and future possibilities. While many recommendations fall in one group or the other and thus employ the strategies we have outlined for that group, some recommendations contain large elements of both groups.

Obviously, recommendations with approximately equal emphasis on present and future will combine the strategies discussed in the preceding two sections of this chapter: they will present and evaluate the current situation, then present the recommendation, and finally identify and evaluate the probable results of the recommendation. Because these arguments consider at some length what currently exists and what could exist, they provide the groundwork for a useful comparative evaluation. After you have examined both the present and future elements of your argument, you may wish to compare the two explicitly—to demonstrate that the probable effects will be preferable to the current situation. If you have an accurate grasp of your audience's needs and values, you should be able to make this demonstration.

SUMMARY

Making Practical Recommendations

- Recommendations emphasizing present conditions will include the following:

    A presentation of the current situation/policy/practice (a factual argument).

    A judgment of this situation in terms of values/needs important to your audience. While the judgment is frequently expressed, the value appealed to is usually implied.

    When applicable, a presentation of the existing effects (causal argument) and a judgment of these effects.

    When applicable, a presentation of the probable future effects (argument of effect) and a judgment of these effects.

- Recommendations emphasizing the future will include the following:

    Presentation of the recommendation. The degree of detail in this presentation is usually dictated by your degree of responsibility for enacting the recommendation.

    Identification of probable effects of your recommendation if it is implemented.

    Evaluation of these effects (both desirable and undesirable) in terms of audience needs and values.

    In some cases, a suggested implementation plan and an analysis of costs.

    Whether or not you include such a plan, those recommendations requiring minor changes to existing structures are generally more acceptable, though not necessarily more valuable, than those requiring radical restructuring.

- Recommendations with approximately equal emphasis on present and future will include the following:

    Presentation and evaluation of the current situation.

    Presentation of the recommendation.

    Identification and evaluation of the probable results of the recommendation.

    In many cases, a demonstration that the probable effects of the implemented recommendation will be preferable to the current situation.

A SAMPLE PRACTICAL RECOMMENDATION

The following sample recommendation report combines an emphasis on the current situation and on future results. The report is an example of what a student might include in a recommendation for a group of students interested in a computer room in their dormitory. The format of the report, outlined here, is one of several possible formats for a recommendation report:

    I. Statement of Problem

   II. Statement of Recommendation

  III. Advantages of Recommendation

  IV. Disadvantages of Recommendation

   V. Costs and Implementation Plan

Many organizations and many professors have a preferred format for such reports; you would be wise to check whether there are such preferred formats before you begin to write this kind of report either at work or for a class.

This recommendation report is briefer and more general than many. If a report with the same proposal were being done by administrators in the Office of Computing, the report would undoubtedly include more detail on scheduling of the project, on the nature of the renovations, and on the kind of equipment that would be purchased. On the other hand, most recommendations by students to administrators would probably not include even a very general implementation plan, though including such a plan can help convince readers that the plan is carefully thought out and feasible. As we noted earlier, many recommendation reports have formats that differ from this sample. To be effective, they must at a minimum include a statement of the problem, a recommendation, a statement about the advantages of the recommendation that appeals to values of the audience, and some indication that the recommendation is feasible. There are, however, many different formats that can contain these elements, the format of this sample being just one of them.

A PROPOSAL FOR A COMPUTER FACILITY IN MARSHALL DORMITORY

Prepared for

Dr. Hector Martinez, Assistant Vice-President for Student Life

by Elaine Weston

Chair, Marshall Dormitory Student Committee

February 13, 1989

STATEMENT OF PROBLEM

Currently many students living in Marshall Dormitory have difficulty getting access to a

computer. The college's main computer facility is located over a mile away on the other end of campus and that facility is often overcrowded; many students find that they can use a computer only after eleven at night or before ten in the morning. Some students bring their own computers with them to college, but not all students here can afford their own computers. I surveyed all students living on the third floor of Marshall and found that only 25 percent had their own computers, while another 50 percent said they use computers at least occasionally for course work. Of this 50 percent, 45 percent said that they have sometimes found it hard to get access to one of the college's computers, and 35 percent frequently had this problem. Clearly, this lack of access to needed computers is a serious problem for Marshall students. When I spoke with Helen Borshoff, the Vice-President for Computing, she confirmed the severity of the problem and said that her organization is trying to deal with the problem within the constraints of its limited resources.

RECOMMENDATION

We recommend that the Office of Student Life work with the Office of Computing to convert the student lounge at the west end of the second floor of Marshall into a computer facility equipped with seven microcomputers, two terminals connected to the main academic computer on the other side of campus, and three printers. Our discussions with the Office of Computing indicate that the number of computers, terminals, and printers is the maximum that would fit into the amount of space available and that this range of equipment would be most appropriate for student needs. Since the need for more computers and more access to computers is so pressing, we recommend that the necessary renovations take place this summer so that the facility will be ready by the beginning of the next academic year on September 6, 1989.

ADVANTAGES OF RECOMMENDATION

If our recommendation is implemented, students who live in Marshall will be able to use college-owned computers without having to go all the way to the college facility. There will also be more computers available than there are now, and students without the means to buy their own computers will be at less of a disadvantage than they currently are. For students, then, there are significant educational advantages if this proposal is implemented.

For the administration, there are several other advantages as well. Construction of this facility will alleviate at least some of the overwhelming pressure on the main computer facility. Since the space for this new facility already exists, renovating this space will be less costly than adding new space somewhere on campus. This new facility will also show the administration's concern for increasing student access to computers, and it will therefore help to reduce the growing tension between students and administrators over this issue.

DISADVANTAGES OF RECOMMENDATION

Our recommendation does have some disadvantages. Probably the most significant is the security risk of having a small facility so far removed from the central computer facility, which means that it would not make financial sense to have someone on duty to guard the equipment. Another disadvantage is that some space devoted to student relaxation would be taken and used for another purpose. The placing of a computer facility in a dormitory also raises some new policy questions for the college, including whether only students in the dormitory could use the facility, or whether the facility would be open to all students of the college.

These disadvantages are real, but they can be dealt with. The Vice-President for Computing assures us that new electronic security devices reduce the need for security personnel. In a poll taken two weeks ago, the Marshall students indicated that they preferred to see the current lounge converted into a computer facility, with 68 percent expressing this preference, 18 percent opposing it, and 14 percent expressing no opinion. Finally, while this proposal does raise some new questions of policy, these questions must be addressed at some point in the near future anyway, as computers and computer facilities become more pervasive in the college.

COSTS AND IMPLEMENTATION PLAN

The following is a tentative and very general outline of the costs of the project as well as an implementation plan. These will have to be refined by the Offices of Student Life and Computing as they begin to work on the project. The Vice-President for Computing has assured us, however, that the costs and implementation plan we have outlined here seem reasonable. At her advice, we have not included personnel costs for the time of administrators, since these costs are difficult to calculate and are not usually included in the budgets for small projects of this kind.

Activity	*Dates*	*Costs*
Initial planning with students, Student Life and Computing Administrators	March	—

Activity	Dates	Costs
Work requests for construction; orders for equipment	April	–
Renovation of lounge	June–July	$15000
Installation of security devices	Early August	$ 3000
Purchase and installation of computer equipment	Late August	$30000
Total initial costs		$48000
Ongoing costs-maintenance on equipment		$ 3000 per year

Suggestions for Writing (9.6)

1. Following the form of the sample recommendation report above, write a recommendation report to improve some aspect of your college or university. Possible areas for improvement could include dormitories or apartments, the library, the curriculum in your major, or the food service. Make your recommendation as realistic as possible by interviewing people with some responsibility for that area. From these people you should try to learn why the situation exists in its current form and how feasible your recommendation might be, as well as some sense of the costs of the project. The length of this report will vary with the complexity of the problem and your recommendation, though it might be wise to limit yourself to a maximum of approximately ten pages.

2. Almost every community has its share of white elephants: elaborate projects or expensive buildings that ultimately had to be abandoned or converted to some alternative use because their cost greatly exceeded their benefit to the community. Look for a white elephant in your community and analyze why the project never met its original intentions. Your professor can help you get started. You will almost certainly have to consult the local newspapers and then perhaps the local archives as well. Since your time is limited and there may be a great deal of documentation, you might have to restrict your research to newspaper accounts of what happened and why. As with Option 1, the maximum length should be approximately ten pages.

Chapter 10

Making Evaluations

All evaluations include a subject to be judged and an evaluative term that is applied to the subject. In the sentence "John is a good writer," **John** is the subject and **good writer** is the evaluative term; in "Ralph Waldo Emerson was a great thinker," **Ralph Waldo Emerson** is the subject and **great thinker** the evaluative term. Some evaluative statements include only partial evaluative terms, but their context suggests the missing parts. If you read the statement "Capital punishment is immoral," you would understand the full evaluative term to be **immoral act**; and in the statement "Rembrandt was a master," you would recognize the evaluative term to be **master painter**.

For an evaluative assertion to be meaningful, writer and reader must agree about the definition of the evaluative term. The basis for arguing that John is a good writer is a mutually acceptable definition of the term "good writer"; John's qualifications for the evaluation cannot be measured until the qualities constituting good writing have been established. In the sentence "John is a good writer; he communicates ideas clearly and gracefully," the evaluative term is defined: the qualities or criteria of a good writer are clarity and grace in the communication of ideas.

Often, evaluative statements are expressed negatively—as in "John is a poor writer," or "Wordsworth's talent failed him in his later poems." A negative evaluation can either imply its opposite as the standard of measurement, or it can establish a definition of the negative term itself. The writer of the judgment "William Faulkner's *The Fable* is a failed novel" could work from a definition of "successful novel," showing how this novel falls short of that definition, or could establish criteria for the term "failed novel" and apply those to the subject.

Not only must readers recognize the definition of the evaluative term, they must also agree with that definition. If their identification of those qualities constituting "good writing" or "great thinker" does not agree with the writer's, the evaluative argument will be useless. Perhaps readers agree that John's writing is clear and graceful, but they find the definition of the term too limited; in their view, good writing also includes richness of ideas and originality of expression. Thus, while they might concede that John's writing possesses the qualities of clarity and grace, they could still object to the judgment that he is a good writer.

In many evaluations, then, you must first argue the definition of your evaluative term, convincing your readers that the criteria by which you define the term are reasonable and complete. Only after successfully arguing this initial proposition can you proceed to demonstrate that that term applies to your subject.

Activities (10.1)

1. What is the evaluative term (implied or stated) in the following assertions?
   a. Mark Twain's *Huckleberry Finn* is an American classic.
   b. When Roger Bannister broke through the four-minute mile barrier in 1954, he accomplished one of the greatest athletic feats of this century.
   c. Calvin Coolidge was a mediocre President.
   d. Calculators are a real boon to mathematics students.
   e. The terrible losses in wars in the twentieth century show the bankruptcy of nations using war as an extension of foreign policy.
2. Write a paragraph giving a brief definition of one of the evaluative terms that you identified in Activity 1.

ESTABLISHING THE DEFINITION OF THE EVALUATIVE TERM

How much space and energy you devote to establishing your term's definition will depend on your audience and the nature of the term. About some terms there is so little dispute that an extensive definition would be unnecessary—a trustworthy bank teller, for example, or a reliable car. And when you are very confident about your readers' values, about what is important to them and why, you may not need to propose and argue a definition. If you were a doctor writing to other doctors about the unprofessional behavior of a certain physician, you could safely assume agreement between you and your readers about the definition of unprofessional behavior. However, when your audience is composed of people with different expertise or values, when your definition is unusual or controversial, or when the term lends itself to a number of possible definitions, you should state and argue your definition of the evaluative term.

Whether or not you explicitly define the evaluative term, remember that very vague or inflated evaluations are usually harder to argue than those that are limited and precise. It would be far easier to convince an audience that "Ralph Nader has served a valuable function in advocating consumer rights" than that "Ralph Nader is a great American."

Proposing the Definition

In most cases, the actual definition of the term can be stated quite briefly, usually as part of or directly following the thesis. "Alison is the ideal management trainee: she is intelligent, ambitious, congenial, and hard-working"; or, "In his highly original and influential reflections on the American spirit, reflections that affected common citizens as well as fellow philosophers, Ralph Waldo Emerson proved himself to be a great thinker."

When defining an evaluative term, you are proposing a stipulative definition—a definition that restricts the term to a particular meaning appropriate to your context. (See Chapter 3 for a fuller discussion of stipulative definitions.) In most cases, your definition will take the shorthand form identified in Chapter 3, although if the term is very difficult you might want to provide an extended definition.

As in all definitions, the defining, explanatory terms you offer must be clear and precise. Your definition will be useless if it offers only broad or abstract generalizations. If you write "The brilliance of the film *Citizen Kane* lies in its wonderful structure," but you fail to define "wonderful," you will leave readers guessing. You should also avoid definitions that include highly subjective terms. If you define "talented soprano" as one whose voice is beautiful at all points of her vocal range, you have not done much to clarify the evaluative term. What is beautiful to one listener may be mediocre or heavy or thin to another; "beauty" is not a measurement that inspires agreement. "Beautiful" requires definition; it can only be useful in this context if it is defined by comparatively objective standards—fullness or clarity or fluidity. While these too are subjective terms, they are more precise, and less a matter of personal taste than a term like beautiful.

Below are some examples of definitions that truly serve their explanatory, illuminating function.

1. A good argument is one that directly identifies its central proposition, supports that proposition with reasonable, relevant, and concrete evidence, and admits the possibility of rival points of view.

2. A dedicated mother devotes herself to her children because she knows she should; a good mother devotes herself to her children because she can't imagine doing otherwise.

3. A good education will prepare a student not only for a career but for a fulfilling life outside of a career. As important as careers are in our lives, they do not and should not occupy all our time and energy. The well-educated person is the one who can view life outside of work with zest, knowing that there are many other interests aside from a career.

While the qualities included in your proposed definition should be as clear and precise as possible, the very nature of evaluations will not always allow you to avoid subjective terms. In the third example above, the term "fulfilling life" is inherently subjective, yet it is not meaningless. There are certain qualities and activities we can identify that can constitute a fulfilling life, including having friends, having hobbies or other recreational interests, and being curious about the past, the future, and the world. It may not be easy to measure precisely each of these qualities or activities, but they do exist, and they can be gauged on some comparative scale.

Activities (10.2)

Using the definitions above as a model, give a brief but useful and reasonably thorough definition for two of the following:

1. A good car.
2. A good teacher.
3. A good politician.
4. A good basketball player.
5. A good movie.

Arguing the Definition

If you have any reason to expect that your readers will not agree with your definition of the evaluative term, you will have to convince them that the definition is just, that the criteria you assign to the term "necessary war," or "master craftsman," or "inspired teacher" are reasonable and complete. In some evaluations, the process of establishing the definition of the evaluative term actually becomes the focus of the argument. You can argue the justness of your definition using any of the methods of argument we have already discussed, including appeal to assumed values, identification of effect, appeal to authority, or comparison.

To illustrate the application of these methods, we'll work with the following example: as a branch manager for a local bank, you are asked to write a formal evaluation of three new management trainees. Your reader will be the bank's vice president for personnel. There is no fixed evaluation form or criteria to work from; *you* must decide which qualities constitute promising performance in a new trainee. The qualities you settle on (in unranked order) are (1) honesty; (2) the ability to foresee the consequences of decisions; (3) attention to detail; and (4) courtesy with customers. Because you have created this list, you will need to justify it, however briefly, to the director. Your justification for each item on the list would probably use the following methods of argument:

1. Honesty: appeal to assumed value. You wouldn't have to say much about this quality. For obvious reasons, bankers place a premium on honesty in their employees.
2. Ability to foresee the consequences of decisions: identification of effect. This criterion may not be as obvious as the first, but bankers must base decisions such as lending money, setting interest rates, and making investments on the probable consequences of the decisions. You could point out briefly the positive results of having this ability, and the negative results of lacking it.
3. Attention to detail: appeal to assumed value. Like honesty, the importance of this quality doesn't have to be argued to bankers.
4. Courtesy with customers: identification of effect. You can easily point out that good customer relations lead to good business. For many bankers, this criterion would be an assumed value.

You could buttress these criteria with other support as well. To bolster the third criterion of attention to detail, you might cite recognized authorities who stress this quality and the grave risks banks run when they hire employees who lack it. And to support the fourth criterion, courtesy with customers, you might use the method of comparison, pointing to the success of a competing bank that stresses good customer relations.

If you can make a reasonable argument for your definition of the evaluative term, your readers are likely to accept the qualities you cite. But they can still object to your definition on the basis of omission: your definition is acceptable as far as it goes, but you have omitted one quality critical to them. Without the inclusion of that quality, they cannot accept your evaluation of the subject. In formulating your definition, try to anticipate the reactions of your readers; if they are likely to be concerned about the omission of a certain quality, you must explain why you chose to omit it. Any of the methods identified above will help you make this explanation. For example, you could justify your omission of knowledge of computer programming as a criterion for judging trainees by using the identification of effect, pointing out that few bank employees do any programming anyway and that it is cheaper and more efficient to hire outside programming experts when they are needed. In this case, you are pointing out that there are no bad effects caused by these trainees' lack of knowledge of programming.

Ranking the Qualities in Your Definition

In some evaluative arguments, it is not enough to establish a list of qualities constituting your evaluative term; often, you will need to indicate the relative importance of these qualities by ranking them. Ranking is almost always necessary in evaluations of multiple subjects. If you were evaluating four models of home coffee brewers, for example, you might establish the following qualities as essential: reasonable price; good-tasting coffee; a quick-brew cycle; and an automatic timer. A reader could agree with every one of these qualities yet disagree with your final choice of brewer. The reason for the disagreement would be that you and your reader rank the four qualities differently. If a quick-brew cycle is most important to you but least important to your reader, he or she will not accept your final evaluation of the three machines.

In some evaluations, particularly those that are likely to directly affect your reader, you may have to justify the relative value you place on each quality. If you were evaluating dormitory life as a valuable freshman experience, you would let your readers (incoming freshmen) know which of the criteria you cite is most important and which is least important. Suppose you rank the qualities as follows: (1) quiet study atmosphere; (2) good social opportunities; (3) proximity to campus; and (4) comfortable surroundings. You could argue the importance of (1), quiet study atmosphere, by a number of familiar methods: appeals to value or authority, comparison, or identification of effect. Regardless of the method you choose, you must be able to demonstrate that without a quiet study atmosphere, one that allows students to work hard and succeed academically, all the other qualities are meaningless. If a student flunks out of school the first year, the other three qualities will have been useless. Thus, the first quality is the most important because, in your view, it is the *essential* quality.

Activities (10.3)

For one of the following subjects, list in order of importance the criteria by which you would judge its quality. Then, for one of the examples, write a one-to-two-page essay justifying your choice and ranking of the criteria. Use whatever methods of argument seem appropriate.

1. A college or university.
2. A musical concert.
3. A newspaper.
4. A church or synagogue.
5. A college textbook.

APPLYING THE DEFINITION TO YOUR SUBJECT

Once you have defined your evaluative term, you must show that the definition applies to your subject. This process constitutes the actual evaluation.

Your evaluation will be largely *factual*; by verifying data and presenting concrete examples, you will demonstrate that your subject possesses the criteria you have cited. Establishing these facts is especially important when the subject is a service—a travel agency, a long-distance phone company—or a functional object—a coffee brewer, a pickup truck. In such cases, where the evaluative term is defined by objectively measurable qualities (for example, speed, efficiency, accuracy, price), your job is to verify the existence of that quality in your subject.

Suppose you were evaluating small portable FM radios with earphones in terms of affordable price, physical convenience, and power of receiver. In your judgment, a good radio of this type is one that costs no more than $40.00 (your definition of affordable price), can be carried and listened to comfortably when you are walking or jogging, and holds the signals of local radio stations without interference. Using these standards, you evaluate the Euphony "Jogmate" as a **good portable radio**. Your evaluation will be convincing so long as you can establish the following three facts: the suggested retail price of the Jogmate is below $40.00; it is easy to carry; it holds local stations firmly.

These facts can be convincingly established through reference to your own experience, provided you present yourself as reliable and objective. (Other supporting sources—the experience of friends or impartial analyses of the Jogmate found in consumer guides—could be referred to as well.) You could cite the actual price of the Jogmate at three local stores to verify the first fact. The second, which is the most subjective, can be verified by your physical description of the Jogmate—its weight, dimensions, earphone style—and a description of your experience running with it: "The small, cushioned earpieces fit comfortably into my ears; there is no connecting band to slip off the head or tighten uncomfortably; the small radio clips easily onto a waistband or can be held comfortably in one hand." The third fact can also be established by reference to your own experience: "I have run distances of four to five miles with the Jogmate at least 20 times. On those occasions, it has never lost the signal of the three stations I like to listen to." As with all factual arguments, the key to success in arguing evaluations is to cite reliable and authoritative experience and observations, and to include specific, concrete examples of general statements.

Not all evaluations are as neat and objective as the preceding example. Let's look at a very different example involving more subjective measurement and see how the principles of factual argument apply. This evaluation argues that your friend Pam Foye knows how to be a good friend: she respects her friends, accepting and loving them for who they are, and she expects the same treatment from them. Because the definition included in the thesis statement is not a standard definition of friendship, it requires some preliminary support (see the preceding section on "Arguing the Definition").

Once supported, the definition must be applied to the subject, your friend Pam. The quality of respecting others—a key criterion of your evaluative term—cannot be measured as objectively or established as definitively as the price of a radio or the fuel efficiency of an automobile. Yet general agreement exists about what constitutes respectful behavior: it is attentive, considerate, accepting behavior. The best way to demonstrate the applicability of the quality to your subject is through specific examples illustrating such behavior. As in any factual argument, you must *describe* the experience faithfully and objectively. Because you want to establish that Pam's respectful treatment of friends is habitual, not occasional, you should cite a number of examples.

Beyond citing the examples, you might also need to point out what is respectful in the examples cited, particularly if your readers might interpret the behavior differently. But in general, the more concrete and immediate your presentation of examples, the less explicit commentary you will need.

FURTHER METHODS OF SUPPORTING EVALUATIONS

Definition and factual argument are central to evaluations, but there are other ways to support these arguments. The tactics we suggest below can be used along with definition and factual arguments or by themselves.

Identification of Effect

Just as you can defend your choice of a defining quality by identifying or predicting the effect of that quality, so too can you support your overall judgment of the subject through pointing to its positive or negative effects. When adopting this supporting tactic, you must be sure that your identification of effect accords with the principles of causality. If the causal link you posit seems improbable, the strategy will fail.

An action, policy, or object is generally considered valuable if its effects are valuable. Freedom of speech is good because it encourages the widest exchange of ideas, which is more likely to lead to the truth or to solutions to problems. Child abuse is bad because it causes physical and mental anguish in children. Judging a subject in terms of its effects is, of course, only useful when your audience agrees with your assessment of the effect. In using this supporting method, you must be prepared to argue your evaluation of the effect if you suspect disagreement from your audience.

Appeal to Authority

Any evaluation can be supported by appealing to the similar judgment of a recognized authority. If Martina Navratilova has publicly expressed her admiration for the tennis game of Margaret Court, this statement would be effective support for your argument that Margaret Court ranks among the finest women tennis players of the last thirty years. When using this method of support for an evaluation, you must be certain that the person whose judgment you cite truly qualifies as an authority on the subject.

Comparison

You can often support your evaluation by comparing your subject with one that would be accorded a similar judgment by your audience. For example, many feminist arguments criticizing sexual discrimination have been supported by reference to racial discrimination. The two forms of discrimination are substantially the same: both base inequitable treatment on irrelevant and immutable characteristics—on race and gender. An audience that would object to racial discrimination would, when the similarities were pointed out, be likely to object to sexual discrimination as well. As with any comparative argument, the similarities between the two subjects must be essential, not peripheral.

Activities (10.4)

For two of the following evaluations, write a paragraph on each describing the most appropriate kind of support: factual argument, identification of effect, appeal to authority, or comparison. Why is this support the most appropriate? You may cite more than one kind of support.

1. Shakespeare is one of the world's greatest writers.
2. Mercedes-Benz makes many of the world's best cars.
3. Failure to build a water treatment plant for the city would be a serious mistake.
4. Strato Airlines has the best customer service record of any airline in America.
5. Military involvements by major powers in small countries are usually unwise in terms of lives lost, money wasted, and the increased suspicion of other small countries.

THE VARIETIES OF EVALUATIONS

By now you realize that different kinds of evaluations demand different kinds of support. Although there are no hard and fast rules in this area, if you can identify the **kind** of evaluation you are making, you should have a better sense of what you need to do to support it. Evaluations usually fall into one of three main categories: ethical, esthetic, or functional.

Ethical Evaluations

The word *ethical* is one of those terms that we all understand in a vague way yet might be hard pressed to define precisely. To avoid confusion, we offer the following definition: *ethical* describes behavior that conforms to an ideal code of moral principles—principles of right and wrong, good and evil. That code may be derived from any number of cultures—religious, professional, national, or political.

All of us operate within many cultures—we are members of families, communities, organizations, religions, professions, and nations. Each one of these cultures has its own set of ethical standards. For example, among the many ethical principles of Judaism and Christianity are the Ten Commandments. As United States citizens, we are subject to other standards of conduct, such as those recorded in the Constitution—including the Bill of Rights—and the Declaration of Independence. Your college also operates by certain standards that it expects its members to follow: respect for school property, respect for faculty, and academic honesty. In most cultures, these standards are formally recorded, but in some instances they remain implicit.

Beyond those ethical codes dictating right or good conduct within a particular culture, there exists a range of powerful standards or values not so obviously tied to any specific culture, but pervasive in most of them, including ideals such as **fair play**, **kindness**, and **respect for others**.

Because each of us is tied to a number of different cultures, clashes between standards are inevitable. Some pacifist groups, for example, see a clash between the religious commandment "Thou shall not kill" and the government's standard that citizens must be prepared to defend their country in time of war. Sometimes conflicts occur between standards of the same culture. Such clashes are commonplace in law. What happens, for example, when the right of free speech collides with the right of a person to be free from libel? Free speech cannot mean that someone has a right to say anything about another person, regardless of how untrue or harmful it is. On the other hand, protection from libel cannot mean protection from the truth being told about mistakes or misdeeds, particularly when they have some impact on the public. Throughout our history the courts have struggled to find a balance between these two competing claims, sometimes slightly favoring one value, sometimes the other, but denying that either value can have absolute sway over the other.

Defining the Evaluative Term in Ethical Arguments

Whenever we evaluate a subject in terms of right or wrong conduct or behavior, we are appealing to certain ethical values or standards held by our audience. When we assert "Hitler was an evil man," or "Ms. Mead is an honorable lawyer" or "The coach used unfair tactics," we are assuming that our readers both *understand* what we mean by the evaluative term and *agree* with that meaning. In ethical and moral evaluations, it is usually pointless to argue a particular definition, because ethical standards are powerful, longstanding, and usually unquestioningly held. In other words, it is extremely difficult to change someone's understanding of what constitutes right and wrong, good and evil.

The exception to this generalization is when your readers are not members of the culture to whose standards you are appealing and when they are not likely to hold a conflicting standard. If you were arguing against the practice of pubic advertising by lawyers and doctors on the grounds that it is unprofessional behavior, and your audience consisted of people from neither profession, you would probably need to define the term "unprofessional behavior." Because your audience is not likely to be committed to a particular understanding of the term, you might be able to convince them to accept a definition not widely held in the professional communities about which you are writing.

The Argument in Ethical Evaluations

Most ethical arguments concentrate on demonstrating what is unethical or immoral about the subject being evaluated. At the center of these evaluations, then, is a factual argument. In arguing that Hitler was evil, your focus would be on documenting the behavior that you identify as evil, and on demonstrating that your evaluative term fits the examples you are citing.

You can also strengthen your evaluation through other supporting methods, including comparison (Hitler was as bad as or worse than certain other dictators) or identification of effect (aside from all the bad he did in his life, the war Hitler started led to the division of Europe into two opposing camps, or to a pervasive sense of victimization among Jews of later generations).

Activities (10.5)

Write an essay of approximately two pages supporting one of the following ethical evaluations. If you disagree with the evaluation, you could write an essay supporting the opposite statement (perhaps you believe, for example, that playing a radio at full volume in a public place does not constitute an act of aggression).

1. Recruitment violations in collegiate athletics are contrary to the ideals of higher education.
2. Playing a radio at full volume in a public place constitutes an act of aggression.
3. Volunteer workers are the unsung heroes of American life.
4. Regardless of the product they are selling, merchants have a right to charge as high a price as they can get for their product.
5. John Glenn, the astronaut turned senator, is a perfect example of the American dream.

Aesthetic Evaluations

Writing a convincing evaluation of a work of art—a poem, an opera, a painting—is not as futile a task as many believe, provided you understand the goals of such an argument. Just as personal tastes in clothes or food are usually immune to reasonable argument, aesthetic preferences—liking Chopin's music and despising Mahler's—are often too much matters of personal taste to be arguable. There is much truth in the Latin saying *de gustibus non est disputandum:* there is no arguing about taste. Nevertheless, while changing aesthetic tastes or opinions is difficult, it is possible and often useful to convince an audience to *appreciate* the strengths or weaknesses of a work of art by giving them a greater understanding of it. A successful aesthetic evaluation may not convince a reader to like Rubens or to dislike Lichtenstein, but it will at least give a reader reasons for approving of or objecting to a work.

All artistic fields have their own set of standards for excellence, standards about which there is surprising conformity among experts in the field. Most literary critics, for example, would agree about standards for a successful short story: coherence of the story, careful selection of detail, avoidance of digression, an interesting style. When critics disagree, and of course they do so regularly, they usually disagree not about identified standards of excellence but about the application of those standards. Such disagreements are often matters of personal preference for one kind of artist over another. Even professional critics are not immune to the influence of their personal tastes.

When you argue an aesthetic evaluation, you should work from standards currently accepted within the field, though you may not have to do more than briefly or implicitly refer to them. Your evaluation is likely to fail if you ignore these standards, or if you try to effect an overnight revolution in them. As with ethical standards, esthetic standards usually change gradually, though there can be periods of revolutionary change, as occurred in artistic tastes in the early twentieth century.

Usually, then, your chief task is to demonstrate that these standards apply (or don't apply) to your subject. This demonstration consists of careful description and concrete examples. In the following review of the performance of Torvill and Dean, the British ice dancing couple, Anna Kisselgoff supports her judgment that the team has achieved "technical perfection" and the status of "the great romantic team of the 1980's" with effective description and examples:

> The music [from the dance "Paso Doble"] is taken from Rimsky-Korsakov's "Capriccio Espagnol," and as both skaters stand at the center of the rink, the surprise to come is kept literally under wraps. Miss Torvill clings to Mr. Dean's back, a hand draped over his right shoulder from behind. Dressed in a bullfighter's costume, he reaches across his chest as if holding a cape. Then, in a second, this is what Miss Torvill "becomes." Her black, winglike sleeves held out, she spins off—flung away by her partner.
>
> As both skaters move continuously in serpentine paths around each other, Mr. Dean whirls, twirls and twists the shape that is his partner. The most spectacular moments are those when the matador drags his cape behind him—that is, Mr. Dean pushes forward emphatically to an insistent rhythm, as Miss Torvill is pulled along, gliding on one knee. . . .
>
> The final moment, no matter how frequently seen, preserves its power to surprise. Mr. Dean, eyes flashing, suddenly throws his "cape" to the ice. Miss Torvill falls prone, revolves on her stomach and comes to rest. Like the grandest of all toreadors, her partner salutes the crowd, one arm raised in triumph.

Kisselgoff's graphic description and detailed language demonstrate how Torvill and Dean achieve the standards of "technical perfection" and being a "great romantic team"—two standards Kisselgoff explicitly mentions in her article. The description also points to other implicit standards as well, including originality of artistic conception and close artistic cooperation between the two partners.

If you wish to convince an audience of the excellence of a work of art, you would be wise to consider carefully how much that audience knows about the work in particular or the field in general. If you suspect inexperience or ignorance on the part of the audience, you should offer a lucid and deferential *explanation* of the standards you are applying and of the work in question. The principle behind this suggestion is that people often fail to appreciate what they don't understand; if your evaluation can teach them about excellence in the field, it may have a better chance at convincing them that your subject represents that excellence.

Another useful tactic when arguing a positive evaluation to an inexperienced audience is to relate your subject to one with which they are more familiar. If, for example, you wanted to convince an audience familiar with and appreciative of modern abstract art that the art of ancient Egypt is also interesting, you might point out the similarities between the two: "Although they are widely separated in time, modern abstract art and ancient Egyptian art both concentrate on the essence of a person or object, not the surface appearance." In taking this approach, you are borrowing from your readers' appreciation of modern abstract art, shining its positive light onto the subject of your evaluation.

Activities (10.6)

For each of the following forms of art or entertainment, list at least three standards by which you would judge the quality of a specific work of this type. Then, for one of the categories, write a two-to-three-page essay demonstrating how a specific work of that type does or does not fit your standards of excellence. (You should make these standards explicit in your essay.)

1. A film.
2. A detective novel.
3. An album (or tape or compact disc) of popular music.
4. A photograph.
5. A painting.

Functional Evaluations

Functional evaluations stand a better chance of changing readers' minds than do ethical and aesthetic evaluations. It is easier to convince a reader that her views about turbo engine cars are inaccurate than that her views about abortion are wrong. While people do form sentimental attachments to objects and machines, they can usually be convinced that however powerful that attachment, it has nothing to do with the subject's actual performance; an audience's preconceptions about performance quality are less matters of cultural values and personal tastes than of practical experience, assumptions, or hearsay.

Functional evaluations always work from a definition of ideal standards: you cannot demonstrate that Sony makes a superior compact disc player in the absence of standards against which to measure the Sony player's performance. You must use your judgment to determine which arguments require an explicit presentation of standards and which can assume audience recognition of the standards. Certainly, if your list of standards is for some reason unusual or innovative, you will need to state it directly in the argument and to argue its relevance and completeness (using any of the methods discussed earlier in this chapter).

When writing a functional evaluation, you must consider ranking the standards from which you work. Functional evaluations typically work from a number of different standards that are rarely viewed as equally important. A reference book's function could be evaluated in terms of its thoroughness, its physical format, and its accuracy, but the three are not equally important. In order to justify your final judgment, you must first explain and support the relative weights you have assigned to each standard.

Most successful functional evaluations focus on factual arguments. In the factual argument, you will demonstrate to what degree the standards of performance apply to your subject. As in all factual arguments, the facts and examples you provide must be well documented. Personal experience—your test-drive of a new car, for example—can be useful and convincing, but in most cases, that experience needs support from authoritative, unbiased sources (for example, an article on the car in a reputable magazine like *Road and Track* or *Consumer Reports.*)

Any of the other supporting methods discussed earlier in this chapter (identification of effect, appeal to authority, comparison) can also be used in a performance evaluation. Of these, the most valuable is identification of effect. The crucial question in evaluating performance is almost always whether the person or object achieves its intended effect: Did the governor's administration achieve most of its goals? Did the camera produce good pictures? The argument will be largely factual if the effect has already occurred, and your primary job will be to document and evaluate the effect. In arguing that "Betsy Turner is a good violin teacher," you would cite the number of fine players she has produced (the effect of her performance as teacher) and briefly support your positive judgment of those players. In other cases, where the effect has not yet occurred, your argument is necessarily more speculative: "Based on all the evidence we have, this car is likely to give you years of reliable service."

Activities (10.7)

List in ranked order at least three standards by which you would judge the performance of the following. Then for one of the categories, write a two-to-three-page essay demonstrating how well one person or object in that category meets your standards of performance.

1. An automobile for a family with three small children.
2. A president of a college or university.
3. A personal computer.
4. A United States Senator.
5. A college reference librarian.

Interpretations

The subject of an interpretive argument is the visible surface we wish to understand or explore further; it is the behavior or event or data that openly exists for all to observe. The interpretive term is the summarized explanation of the reality beneath the visible surface. In the interpretation "The iconoclastic world view of the brilliant physicist Edward Fredkin derives from his lifelong anti-authoritarian bias," the subject is Fredkin's "iconoclastic world view," and the interpretive term is "lifelong anti-authoritarian bias."

To write a solid interpretation, you must satisfy the following requirements: (1) the interpretive term must be clearly defined; (2) the interpretive term and the subject must be linked—not merely parallel or congruent, but attached according to some recognized principle; and (3) evidence must be supplied to support the interpretation.

Defining the Interpretive Term. Like evaluative arguments, interpretations work from assumptions about definition—about what elements constitute a certain condition or reality. In interpretations, we are stating that X (the subject) is Y (the interpretation). To prove or support this assertion, we must define Y in such a way that it restates X, or restate X in such a way that is coincides with Y. In the interpretive thesis "Television news broadcasting is no longer news, it is entertainment," we must demonstrate the coincidence of our definition of entertainment on the one hand with what we see of television news on the other.

In the following passage, we see a similar assertion of coincidence, where Sigmund Freud equates literature (the subject) with the play of children:

> Now the writer does the same as the child at play; he creates a world of phantasy which he takes very seriously; that is, he invests it with a great deal of affect, while separating it sharply from reality. Language has preserved this relationship between children's play and poetic creation. It designates certain kinds of imaginative creation, concerned with tangible objects and capable of representation, as "plays"; the people who present them are called "players."

The first step in assembling an interpretive argument is to consider whether to define and argue the interpretive term. As with evaluative arguments, you should define the term if you are using it in an unusual or controversial way, and you should justify that definition if you think your audience is likely to object to it. In the first example above, the term "entertainment" probably should be defined, as it is a very broad and even subjective term: you might define the term as "any brief, self-contained, sensually pleasing performance that amuses but does not challenge." If your audience is likely to disagree with this definition, you will have to support it with the methods discussed in the preceding section on "Arguing the Definition" in this chapter.

Of course, you can work from an unstated definition, provided your argument clearly reveals the elements of that definition. The following example illustrates this tactic:

> "Much of television news broadcasting is no longer news; it is entertainment. Most local and national news broadcasts, news shows like '60 Minutes,' '20/20,' even public television news are putting out slick, superficial performances that are usually neither challenging nor controversial, but capture huge audience shares."

Here the definition of entertainment is contained in the characterization of television news.

Extensive interpretations of a series of events or continuing behavior work somewhat differently, although the basic principles are the same. In these cases—for example, an interpretation of a character's actions in a novel or of quarterly stock market activity—the subjects are usually explained in terms of a coherent and pre-established theory, system of thought, or belief. Instead of demonstrating the coincidence or equivalence of the subject and a single concept (like children's play or entertainment), these more ambitious interpretations reveal the existence of a series of related concepts—an entire system—behind the visible activity of the subject. The system identified could be Christianity, Marxism, Jungian psychology, feminism, Freudian drive theory, capitalism, semiotics—virtually any set of facts or principles logically connected to form a coherent view of the world.

Examples of this kind of systematic interpretation are especially prevalent in artistic and literary interpretations, although they are not limited to this context. A feminist interpretation of a literary figure like Emily Dickinson would work from a thorough understanding of feminist theory. The interpretation might explain Dickinson's poems in terms of the tension between her vocation as a poet and the very different expectations that nineteenth century society had for women.

However compelling such an interpretation, readers are not likely to be swayed if they strongly object to the interpretive system—to the Freudian or Marxist or feminist model of human behavior. Even if the construct used to explain the subject is not formally named, the principles contained in that construct must seem at least plausible to your readers. If you interpret modern American history on the basis of tensions and conflicts between different social and economic classes, your readers may not give your interpretation fair consideration if they are opposed to this set of principles. On the other hand, a good interpretation can often help readers gain sympathy for a philosophy or point of view they were previously hostile to or ignorant of. When you write interpretations, you should be sensitive to your audience's beliefs and be prepared at least to acknowledge their probable objections as you proceed. If you do so, you may convince some hostile readers, bringing them to accept not only your interpretation but also at least some aspects of your underlying point of view.

Establishing Coincidence. All interpretations must demonstrate coincidence between the subject and the interpretive term. Coincidence in this context can mean equivalence (as in "Television news is the same as entertainment"), substitution ("Although marriage looks like a romantic partnership, it is often a formalization of female dependence"), or revelation ("Behind his warmth and friendliness is a cold and impenetrable shield of defenses"). The challenge of interpretations is in demonstrating these coincidences.

When the interpretive term is concrete, this task is comparatively easy. We can recognize such concepts as entertainment or economic dependence; they are verifiable. Once we agree on the meaning of the term, a simple factual argument will demonstrate the applicability of the term to the subject. If we know what economic dependence is, we can detect it in a relationship with little difficulty or little guesswork, provided we have necessary facts.

But what about detecting "a cold and impenetrable shield of defenses," or "an unresolved Oedipal conflict"? These descriptions are legitimate and typical interpretive terms, yet no one ever saw a defense mechanism or an Oedipal conflict. How do we argue the operation of an essentially unverifiable concept? The answer is that we proceed in much the same way as with causal arguments. Just as a cause and its effect must be linked by some acceptable motivational principle that accords with human experience and observation, so must the interpretation (the less visible reality) relate to the subject (the visible reality) according to an acknowledged principle of experience.

If we argue that an apparently ambitious student's hesitancy to apply for a glamorous, high-pressure job reflects her ambivalence about success, we are assuming that our readers would accept the principle of ambivalence and recognize its symptoms—in this case, behavior guaranteed to threaten one's stated goals. This interpretation will be meaningless to a reader who knows nothing about these ideas. Because few interpretive arguments can afford the space necessary to educate a reader about its assumptions, you must carefully consider what principles of experience your audience is likely to acknowledge.

Documenting the Interpretation. Interpretations need documentation or evidence. As well as explaining your subject through an acceptable principle of experience, you will need to document your interpretation through examples taken from your subject. Even when your subject and interpretation are very narrow, you must offer such evidence. In the earlier example of the student's hesitancy to apply for a job, you could support your theory of ambivalence by describing the student's professed ambitions, the nature of the job, and her chances of getting it if she applies, plus her refusal to apply. Different arguments will provide different kinds of evidence, so it is difficult to generalize about the best kind of evidence. But your interpretation must point to a number of concrete examples drawn from the condition or behavior of your subject.

The Possibility of Multiple Interpretations. Most subjects lend themselves to a number of different interpretations, and these interpretations are not necessarily mutually exclusive. This becomes obvious when we think of the many theories that could be offered to explain why you skipped breakfast this morning: maybe you simply had no time to eat; maybe you weren't hungry; maybe you were punishing yourself by depriving yourself of food; maybe you resent paying outrageous prices to food service. We would need more evidence to know which, if any, of these theories apply to your situation, but it is perfectly conceivable that a number of them could apply.

Because of the likelihood of multiple interpretations, you should try to resist a strongly dogmatic and inflexible tone in interpretive arguments. You do not need to acknowledge constantly the possibility of other explanations, nor should you sound tentative about yours, but don't present your argument as if it were immutable, inarguable dogma.

Activities (10.8)

1. Write a brief interpretation (approximately 250 words) of a recent event or activity. Your interpretation should include the interpretive term, the kind of coincidence, and the supporting evidence. Then write a different interpretation of this same event or activity, again including all the necessary elements of an interpretation. When you have completed these two essays, write an essay of approximately 250 words explaining which interpretation you find more plausible and why. Some possible events or activities: a recent election, a political scandal, a friend's recent success or failure in some endeavor, or an athletic contest.

2. Find in newspapers or magazines two different interpretations of a film that you have seen recently. Write a two-to-three-page essay describing the different views, stating which interpretation you find more plausible and your reasons for that view. You may have reservations even about the interpretation you favor. Be sure to state those as well. (Give your instructor a copy of the two reviews.)

SUMMARY

Supporting Evaluations

- All evaluations include a subject to be judged and an evaluative term that is applied to the subject.
- Before you argue the evaluation, you must ensure that your readers recognize and accept your definition of the evaluative term. When automatic acceptance seems doubtful, you must argue your definition.

  Definitions can be argued by appeals to assumed reader values, appeals to authority, identification of effect, and comparison.

  In evaluations of multiple subjects, you may have to rank the qualities defining your evaluative term and justify that ranking.
- Evaluating your subject consists of demonstrating, through a largely factual argument, the applicability of the evaluative term to your subject. Evaluations can also be supported through appeals to authority, identification of effect, and comparison.
- Evaluations are made in ethical, aesthetic, functional, and interpretive terms.

  In ethical evaluations, the focus is on applying the ethical standard (evaluative term) to the subject, not on defining that standard.

  Aesthetic evaluations typically work from standards currently accepted within the field, demonstrating the applicability of these standards to your subject.

  Functional evaluations typically work from a number of ranked standards in terms of which the subject is measured.

  Interpretations establish a coincidence between the subject and the interpretive term by linking them through an acknowledged principle of experience.

SAMPLE ETHICAL EVALUATION

The following essay on euthanasia, based on an essay written by college student Robert Conway, is an example of an argument of ethical evaluation. The argument contains a stipulative definition of the subject (euthanasia) and an evaluative term ("moral rightness"). It appeals to authority in its references to traditional religions and ethical systems, and it employs identification of effect in discussing what could happen if euthanasia were not allowed. It also refutes one counterargument. This evaluation is somewhat unusual in that its thesis ("I wish to argue the moral rightness of euthanasia") comes in the middle of the essay. As we noted in Chapter 3, theses can be found in the beginning, middle, or end of arguments, or they can be merely implied. The placement of the thesis in the middle of the essay is effective here because the definition of one of the terms of the thesis (euthanasia) is one key support for the argument; the thesis is immediately more acceptable to potentially hostile readers if they accept the stipulative definition that has preceded it.

THE MORAL JUSTIFICATION FOR EUTHANASIA

Euthanasia is usually defined as the act of allowing death to occur in someone who is terminally ill but whose life may be prolonged through continued medical treatment. Despite the frequent equation of the terms, euthanasia should not be confused with mercy killing. Mercy killing involves an action which *causes* death. It is the direct and intentional taking of a human life, and that is murder. Tacking the word ''mercy'' onto ''killing'' is really an inexcusable attempt to justify murder by stressing the motive rather than the act itself.

We should restrict the use of the term ''euthanasia'' to simply *allowing* death to occur through the witholding of life support systems. Free of life maintained by drugs and machines, the body simply dies in a natural, inevitable way. For those unfortunate people who suffer from terminal diseases or horrific accidents, and the loved ones of those people, this natural death comes as a great relief and a welcome end.

Often writers on this subject divide euthanasia into two categories: positive or active and negative or passive, with active meaning mercy killing and passive meaning euthanasia as I have defined it (Ladd, p. 164). But the meaning of the term should not be stretched so far, because the positive and negative versions are so different that it is necessary to have a clear and unmistakable line drawn between them. Using the same term for both acts makes it far too easy to confuse them.

That said, I wish to argue the moral rightness of euthanasia. To my knowledge, none of the world's great religions or ethical systems would dispute the appropriateness of euthanasia for terminally ill patients. According to my limited study, these creeds and systems accept the inevitability of death, with caution to humanity about the folly of trying to prolong life beyond its natural limits. The Book of Ecclesiastes in the Bible tells us:

To every thing there is a season, and a time to every purpose under heaven:
A time to be born, and a time to die; a time to plant, and a time to pluck up that which is planted (3.1,2).

And classical Greek mythology warns us of the folly of desiring immortality without also securing perpetual youth in the story of Tithonus, who aged into a mere shell of a human being, in one version of the myth finally being turned into a grasshopper (Hamilton, pp. 289-290). Those who make immortality possible are also punished in Greek mythology, as we see in the story of Aesculapius, the healer whom Zeus punishes by death for bringing a dead man to life (Hamilton, pp. 280-281).

Closer to our own time, in a work of the eighteenth century, the Struldbruggs in Swift's *Gulliver's Travels* are still another caution against the folly of trying to surpass human limits. The Struldbruggs are immortal but continue to grow older and older, leading miserable lives, a burden to themselves and to their society (Swift, pp. 167-173; pt. 3, ch. 10).

We must also consider the incredible psychological and financial stress on families of patients whose lives are prolonged even though there is no hope of restoration to a reasonable life. Often these families must devote much or even all of their financial resources to this effort, while also undergoing the stress of watching the prolonged suffering of a loved one—with no real hope that this suffering might lead to a cure of the illness. Perhaps even worse than the strain on the families is the strain on the patients themselves, who, if aware of what is going on around them, are often experiencing great pain and are terribly frustrated by their own incapacity. For these patients, the natural outcome of their illness is far more humane than an artificial extension of a life that can no longer be satisfying.

Some opponents of euthanasia will counter that no illness is truly hopeless, since some day science may find a cure for all terminal illnesses, for death itself. Wouldn't it make sense to keep patients alive until that day? Perhaps it would, if society could bear the tremendous cost, and if we had the slightest shred of evidence that such a day were even possible. So far we do not: what science shows us is that individual organisms are mortal and that immortality, if it exists at all, belongs to the species. Those who look to scientific research as an argument against euthanasia seem to have a quarrel not so much with euthanasia as with death itself.

Of course, anyone who studies this issue soon discovers numerous questions with no simple answers, including, as the theologian Roger Shinn notes, questions about infants born with serious disabilities and about the definition of a meaningful life (pp. 23-30). Even the distinction between killing and allowing life to end must be examined in the context of specific decisions, as the philosopher John Ladd points out (pp. 164-186). Nevertheless, though we must be cautious, we can reach some conclusions. Euthanasia, as I have defined it and as I hope others will define it in the future, is consonant with traditional morality and with the acceptance of human mortality that traditional morality requires. Furthermore, it is the

most humane and realistic approach to the suffering of terminally ill patients.

WORKS CITED

Hamilton, Edith. *Mythology.* New York: New American Library, 1969.

The Holy Bible. Authorized King James Version. New York: Harper and Brothers n.d.

Ladd, John. ''Positive and Negative Euthanasia.'' *Ethical Issues Relating to Life and Death.*
    Ed. John Ladd. New York: Oxford University Press, 1979, pp. 164-186.

Shinn, Roger L. ''Ethical Issues.'' *New Options, New Dilemmas: An Interprofessional Approach*
    to Life or Death Decisions. Ed. Anne S. Allen. Lexington, Mass.: Lexington-Heath, 1986,
    pp. 23-30.

Swift, Jonathan. *Gulliver's Travels.* Ed. Louis A. Landa. Cambridge, Mass.: The Riverside
    Press-Houghton Mifflin, 1960.

SAMPLE INTERPRETATION

In her essay *"Fifth Business:* Childhood Fathers the Man," student Deborah O'Reilly interprets the behavior of three characters in the novel *Fifth Business*, by Canadian writer Robertson Davies. The subject of her interpretation is the adult lives of these three men, and the interpretive term—that summary of the operating reality beneath the visible surface—is the influence of childhood experience on these lives. Deborah argues that although each character is renamed as a young adult, a significant coincidence exists between these reborn, adult identities and the childhood identities. The principle linking the subject with the interpretive term is a familiar tenet of psychological development: the powerful force of childhood experience on adult behavior. In the section of the essay excerpted here, ample evidence supports the interpretation of the book's narrator and protagonist, Dunstan Ramsay; Deborah cites Dunstan's loathing of his mother, his choice of career, his fascination with magic. As in all good literary interpretations, textual passages are used to document the writer's reading of the work.

FIFTH BUSINESS: CHILDHOOD FATHERS THE MAN

WHAT'S IN A NAME? In the novel *Fifth Business,* by Robertson Davies, the three central char-

acters seem to believe that taking on a new name will dissociate them from their origins and

mark the beginning of new lives. Dunstable Ramsay sheds the family name of the mother he loathes and becomes ''Dunstan.'' Percy Boyd Staunton opts for the fashionable name ''Boy'' as a more appropriate reflection of his new image. And finally, the frail, victimized little boy Paul Dempster becomes the grand ''Magnus Eisengrim.'' While adopting a new name may provide a sense of rebirth, of new identity, neither Dunny, Boy, nor Magnus can escape the powerful influence of their early lives.

Let us look first at Dunstable ''Dunstan'' Ramsay. Dunny's new name did not originate with him; it was a parting gift from Diane on the night they agreed not to marry. '' 'Let me do one thing more for you,' she said. 'Let me rename you. . . . St. Dunstan was a marvelous person and very much like you—mad about learning, terribly stiff and stern and scowly, and an absolute wizard at withstanding temptation' '' (pp. 92-93). Dunstan ''liked the idea of a new name; it suggested new freedom and a new personality'' (p. 93). Since Dunstable was his mother's maiden name, it is easy to understand how Dunny could so readily give it up. His loathing for his mother is most evident when he recalls his reaction to the news of his parents' death: ''But as I lay in that hospital I was glad that I did not have to be my mother's own dear laddie any longer. . . . I knew she had eaten my father, and I was glad I did not have to fight any longer to keep her from eating me.'' (p. 81).

But Dunstan's beginnings in Deptford had an impact on his life that a mere name change could not erase. The most obvious link to the past is his continuing obsession with Mary Dempster. Since the day she was hit by a snow-covered rock intended for the young Dunstable, he has been unable to relinquish responsibility for her. Indeed, at the time of her death, decades later, he is in effect her guardian—the only person accepting responsibility for her.

In addition, Dunstan's choice of a teaching career had its beginnings in the Deptford library, where he used four-year-old Paul Dempster as audience for his inept magic tricks. According to Dunstan, ''my abilities as a teacher had their first airing in that little library, and as I was fond of lecturing I taught Paul more than I suspected'' (p. 37). Dunstan also remains fascinated with magic long after his performances for Paul, although he never mastered the techniques. In fact, it is that fascination that leads him into his important friendships with Magnus and Liesl.

Much as Dunstan wishes to turn his back on the troubles and perversities of his childhood in the little town of Deptford, he realizes late in life that total dissociation from that childhood is impossible: ''I boarded the train . . . and left Deptford in the flesh. It was not for a long time that I recognized that I never wholly left it in the spirit'' (p. 107).

The man that Dunstable Ramsay became was irrevocably indebted to the boy that Dunstan Ramsay

once was.

WORKS CITED

Davies, Robertson. *Fifth Business.* New York. Penguin Books, 1970.

Suggestions for Writing (10.9)

1. Write a two-to-three-page evaluation of a course you have taken or are taking in college. Your evaluation will be primarily a performance evaluation, with one of the crucial questions being whether the course actually achieves its intended goals. The evaluation can also include an ethical component: was the course good for your soul whether or not it achieved its intended effects?

2. Write a three-to-four-page argument for or against euthanasia based on your reading of the sample student paper at the end of the section on evaluation. Do you agree with the definition of euthanasia given there? What about the other supporting arguments? Are there other arguments for euthanasia, or do you have what you believe are more powerful arguments against it?

3. Write a combination interpretation and evaluation (three to four pages) of a recent artistic or entertainment event that you enjoyed: a film, play, novel, concert, or something similar. Your evaluation will be primarily aesthetic, but it may be ethical as well.

4. Write an essay of approximately five to six pages on the issue of whether capital punishment is morally justified. You may consider issues other than ethical ones, but your emphasis should be on the ethical aspects of this question. Be sure to cite and refute viewpoints opposed to your own.

Chapter 11

Openings and Closings

An argument's opening and closing—the first and last impression you make on the reader—require careful attention. Closings—whether a general conclusion or a specialized summary—are, of course, almost always written late in the process, when you know exactly where your argument has gone. Some writers compose introductions before the body of the argument, but many delay them until the end of the first draft, when they know more clearly what is to be introduced. In the following pages we discuss the importance of effective openings and closings and make some suggestions for beginning and ending your arguments.

INTRODUCTIONS

Because it is the readers' initial experience with your argument, your opening—whether a formal introduction or the first paragraphs of your document—must be particularly appealing to your readers. Unless circumstances compel your readers to read your argument, they are not likely to finish it if its beginning is murky or trite or generally uninviting.

The context of your argument—the occasion and audience for which it is written—as well as its length, tone, and level of complexity will influence the style and content of your introduction. Regardless of how you choose to introduce your argument, the basic purpose of any introduction is the same: to engage the reader. In most cases, introductions will successfully engage readers if they are clear and inviting. Of these two features, clarity—the precise and accurate transmission of carefully considered ideas—is probably the easiest to achieve, although for many writers it comes only with careful thought and considerable revision. To be inviting, an introduction must contain material that by itself stimulates the reader's interest, as well as arousing curiosity about the rest of the document. Because being inviting does not come naturally to everyone, we offer some opening tactics that can make your arguments appealing to readers.

Tactics for General Introductions

Introduction by Narrative. Writers of "general interest" manifest arguments (nontechnical arguments, such as newspaper editorials, intended for a broad audience) often gain their readers' attention by opening their essay with a specific anecdote or short narrative. This kind of opening contains two appeals to which most readers are susceptible: first, in its narrative approach, it satisfies our delight in being told a story; and second, it gains our interest by its *particularity*. Particularity—details about people, places, and events—gives readers a firm context as they begin exploring an unknown text. A *Time Magazine* "Essay," "The Demagogue in the Crowd," begins with the following paragraph:

> The audience leaped to embrace the speaker while sitting still. They ate him up. His words were devoured the ways seals snap at fish. You could see the words settle in the crowd's bellies: 25,000 satisfied customers packing New York City's Madison Square Garden last Monday night to hear Minister Louis Farrakhan, head of the Nation of Islam, bring his dual message of self-help and hate. The message of hate predominated. How the crowd hungered for that meal. At the words of defiance they stood and roared. At the in-jokes they laughed joyfully. At the derisive words they smiled and sneered. The converted attended the preacher.

The writer of this essay, Roger Rosenblatt, begins his largely reflective, philosophical essay with an active narrative paragraph, securely set in time, place, and principal characters. While his essay refers to Minister Louis Farrakhan repeatedly, Rosenblatt's real subject is the danger of hate, a thesis he gives the reader at the beginning of his fifth paragraph. References to Farrakhan serve a unifying and specifying function in the essay, but the essay's scope is wider than the first paragraph suggests. The particularity and the narrative quality of the opening capture a reader's attention more completely than would an abstract and generalized statement about the dangerous combination of hate and demagoguery.

Introduction to Generalization. Good introductions can also begin with a strong, unambiguous generalization related to the readers' experiences, as in the following opening paragraph of an article by David Brown published in a medical society journal:

> Few honorable professions have as much inherent hostility toward one another as medicine and journalism. Ask a doctor to describe journalists and you are likely to

hear adjectives such as "negative," "sensationalistic," and "superficial." Ask a journalist about doctors, and you will probably hear about "arrogance," "paternalism," and "jargon."

Broad statements such as this can and probably should be limited and developed in succeeding sentences or a succeeding paragraph. In the second paragraph of this essay, the writer both justifies and develops the generalization made in the first paragraph:

> The descriptions are the common stereotypes and not wholly inaccurate, for the two professions occupy distant worlds. Physicians are schooled in confidence and collegiality; journalists seek to make knowledge public. Physicians speak the language of science; journalists are largely ignorant of science. Physicians inhabit a world of contingencies and caveats; journalists inhabit a world where time and audience require simplification. Physicians are used to getting their way; journalists are used to getting their story.

This paragraph's development of the idea contained in the initial paragraph is echoed by the writer's syntax (the arrangement of his words): the last four sentences, neatly divided by semicolons into opposing clauses, emphasize the focus on this professional opposition.

Introduction by Quotation. Some introductions begin with quotations that are eventually connected to the topic of the essay. While perhaps overused and overtaught, this technique *can* work if practiced thoughtfully. The writer using an opening quotation must be sure that it can be made to apply to the subject in an interesting way, and that the quotation is interesting, provocative, or well written (preferably all three). The following paragraph in an essay by Marilyn Yalom is a successful example of this technique:

> When Robert Browning wrote his famous lines "Grow old along with me!/ The best is yet to be, /The last of life, for which the first was made," he was undoubtedly not thinking about women. The poet's Victorian optimism is difficult enough to reconcile with the realities of old age for men, and virtually impossible when we consider the condition of older women in the nineteenth century.

As in the article about the antagonism between the medical and journalistic professions, the initial statement is immediately explained and developed in the succeeding sentence. Here, in fact, the explanatory sentence is also the thesis statement of this essay on the older woman in Victorian England and America.

Other Types of Introductions. Many other tactics can be used to make an essay inviting to a reader: the use of startling statistics, a brief historical survey of the topic (which can have the same charm as the narrative introduction), a particularly startling or shocking statement (provided it has something to do with the essay's content), or even a direct announcement of the essay's subject (as in "This article is about bad writing"). Any of these tactics can work so long as they are finally relevant to the rest of the essay.

Introductions in Professional Writing

Introductions written in a professional context according to an established format do not need to be as inviting as our examples above. Because audiences of professional reports are usually more captive than the casual reader of the "Essay" on the back page of *Time Magazine*, writers of these reports have to worry less about being original in their introductions. Rather than trying to attract potential readers to their argument through an effective introduction, these writers are more concerned with serving the needs of a known audience that can use the report for their jobs. Introductions in such cases will usually be successful if they are precisely representative of the content of the report. Company policy often dictates the form of a preliminary summary: some companies require an initial outline, others an abstract, still others an executive summary reflecting both structure and content. When the form is not dictated, the most useful is the summary of structure and content.

We'll use as an example an analysis of problems in customer relations assigned to Carrie Quill, the customer service representative of a local grocery chain. In her report, Carrie first identifies, describes, and documents the different conditions that she has found to be damaging to good customer relations: inadequate customer check cashing privileges, a time-consuming refund policy, impolite carry-out personnel, and inaccurate advertising of sale prices. She then estimates the loss of business resulting from each problem. Finally, she recommends possible solutions to the problems she has identified. Her report is clearly written and organized, but it is also lengthy and complex; unquestionably, it needs an introduction that will prepare her readers not only for the content of the report but also for the arrangement of the report's material. Her preliminary summary will prepare her readers for the sequence of the argument's main points, and it will serve as a useful reference should the readers become confused while reading the body of the report.

A structure and content introduction to the report about difficulties in customer relations might read as follows:

> This report examines the recent quarterly decline in business at the seven Good-belly stores. It attributes this loss of revenue to at least four remediable problems in the area of customer relations: (1) inadequate check cashing privileges; (2) a time-consuming refund policy; (3) lack of concern for customers by carry-out personnel;

and (4) inaccurate advertising of sale prices. It is estimated that these difficulties may have cost Goodbelly's as much as $300,000 in revenue in the past three months. This report concludes by recommending specific personnel and policy measures to be taken to ease these difficulties and to regain the lost business.

Without being painstakingly mechanical, this brief paragraph identifies the central thesis of the report (that the decline in revenue is due to poor customer relations) and prepares the reader for the structure and content of the argument. While an introduction such as this one may not engage a reader who has neither an interest in nor obligation to the company, its concise and accurate representation of the report's content will be extremely useful to the obligated reader.

General Suggestions About Introductions

We conclude our discussion of introductions with a list of suggestions:

1. Try writing your introduction *after* you have written a first draft of the argument. Often, there's no point in agonizing over a preliminary summary for business or technical reports or a more catchy introduction for a general interest argument before you know exactly how the argument is going to unfold. Even if you are working from a fairly detailed outline, structure and content will change as you compose. On some occasions, a catchy introductory sentence or group of sentences may come to you early, which gives you a hold on the overall structure, tone, and style of your essay. Don't let these sentences get away!

2. Don't make your introduction too long. Even the most interesting, captivating introduction is going to seem a little silly if it's twice as long as the argument itself. The turbot, a variety of anglerfish, has a head that takes up half of its total body length and is one of the most ridiculous-looking fish to swim the seas. Don't follow its example.

3. Make sure that your introduction is truly representative of the entire argument. If you are writing a preliminary summary, be sure all the main points of the argument are referred to in the introduction. In a less formal argument, don't let your desire to be engaging lure you into writing an introduction that is stylistically or tonally inconsistent with the rest of the argument. In short, the opening paragraph should never look as if it has been tacked on merely to attract reader interest, with no thought about its relationship to what follows. Rather, it should resemble an operatic overture, beautiful in its own right, but always preparing its audience for what is to follow.

Activities (11.1)

1. For one of the following writing tasks, write two different introductory paragraphs using two of the tactics discussed in the preceding section: narrative, generalization, quotation, startling statistics, a brief historical survey, a startling statement, or an outright announcement of thesis. Then write a two-to-three-sentence description of the different effects of the two introductions.
   a. An essay on a relative whom you admire.
   b. An essay on a law or policy of the federal government that you strongly support or oppose.
   c. An essay on your favorite food.
   d. An editorial in your local newspaper advocating lower local taxes.
   e. A report to your supervisor (or a parent or a friend) explaining why you have failed to accomplish all the goals you set for yourself six months ago.

2. For one of the following theses, write an introductory paragraph, as in the following example:
   Thesis Sentence: Biking is both enjoyable and good for our health.
   Introductory sentences and thesis: Too often in life we learn that what we enjoy is bad for our health. When we are children we learn that too much candy is bad for us. We also learn that certain foods or activities we don't especially like, such as eating spinach or going to the dentist, are good for us. Sometimes we may feel that enjoyment and good health are incompatible, but that despair arises only for those who have not discovered the joys of biking. Biking is one activity that is both enjoyable and good for our health. (Note: These introductory sentences are general, but you could introduce your thesis with a specific anecdote or illustration. Also, although in this case the thesis sentence comes at the end of the paragraph, it does not have to be included in the paragraph.)
   a. Reading fiction is not an escape from life; it helps us to understand life's complexities.
   b. Jogging may be healthy for many people, but it can be dangerous for those with certain cardiovascular diseases.
   c. Today's generation of young people is realistic about the world of work and the economic difficulties our society faces, but it is also idealistic in its hopes for the future.
   d. Despite the tremendous changes in our society in the last thirty years, baseball is still an enormously popular sport.
   e. If costs keep rising as they have been, a college education may become an impossible dream for most young Americans.

3. The following sentences are first sentences of opening paragraphs of essays. These paragraphs could end with a thesis sentence, though they do not have to. For one of these sentences, write the rest of the paragraph.
   Example of an opening sentence: Aside from death and taxes, Americans share one other inevitable experience: being caught in a traffic jam.
   Sample opening paragraph: Aside from death and taxes, Americans share one other inevitable experience: being caught in a traffic jam. Despite energy

crises, pollution alerts, the trend toward smaller cars, and the development of expressways, traffic jams are still a common experience in all large metropolitan areas and even in smaller towns and cities. Americans may see themselves as problem solvers, but they have not yet solved this problem of traffic jams. America still needs a coherent and workable policy on the automobile's role in mass transit.

a. Unsolicited mail, popularly known as junk mail, arrives in my mailbox daily.

b. Despite our enormous technological advances, many age-old problems remain unsolved.

c. When you are driving in the Northeast or the industrial parts of the American Midwest, you don't have to search too long to find an abandoned factory or mill.

d. I remember almost fondly the worst class I ever had.

e. Individuals vary enormously in what they look for in friendships with other people.

CONCLUSIONS

Once you have selected and presented the best possible support for your argument, you may feel that you have exhausted all the material relevant to your position, that you have nothing more to say on the subject. But you cannot consider your argument finished until you have provided a final closing, a conclusion that rounds out your argument, giving your readers a satisfying sense of closure. Most readers feel uncomfortable with open-ended writing, with writing that is not somehow rounded off at the end. Readers expect this closure in all kinds of writing—in letters, in imaginative literature of all kinds, and in written arguments.

Closings are not always easy to write, particularly because by the time we get around to thinking about writing an ending, we are often tired of the whole argument. But you don't need to be a master rhetorician to write an effective ending. A conclusion that is direct, precise, and appropriate to the occasion will serve its purpose well. Depending on the context, the length can be as short as a paragraph or as long as a chapter in a book.

Types of Conclusions

General arguments can have three basic types of conclusions: the findings or results of an investigation; a recommendation or a set of recommendations; or a more general closing that looks back to the essay or points to other considerations related to the central thesis.

Findings. The first of these types, the findings or results of an investigation, usually ends an argument of fact, such as the reporting of a scientific experiment or a case study. Some causal arguments, such as certain historical studies, also end with results or findings. In reality, these findings or results are the argument's thesis, which may be given in general form early in the argument and then with more detail at the end, or they may be given only at the end. An example of a findings or results conclusion is the second-to-last paragraph of an essay entitled "Particle Accelerators Test Cosmological Theory":

> Preliminary results from the machines indicate that there are at most five families of elementary particles. David B. Cline of the University of California at Los Angeles and the University of Wisconsin at Madison . . . has shown that the lifetime of the $Z°$ boson [a subatomic particle] is approximately what one would expect with just three families. Experimental uncertainties, however, allow for two additional kinds of neutrinos [another subatomic particle] and hence two additional families. . . . For the first time accelerators are counting neutrino types and getting a small number, one that was predicted by cosmological theory.

Recommendation. A second common type of conclusion is a recommendation or a set of recommendations, typically found in a practical recommendation report. This type of conclusion tells the readers exactly what the argument expects of them. If the first type of conclusion tells the readers what they should *know*, the second tells them what they should *do*. An example of this type of conclusion is found at the end of "A Proposal for a Computer Facility in Marshall Dormitory" in Chapter 7 of this book. The proposal ends with a "Costs and Implementation Plan" section that spells out in some detail the actions that need to be taken. In the case of this proposal, the more general recommendations came earlier, so ending with more specific steps is a suitable way to conclude. In many other cases, the most appropriate conclusion will be a general recommendation, as in this last paragraph from an essay entitled "U.S. Economic Growth":

> Only if we increase investment in both capital and technology in all sectors of the U.S. economy (particularly manufacturing) and improve the quality of labor at all levels can the American standard of living rise at an acceptable rate. In the present highly competitive world market the U.S. has some historically demonstrated advantages, but it must take the longer view and pursue those seemingly trivial increases of a few tenths of a percentage point in growth rate each year.

General Closing. The general closing is what we usually think of when we think of conclusions. This type of conclusion can work in several ways: it can move from the specific argument to a statement of the argument's broader significance; it can suggest future directions for research; or it can raise related issues. The general closing suggests a movement *onward* (where we go from here) or a movement *outward* (how this specific argument relates to other arguments), though the emphasis in any case will vary between these two elements.

The following paragraph (the closing of Janet Sternburg's opening essay in her collection entitled *The Writer on Her Work: Contemporary Women Writers Reflect on their Art and Situation*) exemplifies a conclusion that moves to a statement of an argument's broader significance:

> This collection offers, I believe, an expanded version of what is central to women writers. Against crippling and mutually exclusive definitions, these essays suggest that multiple choices are possible. Against the fragmentation caused by conflicting demands, they suggest that the various parts of the self can nourish one another. This book stands in relation to a well-documented history of women whose artistic gifts have been damaged by prevailing circumstances. Against the need to justify the worth of our experience . . . women writers are claiming the truths of that experience. Against the silence of the past and of immediate forebears, we are speaking for those who did not speak. Against the fear of stopping, we are trusting in our continuity as artists. Nor is our situation truly solitary; it can be richly populated, as it is here in this book which is, most simply, women writers in each other's company.

A conclusion pointing to new directions and future possibilities is the last paragraph of the essay cited previously, "Particle Accelerators Test Cosmological Theory":

> The next step promises to be even more exciting. As new accelerators are completed and begin producing more data with fewer uncertainties the cosmological limit of three or at most four families will be checked with extreme accuracy. . . . The machines will probe the early universe with an effectiveness that no telescope will ever match.

A conclusion that raises related issues is the last two paragraphs of a famous essay by José Ortega Y Gasset entitled "The Dehumanization of Art," an essay on the tendency of modern art to move away from portraying the human figure and move toward a "pure" art of form and color:

> Should that enthusiasm for pure art be but a mask which conceals surfeit with art and hatred of it? But, how can such a thing come about? Hatred of art is unlikely to develop as an isolated phenomenon; it goes hand in hand with hatred of science, hatred of state, hatred, in sum, of civilization as a whole. Is it conceivable that modern Western man bears a rankling grudge against his own historical essence? Does he

feel something akin to the *odium professionis* of medieval monks—that aversion, after long years of monastic discipline, against the very rules that had shaped their lives?

   This is the moment prudently to lay down one's pen and let a flock of questions take off on their winged course.

In raising related issues, as Ortega does, you need to be careful that the issues are not too far afield from the main thrust of your argument. Ortega is asking questions about the meaning of the modern quest for a pure, abstract art; thus he is staying close to the main point of his essay, which is to describe some characteristics of this type of art.

   These three subcategories of a general closing—significance, future directions, and related issues—can of course overlap. Ortega's related issues are issues of significance, presented as questions to ponder. In addition, a conclusion can contain more than one of our three basic types. The second to last paragraph of "Particle Accelerators Test Cosmological Theory" presents the results of the research, while the very last paragraph presents a statement on future directions of this research. Generally speaking, any results or recommendation conclusion could also have added to it a more general conclusion that opens the argument outward. However, with arguments aimed at restricted audiences, such a strategy may not be necessary.

   A word of caution about all conclusions: the conclusion must not lie outside the boundaries of what you can legitimately claim in your argument. You should not, for example, turn an argument about the weakness of a certain school's curriculum into a conclusion uniformly condemning all schools, though your conclusion could suggest that the case you have examined may not be an isolated one. You should not, in other words, overgeneralize from the evidence you were able to use to support your argument. Nor should you use your conclusion as the place to launch a whole new argument or make claims that do not have some basis in what has preceded. In his conclusion to "The Dehumanization of Art," Ortega makes some suggestions about the significance of "pure art," but these suggestions will not come as a surprise to a careful reader of his essay, and they are presented as no more than possibilities, not as bold new claims.

SUMMARIES

A conclusion differs from a *summary*, which is a restatement of the main points of your argument. In writing most short or medium-size essays (500 to 5000 words), you will not need a summary at the end of your argument; final summaries are typically found in very long essays, essays with difficult subject matter, or in books. We have, for example, used sentence summaries at the end of each chapter of this book because we want to stress certain key points to an audience new to much of this material.

Writers of written arguments or their editors sometimes provide a summary of the basic points preceding the essay. These summaries are usually either separate from or at the very beginning of the arguments and usually take one of two forms: the *abstract*, often used in academic or technical research, and the *executive summary*, often used in business reports and proposals.

An abstract is a summary, typically in paragraph form, that states the essential points of the essay so that readers can grasp these points without having to read the essay; in other words, the good abstract can stand alone, meaningful by itself. If the readers can read only the abstract, they will of course miss much of the argument, especially its support, but they will at least know what the argument's main claims are. With the flood of information confronting us all, abstracts have the obvious value of helping us decide what research needs further investigation and what can be left alone.

The following summary by King-Kok Cheung of her essay on Alice Walker's *The Color Purple* and Maxine Hong Kingston's *The Woman Warrior* is a good example of an abstract:

> *The Color Purple* and *The Woman Warrior* exhibit parallel narrative strategies. The respectively black and Chinese American protagonists work their way from speechlessness to eloquence by breaking through the constraints of sex, race, and language. The heroines turn to masculine figures for guidance, to female models for inspiration, and to native idioms for stylistic innovation. Initially unable to speak, they develop distinctive voices by registering their own unspoken grief on paper and, more important, by recording and emulating the voices of women from their respective ethnic communities. Through these testimonies, each written in a bicultural language, Walker and Kingston reveal the obstacles and resources peculiar to minority women. Subverting patriarchal literary traditions by reclaiming a mother tongue that carries a rich oral tradition (of which women are guardians) the authors artfully coordinate the tasks of breaking silence, acknowledging female influence, and redefining while preserving ethnic characteristics.

Executive summaries are often longer than abstracts, though they should not usually be longer than a page. Like abstracts, they give the main points of an argument, but they may also contain some background on why the report was written and on the scope of the original study. If the executive summary is of a recommendation report, the major recommendation should be included in it. Like abstracts, executive summaries should be written to stand alone; the readers should be able to get the major points of the report without referring to the report itself.

The following is a sample executive summary with a format that might be used by a group auditing the overall effectiveness of a university computer center:

> Audit completed a review of the Johnston Computer Center in February 1989. The Johnston Computer Center is one of three academic computing centers at the University and contains terminals and microcomputers for up to 200 onsite users, with access also available for up to 50 offsite users, making it the second largest of such centers at the University.
>
> The objectives of our review were to determine whether present and planned Center operations are fulfilling user needs and in compliance with University policies and procedures for computer security.
>
> In our opinion, the Center's operation is satisfactory in meeting the needs of its users and in using its internal resources to meet these needs, but unsatisfactory in meeting security policies and procedures.
>
> Our survey of Computer Center users indicated that user satisfaction is high and that Center personnel are responsive to user needs. While system response time has deteriorated in the last six months because of an unexpected increase in user demand, Center management has addressed this problem by encouraging users to use the system during nonpeak hours and by recommending a hardware upgrade to the Vice President for Systems and Computing.
>
> Our review of security showed that unauthorized users could gain access to and change another user's files. Since the Center's computers are not directly connected to the University's administrative computers, which do contain other security safeguards, the University does not face a risk to its financial and personnel records because of these deficiencies. The student and faculty academic files contained in the Center's computers are at risk, however. The Center has reported three such instances of tampering in the last six months. Center management is eager to address this problem but will need additional resources to purchase software and to obtain the necessary technical assistance.

Executive summaries have become increasingly common as business executives and other managers find themselves confronted with an overwhelming number of reports to read. The executive summary allows readers to decide if they want to read further, or if the summary alone provides enough information. Unlike abstracts, which are often intended for a specialist audience, executive summaries usually have a nonspecialist audience of higher managers who may be very far removed from the technical details of the report. The executive summary should allow for the audience's lack of familiarity with these details by avoiding specialized vocabulary whenever possible and by defining any specialized terms that are used. Executive summaries can be very difficult to write because they demand great attention to the readers' needs and great precision in wording. They are also typically written after the report or essay is finished, when the writer wants to relax or move on to a new project, not concentrate on writing a summary of something already finished. The writer of the executive summary needs to remember, however, that for some important readers this summary may be the only part of the report they will ever see.

SUMMARY

Openings and Closings

- The context of your argument will influence the style, content, and length of your introduction, but all introductions should be clear, engaging, and appropriate to the occasion.
- Some useful tactics for general introductions are:

  Introduction by narrative.

  Introduction by generalization.

  Introduction by quotation.
- Introductions of arguments in formal, professional writing should be precisely representative of the content of the report.
- Conclusions are usually one of three basic types: findings or results; a recommendation or set of recommendations; or a general closing. Which type of conclusion you use depends on the type of argument.

  Findings or results typically conclude reports of scientific experiments or case studies.

  Recommendations conclude practical recommendations.

  General closings are used for other types of arguments, especially interpretations and evaluations. The general closing has three subtypes: a statement of significance; suggested directions for research; and a raising of related issues.
- Do not confuse a conclusion with a summary. A summary is a restatement of the main points of your argument.

  There are three types of summaries: the ending summary; the abstract; and the executive summary.

  Ending summaries are typically found in books and in very complex or very long essays or reports.

  Abstracts and executive summaries are typically found at the beginning of or separate from the arguments on which they are based.

  Readers should be able to understand an abstract or an executive summary without referring to the report or essay on which it is based.

Suggestions for Writing (11.2)

1. Write a one-to-two-page essay that describes the kind of introductions you used in your last two or three essays. Were the introductions engaging? Would the essays have been substantially different if you had used a different type of opening? Would they have been better? Why? Be sure to give your instructor a copy of each of the essays you discuss.

2. Locate a section of a newspaper or magazine that presents several editorial or opinion essays (the Sunday *New York Times* Op Ed page is an excellent source; your local Sunday paper may have its own version). Examine the types of conclusions used for the three pieces and write an essay of two to three pages describing the type of each conclusion, its effect on readers, and its overall effectiveness. Which of the three do you find the most effective? Why? Be sure to give your instructor a copy of the Op Ed page that you use for this assignment.

3. Write a one-paragraph abstract of one of your last papers, making sure that readers will be able to understand the abstract without reading the paper. When you hand in this assignment, give your instructor both the abstract and the paper on which it is based.

Chapter 12

Revising

Revising your argument means stepping back from the argument and seeing it whole. *Revising*, as its Latin roots ("re"—again; and "visere"—to look at) indicate, is to see again, to have a new vision of the entire work. Sometimes this new vision can lead to dramatic changes in the introduction, the thesis, the support, or the style of your argument, though close attention to these issues while you are writing the first draft can greatly reduce the need for such changes. Even the most careful work on the first draft, however, cannot prevent your having to make some changes. Good writers know that they must allow time and attention for revision.

WRITING A FIRST DRAFT, REVISING, AND EDITING

Some college students, knowing that revising could mean serious changes in their draft, avoid the process altogether or reduce it to a perfunctory check for poor spelling or grammar. These students confuse revising with editing. Editing is a careful check of language usage, spelling, grammar, punctuation, and consistency of a manuscript. Revising, as we have noted, is a more profound look at the manuscript's entire content, shape, and style. Revising involves a great deal of judgment on your part, because questions about thesis, support, and style rarely have simple black or white, right or wrong answers. Most questions about editing do have right or wrong answers. There are only so many ways to spell a word or punctuate a sentence correctly.

Writing your first draft, revising, and editing require different attitudes and employ somewhat different skills. Writing the first draft requires energy and egoism to keep you going through the bumpy parts; revising calls for detachment and reflection; and editing demands close attention to detail. Attempting a "perfect" first draft is actually one of the most dangerous and laborious ways to write. It is dangerous because you will lack the necessary distance to judge the quality of your argument, and laborious because you are trying to combine these three separate tasks. To some extent, of course, revising and editing occur during the writing of any draft; we all make minor changes in wording, organization, and mechanics even in the early stage of writing, and sometimes we decide on major changes as we write. Inserting these changes then makes sense, but you still need to set aside time for revising and editing, making each your major preoccupation in separate reviews of the manuscript.

Many college students feel that they don't have time for anything but a first draft, but in fact they usually do. Students of roughly equal ability and with roughly the same amount of time available work in amazingly different ways, some finishing their work with plenty of time to spare, others doing everything at the last minute. Most students who claim that they were forced to write their papers just before the due date mean that writing the paper was not their highest priority and they could get motivated to write it only by the pressure of a deadline. Especially with word processing, writers who write a first draft, leave it for awhile, and then revise it do not spend any more time writing than those who try to write just one polished draft.

SOME SUGGESTIONS FOR SUCCESSFUL REVISING

We offer here some arguments that should help you to revise your arguments more effectively. These are not ironclad rules, but our own experience and the experience of many other writers indicate that following these rules can make revising easier and more effective.

Suggestion 1: Give Yourself Some Breathing Space

Whenever possible, allow some time between finishing the draft and beginning to revise, usually a minimum of twenty-four hours. This "breathing space" will provide the necessary distance between you and your work, allowing you to view the manuscript more objectively and thus be ready to make major changes if they are needed. Setting aside time also allows the more recessed parts of your mind to churn the material over, giving you new perspective and allowing you to become more comfortable with what you feel is worth keeping and less comfortable with those parts of the manuscript you will change or discard. Even when you are not consciously thinking of the manuscript—and the smart thing to do is to try not to think about it too much—your subconscious will be active, working for you even when you have stopped consciously working. This "churning" process can be enormously valuable. If you do not take advantage of it, you are denying yourself an opportunity to improve your work simply by waiting.

Suggestion 2: Avoid the Red Pen

As you are reviewing the draft, you need to avoid the lure of the red pen—the temptation to make small mechanical changes even before you have read and assimilated the entire manuscript. When you begin revising, you need to figuratively tie your hands behind your back and *just read*. Read the entire draft through, asking yourself how the draft works as a whole: Does the introduction catch the reader's attention and give the reader a sense of what will follow? If there is a thesis, is it clear? Does the rest of the argument support the thesis? Is the organization the most effective for this argument?

Suggestion 3: Review Your Original Purpose and Audience

In writing a first draft, writers risk losing touch with their original purpose and their intended audience, becoming so fascinated by the composition itself that they lose track of why they started the composition in the first place.

When you revise, you need to make sure that you have successfully fulfilled your original purpose for your intended audience (your purpose and audience could change, of course, but that should be your conscious choice). Part of distancing yourself from your manuscript is putting yourself into the mind of your readers, trying to see your argument through their eyes. Have I met my original purpose? If I intended, for example, to recommend a course of action, have I done so? Are my vocabulary and use of specialized terms appropriate for my readers? Have I understood and appealed to what is likely to motivate them? Will they know what I want them to do after they have finished reading the argument?

Suggestion 4: Review Your Overall Organization

In making sure your argument works, you need to review not only your purpose and audience but your overall structure as well, making sure that the parts fit together well, that nothing crucial is omitted, and that the structure is lean, with a minimum of repetition. If you find it hard to keep the structure in mind, you might try reproducing it in an outline form like the one below. This outline should reflect what you actually wrote, not what you intended to write.

    I. INTRODUCTION (if appropriate)

   II. THESIS (if appropriate)

  III. SUPPORTING ARGUMENTS:
     A.
     B.
     C.
     D.

  IV. CONCLUSION OR SUMMARY (if appropriate)

If you actually wrote the argument from an outline, you should not look at it until you have completed this new one. If you have trouble constructing this outline, your manuscript almost certainly has structural problems that need correction.

At this stage you need to review the issues raised in Chapter 3 on theses and introductions: If I have a thesis, is it clearly stated? If I have an introduction, does it adequately program the readers for what will follow? Is my introduction interesting if it needs to catch the readers' attention? You also need to deal with the issues raised in Chapter 5 about organization: Should I include a refutation of one or more opposing arguments? Is my ordering of the support most effective for the essay?

Suggestion 5: Review Your Argument's Coherence

Even the most carefully organized argument can puzzle readers if the relationship between its parts is not indicated in some way. In certain professions and businesses, standard formats include headings like "Introduction," "The Problem," "History," and so on. But such headings are inappropriate in many settings. You can make the elements of your argument *coherent*—establish their relationship to each other and to the whole—by using simple transitional words and expressions that indicate the nature of the relationship.

Words like "therefore," "thus," "so," and "consequently" identify a conclusion and its evidence. Words like "but," "however," and "on the other hand" indicate exceptions to a stated point. You can alert your reader to the introduction of each new piece of support by using indicators such as "first . . ., second . . .," "and," "furthermore," and "finally." Transitional words and expressions such as these are enormously useful to readers of arguments, particularly when the argument is long or elaborate. They help readers understand how one statement or section that might otherwise seem a digression or irrelevancy relates to what has gone before or what might come later.

As well as using such brief signposts, you can also be quite direct about the role of different parts of your argument. Public speakers are often very explicit about the function of crucial parts of their speechs: "Let me give you two reasons why this land should be developed," or "To conclude, I'd like to remind you of a few lines by Walt Whitman." Such obvious signs are crucial when there is no written text for an audience to follow and ponder. But indicators such as these can be used in written argument as well, especially when the parts are many and complex.

Suggestion 6: Review Your Style

During revising you also need to examine the style of your argument, and when necessary, modify it. As we discussed in Chapter 6, style is an important component of the argument's total image, and image plays a major role in an audience's acceptance or rejection of the argument. The writer who complains that readers failed to appreciate his strong argument because of poor style doesn't really understand that style is a part of good argument. Poor style can be just as damaging to an argument as a vague or unsupported thesis, and compelling style just as helpful in convincing an audience as abundant evidence.

The appropriateness of voice in your argument is a question of style. In Chapter 6 we discussed the crucial role of a credible voice in winning over a reader. You need to review the voice of your argument to ensure that it presents a positive ethos and a reassuring confidence in your position.

In reviewing the style of your manuscript, you should ask yourself if you have followed Orwell's rules for clarity in writing along with the friendly amendments offered in Chapter 6. You should also check to see if you have (1) used connotation effectively; (2) avoided slanting; (3) used metaphor and analogy effectively; and (4) paid attention to the sounds of words. Some of these questions will naturally occur during your consideration of a thesis (if you have one) and the organization of its support, as well as during your review of audience and purpose.

Suggestion 7: Use a Word Processor

As you begin to revise, you may be disheartened to know that revising can lead to drastic overhaul of your argument, but if you want to create the most effective argument possible, you will not forsake the opportunity to make improvements. As a growing number of writers know, using a word processor can make revising much easier than it used to be. With word processing, you can switch entire sections of a draft around with relative ease, change words swiftly and even "globally" so that one word replaces another throughout an entire essay, and make corrections with no trace of crossed-out words and letters, no tell-tale blotch of white ink. Because revision can mean not just a second draft of an argument but a third or even a fourth draft as well, word processing can save you a great deal of time as you move from one draft to the next. If you own a computer with word processing software or if you have access to one, you should use this valuable tool. The computer will not make you a better writer, but it will give you the chance to make yourself a better writer.

Suggestion 8: Review Your Support for Adequacy, Appropriateness, and Logic

To review your support, you need to ask yourself the kinds of questions addressed in Chapters 5 and 7 through 10: Is the amount of support adequate to defend my argument? Is it appropriate for the kind of argument? Is its presentation consistent with logical principles? At this point you should make sure that your argument does not commit the kinds of logical fallacies that we discuss in the next section of this chapter.

Activities (12.1)

1. Write an outline of a paper or a draft of a paper that you have written for this class, using the format given above in Suggestion 4. Then exchange this paper or draft with one of your classmates, while keeping your outline. Now prepare an outline of your classmate's paper, again using the same format, and then exchange outlines with your classmate. Compare your classmate's outline with your own. Do the two outlines agree on what the thesis is and what the supporting arguments are? If there are disagreements, discuss these with your classmate. Find out why he or she saw your argument working in a different way than you did. Remember that if there is disagreement, you cannot simply assume that your classmate is wrong and you are correct: the purpose of your argument is to convince the reader, not yourself. After this discussion, make a list of the changes or possible changes you would make in your paper in a next draft.
2. Write a one-to-two-page essay describing the voice you created in one of your earlier essays. What means did you use to create this voice? How credible is this voice?

PRINCIPLES OF LOGIC

The principles of traditional logic discussed in this section should be an important part of everyone's education. Nevertheless, these principles, as valuable as they are, do not provide much help in trying to produce your own arguments. Students and other writers quickly discover that there is a vast gap between the principles of reasoning and the necessities of particular arguments. As Stephen Toulmin, Richard Rieke, and Alan Janik observe in their *An Introduction to Reasoning:* "Reasoning . . . does not create ideas and does not answer once and for all whether those ideas are good or bad, true or false."

The principles of logic *can* be valuable to you in two ways: they can help you analyze the strengths and weaknesses in arguments written by others, and they can help you analyze and review your own arguments to make them as convincing as possible. These principles may not help you create your argument, but they can be enormously valuable in helping you to revise it.

INDUCTIVE AND DEDUCTIVE REASONING

The two basic types of logic are *inductive* and *deductive.* Inductive logic involves reasoning from observed evidence to a general statement; deductive logic involves reasoning from premises (assertions of a condition or activity) to a conclusion.

Inductive:

Observed Evidence: In the twenty years I've lived in New York State, warm weather has begun every year between March and May.

General Statement: In New York State, warm weather begins between March and May.

Deductive:

Premise: All human beings are mortal.

Premise: Jane is a human being.

Conclusion: Jane is mortal.

Notice in our first example that we conclude from specific examples that a situation is generally true or will remain true. Yet we cannot be absolutely sure that this situation will continue: it is not *necessarily* true but only *probably* true that warm weather habitually arrives between March and May. In our deductive example, on the other hand, the statement that Jane is mortal is necessarily true if the premises that precede it are true. Deductive arguments involve a process that if followed in certain ways leads to necessary conclusions.

We have already discussed inductive reasoning in Chapter 7: Factual Arguments. Consulting the summary at the end of that chapter will refresh your memory of the chief points to keep in mind for inductive arguments, including establishing the credibility of the facts used to support your general thesis, ensuring that you have a sufficient number of facts, and making sure that the facts cited are representative of the available evidence. The same principles hold for statistical samples—a large-scale version of inductive reasoning. The sample must be known, sufficient, and representative of the larger population.

SYLLOGISMS

The basic form of the deductive argument is the *syllogism*—a three-part argument consisting of a *major premise*, a *minor premise*, and a *conclusion*. We have already given one example of a syllogism in our sample deductive argument above:

Major Premise: All human beings are mortal.

Minor Premise: Jane is a human being.

Conclusion: Jane is mortal.

This syllogism is an example of thinking in terms of classes. The major premise establishes two classes, a larger one of mortal beings and a smaller one of human beings, and it asserts that the smaller class belongs in the larger. The minor premise establishes that a still smaller class, in this case one individual (Jane), belongs in the smaller class of the major premise. From there it necessarily follows that Jane will also be a member of the largest class, mortal beings. The syllogism can also be displayed visually:

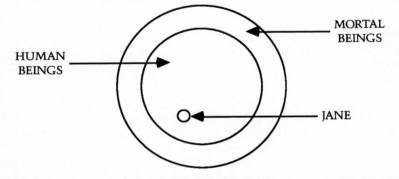

Thinking in terms of classes can be misleading if the process is done incorrectly. Examine the following syllogism:

All communists advocate the abolition of private property.

Jane advocates the abolition of private property.

Jane is a communist.

At first glance this argument may seem plausible, but as the following diagram shows, the argument is seriously flawed because the minor premise puts Jane in the larger group of those who advocate the abolition of private property but not in the smaller group of those who are communists. All that the argument can really tell us is that Jane and communists share this one trait. They may differ in everything else.

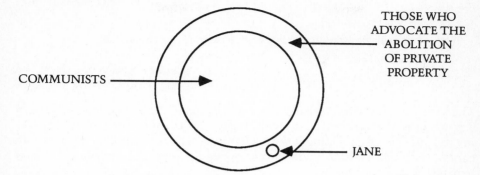

This sample syllogism is *invalid* because the process of reasoning it uses is flawed, while the first sample syllogism is *valid* because the process of reasoning used there is correct. Validity, however, should not be confused with *truth*, or invalidity with falseness, because truth is a matter of a statement's correspondence with the facts, not a question of the process of reasoning. To cite the example above, even if Jane were a communist, and thus the conclusion of the syllogism were true, the syllogism would still be invalid because of the flawed process. On the other hand, an argument can be valid but untrue because at least one of the premises is false:

All human beings have wings.

Jane is a human being.

Jane has wings.

Deductive arguments that are both true and valid are *sound*. Deductive arguments that are untrue, invalid, or both are *unsound*. Obviously, sound deductive arguments should be your goal as a writer. As a reader and analyzer of others' arguments, you need to be on guard against the seductions of the valid argument built on false premises, or the invalid argument luring us with the truth of its premises or conclusion.

In addition to the syllogism involving classes, you will frequently encounter two other types of syllogism: the "if–then" syllogism and the "either–or" syllogism. The "if–then" syllogism takes the following form:

If John drops the glass on the sidewalk, then the glass will break.

John will drop the glass on the sidewalk.

The glass will break.

This syllogism is valid, and if its premises are true, it is also sound.

With "if–then" syllogisms, however, you need to watch out for a very common error, usually called "affirming the consequent," where the "then" clause of the major premise is turned into an affirmative statement in the minor premise:

> If John drops the glass on the sidewalk, then the glass will break.
>
> The glass will break.
>
> John will drop the glass on the sidewalk.

The argument is invalid because the major premise merely claims that John's dropping the glass will make it break; it does not exclude other ways of breaking the glass, such as hitting it with a hammer. Given this major premise, we cannot conclude that John will have dropped the glass merely from the glass being broken.

The "either–or" syllogism takes the following form:

> Either the doctor gave the patient oxygen or the patient died.
>
> The patient did not die.
>
> The doctor gave the patient oxygen.

Note that this argument is invalid if the alternative is affirmed rather than denied:

> Either the doctor gave the patient oxygen or the patient died.
>
> The patient died.
>
> The doctor did not give the patient oxygen.

The major premise merely asserts that we can assume the first alternative from the non-occurrence of the second; it does not claim that the patient's dying necessarily means that the first alternative (the doctor's giving the patient oxygen) failed to occur.

Another potential problem with "either–or" arguments is our frequent use of these terms in a non-exclusive sense, where "or" really means "and/or." When someone says that "Sarah is either a genius or a saint," she often does not mean that being a genius and a saint are mutually exclusive—she allows for the possibility that Sarah is both. She is not wrong in using "either–or" in this way, so long as she is aware that she is using it in this non-exclusive sense. "Either–or" thinking can also lead to an incorrect form of reasoning: the establishment of two extreme positions as the only choices in a complex situation, a logical fallacy we will discuss in the next part of this section.

How do these types of deductive argument relate to the categories of arguments presented in this book, especially to causal arguments, practical recommendations, and evaluations and interpretations? While there is no simple one-to-one correspondence between these types and our categories, a particular type, though not in pure form, sometimes predominates in a certain category. All practical recommendations, for example, are "if–then" arguments, arguing that if certain steps are taken, then desirable results will occur. "If–then" thinking also plays a role in causal analysis, particularly in helping writers create hypothetical causes to test against the facts. Medical research on the cause of a disease often involves a reverse form of "if–then" thinking as researchers move from known symptoms to possible causes, and then, where appropriate, test these causes in a laboratory setting to see if they produce the predicted effects.

Most evaluations and interpretations involve some classifying by groups, arguing that a particular person or object evaluated belongs in a certain group ("the good," "the bad," "the beautiful," and so on), or that a person, action, or object being interpreted fits into the category of an interpretative framework ("Shakespeare's *Hamlet* is a showcase of unresolved Oedipal tensions"). "Either–or" reasoning can occur in all of these categories and is not usually associated with a particular category. "Either–or" thinking is frequent in practical recommendations, where often one course of action must be chosen over another, even if both alternatives have much to recommend them.

These types of deductive arguments, as we noted, rarely appear in pure form. In fact, written arguments almost always appear not as syllogisms but as *enthymemes*: as deductive arguments with one or more parts—the major premise, the minor premise, or the conclusion—missing. Enthymemes are not inferior syllogisms; as rhetoricians have noted, the very incompleteness of enthymemes helps to convince because it allows the audience to help complete the argument, thus making the audience more likely to identify with the argument and accept it. Advertising works this way by asking us to associate certain desirable ends ("the good life") with a particular product. We are all familiar with ads for cigarettes that display beautiful country scenery in the background or ads for soft drinks that show beautiful bodies cavorting on beaches; in both cases the ads are trying to make us complete the enthymeme by believing at some level that purchasing the product will somehow lead to the life pictured in the ad. Similarly, political slogans demand that we complement their vagueness (the "New Deal," the "New Frontier," and so on) with our own aspirations and values. Even elaborate arguments, when examined closely, are usually enthymemes demanding that we participate in completing them.

LOGICAL FALLACIES

All of us occasionally make mistakes in our own reasoning, and we are all occasionally misled by someone else's false reasoning. Familiarity with certain common flaws or fallacies in reasoning is a safeguard, though not a certain one, against falling into these traps. Unfortunately, the list of logical fallacies is as inexhaustible as human inventiveness. The following list includes only what we believe are the most frequent and flagrant missteps in reasoning. We have also indicated for each of these fallacies the category or categories in which it is most likely to occur in written arguments.

Ad Hominem Argument

An argument against the arguer (Latin *ad hominem*—"to the man") rather than against the argument: "Smith's argument against increasing taxes on the rich is worthless because he himself is rich." This fallacy can occur in any of the four categories of argument, most frequently in practical recommendations or evaluative arguments. The effect of an *ad hominem* argument is to introduce an unnecessary and misleading element of negative evaluation into an argument.

Circular Argument

An argument in which the conclusion is already contained in the premise: "John did not succeed on the track team [the conclusion] because he did not do well in track events [the premise]." Also known as **begging the question**. This fallacy most frequently occurs in evaluations and interpretations ("This film is immoral because it contains immoral scenes") or in causal analysis, such as the explanation for John's failure on the track team.

Distraction

Bringing in irrelevant points to distract attention from the issue being argued: "Sure I cheated on my income taxes, but think of all the money I gave to charity last year." Also known as the **red herring**, from the practice of dragging a dead herring across a trail to distract hunting dogs from the scent of their prey. Distraction is frequently found in evaluative arguments, or, to be more accurate, is frequently used to deflect unfavorable evaluations.

Either–Or

Setting up two extreme positions as the only alternatives and denying any possible middle ground: "The painting is either a masterpiece or trash." The painting could be something in between. Also known as **bifurcation** or the **fallacy of the excluded middle**, this fallacy can occur in any category of argument, though it is probably most frequent in evaluation (as in the statement about the painting) or in practical recommendations, where sometimes extreme solutions are seen as the only options: "Either we build a new computer facility or we give up on using computers at this school."

Hasty Generalization

Making general statements on the basis of a limited sample: "Young professional people tend to be self-centered and materialistic. My friends Eric and Melanie certainly are." This fallacy typically occurs in factual arguments and in the supposedly factual support for evaluative statements on entire groups of people: "Women are sentimental"; "Asian-American students are good in mathematics."

Oversimplification

Failing to consider important aspects of an issue, thereby making the issue appear simpler than it is: "The cure for juvenile delinquency is more homework for students." Oversimplification is especially prevalent in practical recommendations and in causal analysis ("This diet will cure your weight problems").

Non Sequitur

Claiming a logical relationship between a conclusion and a premise where none exists: "Henry should make a good governor because he is tall and handsome." *Non sequitur* in Latin means "it does not follow"; non sequitur reasoning is behind almost all fallacies. The term is really a generic one that has been specifically applied to cases where the relationship between premises and conclusion is seriously askew. The term is also used to cover some fallacies in causal analysis: "I performed poorly on that speech because I wore my green tie rather than my red one," which is an example of our next fallacy—**post hoc ergo propter hoc**. Non sequitur reasoning can occur in any category of argument.

Post Hoc Ergo Propter Hoc

Claiming that because one event preceded another it must have caused the subsequent event to occur: "I performed poorly on that speech because I wore my green tie rather than my red one." *Post hoc ergo propter hoc* is Latin meaning "after this, therefore because of this." This fallacy is at the root of much superstition, as in the case of a pitcher who carries a red handkerchief with him whenever he pitches because he had one with him the day of his no-hitter. It is a serious risk in any causal analysis and can be guarded against by following the principles of causal reasoning presented in Chapter 8.

Straw Man

Attacking a view similar to but not identical with that of an opponent: "How long will America tolerate softheaded opponents of gun control who want only criminals to have guns?" Advocates of gun control vary in their views, but they do not want only criminals to have guns. The use of the adjective "softheaded" is an example of a **loaded term**, a term designed to arouse highly favorable or unfavorable emotional response. Negative loaded terms are frequent in straw man arguments. Straw man arguments are a common but incorrect tactic of evaluative argument.

You can improve your ability to analyze your own and others' arguments by familiarizing yourself with the kinds of fallacies defined above, but you need to remember that what is considered "correct" thinking depends on your context. What may be incorrect in one context may be perfectly acceptable in another: *ad hominem* arguments are frowned on in academic writing (though they do occur), but they are perfectly acceptable in a court of law, where questioning and at least implicitly attacking witnesses' background and motives are frequently practiced. In addition, some of these fallacies are but a slight step off the path of correct reasoning. For example, there is nothing inherently fallacious about "either–or" reasoning, but this kind of reasoning goes wrong when "either–or" alternatives lead to excluding other real possibilities.

Activities (12.2)

1. Examine an essay you wrote recently and present its major argument as a syllogism. What is the argument's major premise, minor premise, and conclusion? Are any of these parts of a syllogism implicit rather than explicit in your essay? Is the syllogism a sound one? Or is it untrue or invalid? Write a one-page essay presenting the syllogism and your analysis of it.
2. Examine a televised or printed advertisement. Is it an enthymeme? If it is, what is the implicit syllogism that the advertisement is urging us to complete? How credible would this syllogism be if it were explicit? Write a one-page essay addressing these questions.

SUMMARY

Revising

- You should plan on spending separate portions of time writing a draft, revising, and editing.
- Allow breathing space between writing a draft and revising it. In your first review of the draft, concentrate on how the draft works as a whole.
- In revising, you need to review your original purpose and audience, organization, adequacy and logic of support, and style.
- Using a word processor makes revising significantly easier.
- Knowing the principles of logic can be a significant help in reviewing your draft.

AN EXAMPLE OF REVISION

Having read your manuscript all the way through at least once and preferably twice, you are now ready to make major changes if they are needed. By avoiding the red pen until you have reviewed the entire manuscript, you are more likely to recognize the need for such major changes, and less likely to get lost in grieving over minor errors.

The following sample student essay (based on an essay written by a student at our institution) is a good example of how revising can correct major problems in an argument. What follows is the first draft of the essay, along with the student's notes for revision, which he wrote in the margins during a second and third reading of the draft.

When we think about computers, we usually think about how helpful they are to us: they enable us to process huge amounts of data, prepare large written documents with an ease undreamt of even twenty years ago, and by acting as the ''brains'' of robots, help us perform dangerous or monotonous tasks. But we often fail to think of the negative side of computers, including the threat they pose to our privacy. Also, in many cases computers are replacing human labor in factories and offices.

Drop - this idea not followed up ‖

One thing computers are used for is to store information about people. These computers contain databases, which are collections of discrete data that are divided into fields, such as age, sex, income, and place of residence. A user of a database can pull information out of the database on everyone who fits a category made up of some or all of these fields, such as every male between thirty and forty who earns between thirty and fifty thousand dollars a year and lives in Florida. An example of a database is the Internal Revenue Service's database, which contains basic information on tax returns along with demographic information on those who pay taxes. Other databases contain credit histories within them. If

OVERSTATED → you have someone's Social Security number, you can find out just about

A separate → anything you want about them. Not just anybody can do this, but there are
point, NOT
Related to A. already too many people who can. *← wordy, vague*
Also, I have
No proof.
If it isn't bad enough to have someone go through all the information about you in one database, databases can even be linked to other databases because of the increased networking power of computers today. Having this ability leads to the potential problem of wrong information being

Two many kept on a person (especially if no written records are kept). Computers
separate
ideas in do fail, but the most important reason why a database would contain wrong
this A:
Networking, information about someone would be because someone typed in incorrect
human error,
lack of paper information. If the police used computer databases to keep track of crim-
Copies. These
need separate inal records without having another record of them on paper somewhere,
treatment.
anyone could input harmful data on innocent people that could cause them a great deal of misery.

If the major problem with the accuracy of information in databases is human error, then perhaps new forms of electronic entry of data will eliminate some of these errors. Our phone bills are one example of a

No evidence. completely electronic system. But these phone bills can tell someone who
Statement
undermines wants to know everybody we called and when we called them. Our phone com-
my credibility.
panies could be recording everything we say as well.

In our society privacy is regarded as a right–a right that is being

threatened by the increasing use of databases to maintain large amounts

Ideas need development. Is situation hopeless?

of information on all of us. A number of privacy bills have been passed

but are almost useless because they are so hard to enforce. Violating

someone's privacy is hard to detect, and successfully prosecuting some-

one for this offense is harder still.

Not relevant to what I've written.

Computers are enormously valuable tools, but they can be misused to

violate privacy and to manipulate people. We have a population explosion

today and yet we replace people with computers. We must carefully examine

Is this conclusion justified by what I've written?

the role of computers in our society and learn to control them before they

control us.

This essay reflects poor planning by the writer: it contains some errors that a careful consideration of the thesis and its support before the actual writing would have probably prevented. Fortunately for the student, he noticed many of these problems during a careful review of the draft and made a list of them:

1. Thesis—I have a combination thesis focusing on the privacy issue and the issue of computers replacing human labor, but I do nothing with the second issue. I should drop the second issue and concentrate on the first.

2. Organization—My ideas aren't clearly presented and organized, especially in the third paragraph, which talks about the three separate ideas of networking, human data entry errors, and lack of paper or "hard copy" backups. All my paragraphs must be clearly tied to the privacy threat.

3. Support—I don't really support my argument because I talk a lot about the threat of invasion of privacy but give no actual cases. I need to distinguish clearly between the potential for abuse and actual cases. Is there a real possibility for abuse? Also, my conclusion about humans controlling computers before they control us isn't warranted by what I've written, since I've offered no suggestions for controlling computers.

4. Style—I undermine my credibility with sweeping statements like "If you have someone's Social Security number, you can find out just about anything you want about them." Some of my writing could be much tighter, including wordy expressions like "If it isn't bad enough to have someone go through all the information about you in one database. . . ."

When writing a second draft, the student tried to correct the problems he saw in the first. This draft still has some problems, but it is stronger than the first. In this draft the student has also added source references.

When we think about computers, we usually think about how helpful they are to us: they enable us to process huge amounts of data, prepare large written documents with an ease undreamt of even twenty years ago, and by acting as the ''brains'' of robots, help us perform dangerous or monotonous tasks. But we often fail to think of the negative side of computers, including the threat they pose to our own privacy. This threat may not seem immediate, but it is growing with the increasing power of computers, and so far society has done little to deal with it (Roszak, p. 181).

One thing computers are used for is to store information about people. Computers often use databases, which are collections of discrete data that are divided into fields, such as age, sex, income, and place of residence. A user of a database can pull information out of the database on everyone who fits a category made up of some or all of these fields, such as every male between thirty and forty who earns between thirty and fifty thousand dollars a year and lives in Florida. An example of a database is the Internal Revenue Service's database, which contains basic information on tax returns along with demographic information on those who pay taxes. Other databases contain our credit histories, our history of contributions to a specific organization, our personnel records with our employers, or a variety of other information. Businesses and other organizations already use this information to bombard us with targeted advertising through the mail; the information could be used to monitor our opinions and activities (Roszak, pp. 182-187).

Databases can be made even more powerful by being linked to other databases through networking. The increasing capabilities of network systems raise the possibility of a wide variety of information on us being shared by numerous databases. Such information on specific individuals would be a boon to marketeers trying to find target audiences, but individuals could end up with their records of contributions to an organization in the hands of the IRS, or their IRS files in their employers' personnel records without their even knowing it.

So far at least, cases of deliberate abuse or manipulation of databases to violate an individual's privacy have been relatively rare. Far greater problems have arisen because of errors in the entry of data in databases, with such undesirable results as individuals

receiving bad credit ratings because of erroneous reports of unpaid bills or even some cases

of innocent individuals being denied government jobs because their names appeared on com-

puter lists of people belonging to subversive organizations (Sherman, p. 344). The risk of

these kinds of errors may increase with the increasing use of ''on-line'' entry of data into

computers, where a paper copy (called a ''hard copy'' in computerese) of the transaction is

not necessary, leaving no trace outside the computer system of the source of the error. These

errors threaten our privacy, because this supposedly ''private'' information can mislead

others, damage our reputation, and enormously complicate our lives. Common sense suggests

that with the increasing amount of ''private'' data being kept on all of us, the likelihood of

harmful errors also increases.

Most such errors are caused by human mistakes, but even computers can develop

''glitches.'' Furthermore, even errorless electronically entered data can pose threats to

our privacy. Our phone bills are one example of a completely electronic system which is almost

always error-free. Yet these phone bills can tell someone who wants to know everybody we

called and when we called them. The information may be accurate, but in the wrong hands it

can be seriously misused.

In our society, privacy is regarded as a right—a right that is being threatened by the

increasing use of databases to maintain large amounts of information on all of us. A number

of computer privacy laws have been enacted in the last fifteen years, including the Medical

Computer Crimes Act of 1984, the Cable Communications Policy Act of 1984, the Financial

Privacy Act of 1978, the Fair Credit Reporting Act of 1974, and the Family Educational Rights

and Privacy Act of 1974 (Organisation for Economic Co-operation and Development, p. 22). One

aspect of all these laws is the protection of individuals from unwarranted use of data about

them. But violating someone's privacy is hard to detect, and successfully prosecuting some-

one for this offense is harder still.

Nevertheless, protecting individual privacy against the threat posed by large databases

is not a hopeless cause. The growing list of computer privacy laws indicates that the public

is not blind to the threats posed by computers, though much needs to be done to make these laws

meaningful. Even consumers can help, by insisting that their names not be sent to others when

they subscribe to a magazine or join an organization. Faced with such insistence and the pos-

sibility of losing customers or members, many groups will stop sharing these lists.

Computers are enormously valuable tools, but they can be misused to violate our privacy. While the threat to our privacy is real, the situation is not yet severe. We still have the time to control this threat before the threat begins to control us.

WORKS CITED

Organisation for Economic Co-operation and Development (OECD). *Computer-Related Crime: Analysis of Legal Policy.* Information on Computer Communications Policy 10. Paris: OECD, 1986.

Roszak, Theodore. *The Cult of Information: The Folklore of Computers and the True Art of Thinking.* New York: Pantheon, 1986.

Sherman, Barrie. *The New Revolution: The Impact of Computers on Society.* Chichester, U.K.: Wiley, 1985.

This second draft attempts to deal with the problems the writer saw in the first. Read it carefully in light of the issues he identified. How did he solve (or at least try to solve) the problems he noted? What further changes do you believe would be necessary in a third draft?

Activities (12.3)

Read the following draft of a student's essay (actually a composite of several essays) and make a list of what you feel the major revisions need to be. Compare your list with those of your classmates, then revise the essay in accordance with your list. Compare your revision with some of those done by your classmates.

STUDENT GOVERNMENT: WHY NO ONE CARES

Being an engineering student here at High Tech, I have very little free time. My time is entirely devoted to academics. Occasionally I will have a few hours free on the weekend, but then I work part-time at odd jobs. Tuition here is very high.

I am one of many busy students here who simply doesn't have the time to take an interest in student government. This same fact is true for most of us. Most of us don't even know one person who is in student government and could not tell you what student government actually does.

We are very ignorant about student government and what role we can play in it. Speaking for myself, even if I saw posters announcing a meeting about student government, I would not attend. Most of my fellow students would not either. What can just one student do? None of us has much of a voice in how things are run. The administration really runs the show here at High Tech, not the students. I believe that if the student government started putting up more posters and getting out more publicity about its activities, students would be more interested in its activities even if they did not attend them.

It is a whole lot simpler to just ignore what's going on and to assume that the student government is looking out for our interests than to take the trouble to get involved. Besides, life isn't all that bad around here, so why should we spend a lot of time and effort trying to improve a situation most of us already find satisfactory? By the time we solved some problem, we would be ready to graduate anyway.

Suggestions for Writing (12.4)

1. Revise a paper that you wrote earlier in this course, following the advice outlined in this chapter. Make a list of the major differences between the original paper and your new version and indicate very briefly why you made these changes.

2. For this assignment the class should be divided into groups of three or four. Each group will collectively write a three-to-four-page paper (750 to 1000 words), starting with a group outline, each student then writing a particular section of the paper. When this first draft is written, the group will get together to discuss the draft and then revise it again in light of the group discussion, with each student revising his or her own section. The group will then discuss this second draft and choose one student to prepare and edit a final version consistent in style and tone. Some possible topics follow.
   a. The uses of word processing in revising papers.
   b. Social life on your campus.
   c. The changing nature of the job market.

3. Write a paper on the steps you usually follow in writing arguments—not the steps you believe you should follow or the ones you would like to follow, but the ones you actually do follow. Start with where you get your ideas and move through writing the first draft and on to whatever steps you take before you arrive at a final edited version. Describe how efficient you find this process in terms of the time you spend, and how effective you find it in terms of creating a convincing argument. Do you believe there are ways this process can be improved so that you could write better arguments in a reasonable amount of time?

Acknowledgments

Page 3. From *The Drowned and the Saved* by Primo Levi, translated by Raymond Rosenthal. Copyright © 1988 by Simon & Schuster, Inc. Reprinted by permission of Summit Books, a division of Simon & Schuster, Inc.

Page 5. Robert Wright, *Three Scientists and Their Gods.* New York: Random House–Times Books, 1988.

Page 8. Eastman Kodak Company, *Filters & Lens Attachments for Black-and-White and Color Pictures.* Rochester, NY: Eastman Kodak–Consumer Markets Division, 1975.

Page 23. Winston S. Churchill, *Blood, Sweat, and Tears.* New York: G. P. Putnam's Sons, 1941.

Page 23. "Three feared kidnapped in Beirut turn up safe," Rochester, NY: *Times–Union*, December 23, 1985. Reprinted by permission of REUTERS.

Page 23–24. Edwin Newman, *A Civil Tongue.* New York: Warner Books, 1976.

Page 24. Ralph Waldo Emerson, *Emerson in His Journals*, edited by Joel Porte. Cambridge: Harvard University Press, 1982.

Page 31–32. "Striving to Formulate a Ticket That Sells" by Michael Oreskes, *New York Times*, July 10, 1988. Copyright © 1988 by The New York Times Company. Reprinted by permission.

Page 34. Art Berman, *From the New Criticism to Deconstruction: The Reception of Structuralism and Post-Structuralism.* Urbana and Chicago: University of Illinois Press, 1988.

Page 36. From *Oxford Illustrated Encyclopedia* by Sir Vivian Fuchs (ed.). Copyright © 1985 by Oxford University Press. Reprinted by permission.

Page 41. Peter Tauber, "Ali: Still Magic," *The New York Times Magazine*, Section 6, July 17, 1988.

Page 50. Franklin Delano Roosevelt, *The Public Papers and Addresses of Franklin D. Roosevelt, Vol. 2, The Year of Crisis, 1933*, 1966.

Page 53. Webster's New World Dictionary of the American Language. Copyright © 1986, 1984, 1982, 1980, 1979, 1978, 1976, 1974, 1972, 1970 by Simon & Schuster. Used by permission of the publisher, Simon & Schuster, Inc., New York, NY.

Page 57. "Playing to Win" by Margaret A. Whitney, *New York Times Magazine* (Section 6), July 3, 1988. Copyright © 1988 by The New York Times Company. Reprinted by permission.

Page 57–58. From *Why We Can't Wait* by Martin Luther King, Jr. Copyright © 1963, 1964 by Harper & Row. Reprinted by permission.

Page 61. Aristotle, *The Rhetoric and the Poetics of Aristotle*, translated by W. Rhys Roberts and Ingram Bywater. New York: The Modern Library, 1984.

Page 63. Excerpt from *The Collected Essays, Journalism and Letters of George Orwell: In Front of Your Nose, 1945–1950, IV,* edited by Sonia Orwell and Ian Angus, copyright © 1968 by Sonia Brownell Orwell, reprinted by permission of Harcourt Brace Jovanovich, Inc.

Page 64. Henry David Thoreau, *The Portable Thoreau,* edited by Carl Bode. New York: Penguin Books, 1975.

Page 65. Marshall McLuhan and Quentin Fiore, *The Medium is the Massage.* New York: Bantam Books, 1967.

Page 65. Donald Hall (ed.), *The Contemporary Essay.* New York: St. Martin's Press, 1984.

Page 66. C. G. Jung, *Contributions to Analytical Psychology,* translated by H. G. and Cary F. Baynes. New York: Harcourt, Brace, 1928.

Page 70. John F. Kennedy, *Public Papers of the Presidents of the United States,* 1962.

Page 71. Michael Herr, *Dispatches.* London: Picador (Pan Books), 1978.

Page 71. "Letter from World Wildlife Fund," *World Wildlife Fund,* 1987.

Page 71. Ralph Waldo Emerson, *Essays and Lectures,* Joel Porte (ed.). New York: The Library of America, 1983.

Page 71. Jerry Vaughn, "Think—before you buy that handgun," Rochester, NY: *Times–Union,* November 20, 1987.

Page 71–72. E. D. Hirsch, Jr., *Cultural Literacy: What Every American Needs to Know.* Boston: Houghton Mifflin Company, 1987.

Page 77. *The Oxford English Dictionary, Volume IV.* Oxford University Press, 1933. Reprinted by permission.

Page 77. Norman Mailer, *The Armies of the Night.* New York: Signet Books, 1968.

Page 78. From *The Concise Columbia Encyclopedia,* Judith S. Levey and Agnes Greenhall, (eds.). Copyright © 1983 by Columbia University Press. Used by permission.

Page 78. Karl Marx and Friedrich Engels, *The Comunist Manifesto,* 1955.

Page 78. Peter Balakian, "Theodore Roethke, William Carlos Williams, and the American Grain," *Modern Language Studies,* Winter, 1987.

Page 78. Harry J. Older, "An Objective Test of Vocational Interests," *Journal of Applied Psychology,* Vol. 28, 1944.

Page 78. Neil Postman, *Amusing Ourselves to Death.* New York: Viking (Elizabeth Sifton Books), 1985.

Page 87. Benjamin Lee Whorf, *Language, Thought, and Reality.* Boston: The Technology Press of Massachusetts Institute of Technology and New York: John Wiley & Sons, Inc., 1956.

Page 108. Michael Useem, "The Corporate View of Liberal Arts," *Journal of Career Planning & Employment*, May, 1988.

Page 142. "Ice Dancers Who Spin Tales of Romance" by Anna Kisselgoff, *New York Times*, January 17, 1988. Copyright © 1988 by The New York Times Company. Reprinted by permission.

Page 145. Sigmund Freud, *On Creativity and the Unconscious*. New York: Harper & Row, 1958.

Page 153–154. Robertson Davies, *Fifth Business*. New York: Penguin Books, 1970.

Page 156. "A Demagogue in the Crowd" by Roger Rosenblatt, *Time*, October 21, 1985. Copyright © 1985 Time Inc. Reprinted by permission.

Page 156–157. "Medicine and the Media: A case study" by David Brown, *The Pharos*. Copyright © 1984 by ALPHA OMEGA ALPHA HONOR MEDICAL SOCIETY, reprinted by permission from *The Pharos*, Volume 47, Number 3.

Page 157. Marilyn Yalom, "The Older Woman" (Introduction), *Victorian Women*. Stanford, CA: The Stanford University Press, 1981.

Page 162. "Particle Accelerators Test Cosmological Theory" by David N. Schramm and Gary Steigman, *Scientific American*, Volume 258, Number 6, June, 1988. Copyright © 1988 by Scientific American. Reprinted by permission.

Page 162. Ralph Landau, "U.S. Economic Growth," *Scientific American*, June, 1988.

Page 163. Janet Sternburg, ed., *The Writer on Her Work*. New York and London: W. W. Norton & Company, 1980.

Page 163–164. Jose Ortega y Gassett, *The Dehumanization of Art*. Princeton University Press, 1948.

Page 165. Abstract of "Don't Tell: Imposed Silences in *The Color Purple* and *The Woman Warrior*" by King-Kok Cheung, *PMLA*, March 1988, Volume 103, No. 2. Copyright © 1988 by PMLA. Reprinted by permission of PMLA: The Modern Language Association of America.

Page 175. Stephen Toulmin, Richard Rieke, and Allan Janik, *An Introduction to Reasoning*. New York: Macmillan, 1979.

Index

A

Abstract, 165, 166
Ad hominem argument, 180, 182
Advertising
  bias in, 76
  connotation used in, 68
  enthymemes in, 179
  implied arguments in, 5
  jingles and catch phrases in, 69
Aesthetic evaluations, 47, 141–143
Agreement, method of, 95–96
Analogy, 65, 66, 173
  cautions about, 67
  domino theory, 67
Appeal to authority, 138, 144
Argument(s), 11–12
  ad hominem, 180, 182
  causal, 11, 42–44
  circular, 180
  definition of, 1–2
  of effect, 104, 121 (*see also* Effects, arguing)
  in ethical evaluations, 140
  factual, 11, 39–42
  focus of, 26, 37
  forming, 9–10
  by image, 7
  implied, 4–5
  levels of, 2–7
    combining, 7–9
  manifest, 2–4
  overview of, 12
  process, 9–11
  reviewing, 11
  review of coherence of, in revising first draft, 172–173
  secondary, 33
  straw man, 182
  supporting, 10–11
  thesis stated at end of, 32–33
  writing of, meaningful to you, 16–17
  See also Causal argument(s); Factual argument(s); Manifest argument(s)
Aristotle, 61, 62
Assumed value(s)
  and needs
    evaluating situation in terms of, 117–118
    judging effects in terms of, 122–124
  in practical recommendations, 112–113
  reader vs. writer, differences in, 113–116
Audience
  composition of, 18–19
  hostile, winning over, 21–22
  identifying, 10
  importance of, 17–24
  level of interest of, 20–21
  reactions of, 22–23
  and revising first draft, 171
Austen, Jane, 16
Authority, appeal to, 138, 144
Average number, defined, 83–84

B

Begging the question, 180
Bias, 76
Bifurcation, 180–181

Brown, David, 156–157
Burke, Kenneth, 70

C

Causal argument(s), 11, 89
  discussion of, 42–44
  evaluating through, in recommendations
      emphasizing present, 117
  sample, 108–110
  supporting, 99–100, 103
      establishing factuality, 100
      identifying acceptable motivation,
          101–102
      qualifying argument, 102–103
      reporting process of determination,
          100–101
  See also Causal constellation; Causality;
      Effects, arguing
Causal constellation, 89–90
  and causal chains, 90–91
  and central causes, 93
  and contributing factors, 93–94
  deciding which causes to argue, 94
  and necessary and sufficient causes, 92–93
Causality, 99
  determining, 95
      method of agreement, 95–96
      method of difference, 96, 101
      method of proportional correlations,
          96–97, 101
  in human actions, 98
  principles of, 105
Central cause, 93
Change, demonstrating probable results of no,
      118
Charles, Mary, 1, 11–12
Cheung, King-Kok, 165
Christian Science Monitor, 76
Churchill, Winston, 23
Circular argument, 180
Citations, 77
Closings, *see* Conclusion(s); Summaries
Coincidence, establishing, between subject
      and interpretive term, 147
Common knowledge (or familiar) facts, 40, 73
Communist Manifesto, The, 14
Comparison, 138, 144
Conclusion(s), 11, 32–33, 161, 164, 167
  and syllogisms, 176–179
  types of, 161
      findings, 162
      general closing, 162–164
      recommendation, 162
  See also Summaries
Connotation, 68, 173
Connotative language, 68–69
Contributing factors, 93–94

Conway, Robert, 149
Counterargument, addressing, 56–58
Court, Margaret, 138
CRC Handbook of Chemistry and Physics, 76
Credibility, establishing, 74–75
Currency of facts, 76–77

D

Darwin, Charles, 41
Davies, Robertson, 152
Declaration of Independence, The, 14, 15–16
Deductive logic, 32–33, 175
  sound, 177
  and syllogisms, 176–177
  unsound, 177
Definition
  applying, to subject, 136–137
  of evaluative term, establishing, 131–132
      arguing, 133–135
      proposing, 132–133
      ranking qualities in, 135
  extended, 35–36, 132
  importance of clarity of, 34–35
  sentence, 35
  shorthand, 35, 132
  stipulative, 36, 132
  types of, 35–37
Denotation, 68
Descriptive writing, 5
Dickinson, Emily, 146
Difference, method of, 96, 101
Dissonance
  defined, 14–15
  value of, 15–16, 28
Distraction, 180
Documentation, of interpretation, 147–148
Domino theory, 67
Dow Jones Industrial Average, 96
Draft
  first, 11
      writing, revising and editing, 169–170
  revision, 11

E

Eastman Kodak, 8, 9, 43
Editing
  first draft, 169, 170
  vs. revision, 11, 169
Effect, identification of, 137–138, 144
Effects, arguing, 104
  comparable situations, 106–107
  determining and supporting probable effect,
      105, 107
      applying principles of causality, 105
      causal chains, 105–106

of practical recommendation, 121–122
Effects, judging, in terms of assumed needs
    and values, 122
    implementation, 123–124
    undesirable effects, 122
Either–or
    fallacy, 180–181, 182
    syllogism, 177, 178, 179
Eliot, T.S., 36
Emerson, Ralph Waldo, 130, 132
Emphasis, 70
Enthymemes, 179
Ethical evaluation(s), 47, 69, 139–140
    argument in, 140
    defining evaulative term in, 140
    sample, 149–152
Ethos, importance of, 61–62
Euphony, 69, 70
Evaluations, 11, 50, 130–131
    aesthetic, 47, 141–143
    applying definition to subject, 136–137
    discussion of, 46–49
    ethical, 47, 69, 139–140
        argument in, 140
        defining evaluative term in, 140
    functional, 47–48, 143–144
    further methods of supporting, 137, 149
        appeal to authority, 138
        comparison, 138
        identification of effect, 137–138
    interpretive, 48 (*see also* Interpretations)
    varieties of, 47–48, 139–148
Evaluative term, 130–131
    defining, in ethical evaluations, 140
    establishing definition of, 131–132
        arguing, 133–135
        proposing, 132–133
        ranking qualities in, 135
Executive summary, 165–167
    sample, 166
Expertise, 76
Extended definition, 35–36, 132

F

Facts
    common knowledge, 40
    currency of, 77–78
    personally experienced, 40–41
        supporting, 73–75
    reported by others, 41
        supporting, 75–78
    supporting, 73–78, 85
    types of, 40–41
    See also Factual argument(s); Factual gener-
        alizations; Statistics
Factual argument(s), 11, 73
    discussion of, 39–42

and functional evaluations, 144
    for practical recommendations emphasizing
        present, 116
    sample, 85–87
    See also Facts
Factual generalizations, 41
    supporting, 78–82
Fallacy of the excluded middle, 180–181
    See also Logical fallacies
Farrakhan, Louis, 156
Faulkner, William, 130
Findings, as type of conclusion, 162
Focus
    of argument, 26, 37
    discovering specific, 15
Forming argument, 9–10
Fredkin, Edward, 66, 145
Freud, Sigmund, 145
Functional evaluations, 47–48, 143–144
Future directions, as subcategory of general
        closing, 163, 164

G

Gallup poll, 83
General closing, as type of conclusion,
        162–164
Generalization(s)
    factual, 41
        supporting, 78–82
    grounds for, 79–81
    hasty, 181
    introduction to, 156–157
    statistics based on, 82
Gould, Stephen Jay, 77

H

Harris poll, 83
Hasty generalization, 181
Hitler, Adolf, 47, 140
Hypothesis, 28, 85–86
    defined, 53–54
    Whorf, 86–87

I

Identification of effect, 137–138, 144
If–then syllogism, 177–178, 179
Image, 72
    argument by, 7, 8
    defined, 7, 60
Implied argument, 4–5, 7, 8
Inductive logic, 32–33, 79, 175–176
Interpretation(s), 145–147
    documenting, 147–148

possibility of multiple, 148
  sample, 152–154
Interpretive evaluations, 48
  See also Interpretation(s)
Interpretive term
  coincidence between subject and, 147
  defining, 145–147
Introduction(s), 11, 155–156, 167
  to generalization, 156–157
  general suggestions about, 159
  by narrative, 156
  other types of, 157–158
  in professional writing, 158–159
  by quotation, 157
  tactics for general, 156–158
  thesis stated in, 31–32
Invalid syllogism, 177

J

Janik, Alan, 175
Journal of the American Bar Association, The,
  76
Journals, reputable, 76
Jung, Carl, 65

K

Kennedy, John F., 70
King, Martin Luther, Jr., 57–58
Kingston, Maxine Hong, 165
Kisselgoff, Anna, 141–142
Kissinger, Henry, 47

L

Language
  connotative, 68–69
  music or sounds of, 69–72
Letter of application, 3–4
Levi, Primo, 3
Loaded term, 182
Logic
  deductive, 32–33, 175, 176–179
  inductive, 32–33, 79, 175–176
  principles of, 174–175
Logical fallacies, 179–180, 182
  ad hominem argument, 180, 182
  circular argument, 180
  distraction, 180
  either-or, 180–181, 182
  hasty generalization, 181
  non sequitur, 181
  oversimplification, 181

post hoc ergo propter hoc, 181–182
  straw man, 182
Lying, avoiding, in writing, 16

M

Manifest argument(s), 2–4, 7, 10
  groups or classes of, 11, 39, 52
  unstated thesis in, 33
  See also Causal argument(s); Evaluations;
    Factual argument(s); Practical recom-
    mendation(s)
Maxwell, James Clark, 19, 34
Mean, defined, 83–84
Median, defined, 83–84
Metaphor, 65–67, 173
  cautions about, 67
Mill, John Stuart, 95, 96
Mode, defined, 83–84
Motives, 14
  for writing, 14–17

N

Nader, Ralph, 132
Narrative, introduction by, 156
Navratilova, Martina, 138
Necessary cause, 92–93
New England Journal of Medicine, The, 76
New Left Journal, 19
Newspapers, reliable, 76
New York Times, 76
Nixon, Richard, 48
Non sequitur, 181

O

Openings, *see* Introduction(s)
O'Reilly, Deborah, 152
Oreskes, Michael, 31–32
Ortega y Gasset, Jose, 163–164
Orwell, George, 63–64
Oversimplification, 181
Oxford English Dictionary, 76, 77
Oxford Illustrated Encyclopedia, 36

P

Parallelism, 70
Particularity, in introduction by narrative, 156
Personally experienced facts, 40–41
  supporting, 73–75
    describing experience, 74

establishing credibility, 74–75
Polling organizations, 83
Pomposity, 64
  avoiding, in writing, 16
Post hoc ergo propter hoc, 181–182
Practical recommendation(s), 11, 50, 111–112, 125, 162
  arguing effects of, 121–122
  assumed value in, 112–113
    differences in reader vs. writer, 113–116
  detailed or specific, 119–120
  discussion of, 45–46
  emhasizing future, 118
    presentation of, 119–120
  emphasizing present, 116
    evaluating situation in terms of assumed needs and values, 117–118
  with equal emphasis on present and future, 124–125
  general, 119
  and if–then arguments, 179
  judging effects in terms of assumed needs and values, 122
    implementation, 123–124
    undesirable effects, 122
  sample, 126–129
Premise, 175
  major, 176–179
  minor, 176–179
Professional writing, introduction in, 158–159
Prohibition, 106
Proportional correlations, method of, 96–97, 101
Proposals, *see* Practical recommendation(s)

Q

Quill, Carrie, 158
Quotation, introduction by, 157

R

Random sample, 83
Reasoning, *see* Logic
Recommendation, as type of conclusion, 162
  See also Practical recommendation(s)
Red herring, 180
Refutations, 22, 57–58
Related issues, as subcategory of general closing, 163–164
Representative sample, 83
Reviewing argument, 11
Revision, 169, 183
  vs. editing, 11, 169
  example of, 183–188

first draft, 11, 169
  writing and editing, 169–170
  suggestions for successful, 170–174
Rhythm, 69–70
Rieke, Richard, 175
Roosevelt, Franklin Delano, 50
Rosenblatt, Roger, 156
Rossiter, Sarah, 47

S

Sagan, Carl, 76
Sample, 82–83
  random, 83
  representative, 83
Sands, Laurie, 17
Secondary argument, 33
Sentence definition, 35
Shakespeare, William, 14, 48
Shorthand definition, 35, 132
Significance, as subcategory of general closing, 162–163, 164
Simile, 65
Slanting, 68–69, 173
Socrates, 14
Sound deductive logic, 177
Sounds, of language, 69–72, 173
Sources
  citing, in text, 77
  determining reliability of, 75–77
Statistics, 82–85
Statt, Michele, 108
Sternburg, Janet, 163
Stipulative definition, 36, 132
Style, writing, 7, 10, 60, 72
  review of, during revising, 173
Subject
  applying definition to, 136–137
  coincidence between interpretive term and, 147
  in evaluations, 130
  in interpretations, 145
Sufficient cause, 92–93
Summaries, 11, 164–167
  executive, 165–167
    sample, 166
  See also Conclusion(s)
Superstition, 182
Support(ing), 53
  and addressing counterargument, 56–58
  arrangement of argument's, 55–56
  facts, 73–85
  introduction to, 53–54
  review of, during revising, 174
  thesis or argument, 10–11, 58
Syllogisms, 176–179

either-or, 177, 178, 179
if-then, 177-178, 179
invalid, 177
valid, 177

T

Tauber, Peter, 40-41
Technical writing, 5
Thesis(es) (or thesis statements), 3, 10
   combination, 49-51
   defined, 26-27
   defining terms in, 34-37
   facts as, 73
   flexibility of, 29-30
   generating, 27-29
   positioning, 31-34
   representative causal, 43-44
   representative evaluative, 48-49
   representative factual, 41
   sample, for arguments of practical recom-
     mendations, 46
   stated at end of argument, 32-33
   stated in introduction, 31-32
   supporting, 10-11
   unstated, in manifest argument, 33
Thoreau, Henry David, 64
Torvill and Dean, 141-142
Toulmin, Stephen, 175
Tuchman, Barbara, 65-66

U

Unsound deductive logic, 177

V

Valid syllogism, 177
Values, *see* Assumed value(s)
Voice, 7
   role of, 61-63, 173

W

Walker, Alice, 165
Wall Street Journal, The, 76
Webster's *New World Dictionary*, 53
Weiss, Betty, 7
Whitman, Walt, 36
Whitney, Margaret, 57
Whorf hypothesis, 86-87
Word processing, and revising, 170, 173-174
Wordsworth, William, 28-29, 130
Wright, Robert, 5
Writing
   descriptive, 5
   meaningful arguments, 16-17
   motives for, 14-17
   plain, virtues and limitations of, 63-65
   professional, introductions in, 158-159
   style, 7, 10, 60, 72, 173
   technical, 5
   See also Revision

Y

Yalom, Marilyn, 157